AF880167

TOWARD AN INFORMAL ACCOUNT OF LEGAL INTERPRETATION

Toward an Informal Account of Legal Interpretation offers a viable account of law, judicial decision-making, and legal interpretation that is as fresh as it is familiar. The author expertly challenges the dominant mode of formalist theorizing and proposes an explanatory account of legal interpretation that can profitably be understood as an 'informal' intervention. Such an informal approach has no truck with the claims of the formalists (i.e. that law is something separate from ideology) or the anti-formalists (i.e. that law is nothing other than ideological posturing). Hutchinson insists that, when understood properly, legal interpretation is an applied exercise in law-and-ideology; it is both constrained and unconstrained in equal measure. In developing this informalist account through a sustained application of the 'no vehicles in the park' rule, this book is wide-ranging in theoretical scope and substance, but also accessible and practical in style.

ALLAN C. HUTCHINSON is Distinguished Research Professor at Osgoode Hall Law School, York University, Toronto.

TOWARD AN INFORMAL ACCOUNT OF LEGAL INTERPRETATION

ALLAN C. HUTCHINSON
Osgoode Hall Law School, York University

CAMBRIDGE
UNIVERSITY PRESS

CAMBRIDGE
UNIVERSITY PRESS

One Liberty Plaza, 20th Floor, New York, NY 10006, USA

Cambridge University Press is part of the University of Cambridge.

It furthers the University's mission by disseminating knowledge in the pursuit of education, learning, and research at the highest international levels of excellence.

www.cambridge.org
Information on this title: www.cambridge.org/9781107152328

© Allan C Hutchinson 2016

This publication is in copyright. Subject to statutory exception and to the provisions of relevant collective licensing agreements, no reproduction of any part may take place without the written permission of Cambridge University Press.

First published 2016

A catalogue record for this publication is available from the British Library

Library of Congress Cataloging-in-Publication Data
Names: Hutchinson, Allan C., 1951- author.
Title: Toward an informal account of legal interpretation / Allan C. Hutchinson.
Description: New York NY : Cambridge University Press, 2016. | Includes bibliographical references and index.
Identifiers: LCCN 2016016032 | ISBN 9781107152328 (hardback : alk. paper)
Subjects: LCSH: Law–Interpretation and construction. | Law–Methodology. | Law–Philosophy. | Comparative law.
Classification: LCC K290 .H88 2016 | DDC 340/.1–dc23 LC record available at https://lccn.loc.gov/2016016032

ISBN 978-1-107-15232-8 Hardback

Cambridge University Press has no responsibility for the persistence or accuracy of URLs for external or third-party Internet Web sites referred to in this publication and does not guarantee that any content on such Web sites is, or will remain, accurate or appropriate.

A2J^3

CONTENTS

PREFACE

In this monograph, I draw together a number of thematic strands from my earlier work – *It's All in the Game: A Non-Foundationalist Account of Law and Adjudication* (2000), *Evolution and the Common Law* (2005), and *The Province of Jurisprudence Democratized* (2009). I have sought to weave these ideas into a more integrated and consistent whole. In the process, I have made certain adjustments and revisions. But this is not intended to be a 'theory' in the grand sense. My ambition is more modest: to provide a viable account of law, judicial decision-making, and legal interpretation that is as fresh as it is familiar.

As well, I have made a deliberate attempt to write this book for law students. Although the themes pursued and explored might hold some value for more specialized and jurisprudentially inclined scholars, it is intended to work as an introduction to jurisprudence and legal theory generally. That said, whatever success that I have managed to achieve in this project, it has been a challenging and richly rewarding experience for me. Because the world of jurisprudence can be all too precious and remote, this book aims to be more accessible and practical, even if it is wide-ranging in scope and substance.

As always, many people have made important contributions to the substance and style of the book. I will not repeat my gratitude to those who played an important role in my earlier works, but simply reiterate my general and genuine thanks. However, some people have made a particular contribution to this volume – I am grateful to David Fraser, Jennifer Leitch, Chris McCormack, Daved Muttart, Hannah Ordman, Vanessa Scanga, Sam Sutherland, and other friends and colleagues for critical assistance and intellectual support. I have benefitted immensely from their generous insights and suggestions – thank you.

1

An Informal Opening

What is a 'vehicle'? and *What is a 'park'?* These seemingly prosaic queries beg simple and straightforward answers. They hardly seem to be the stuff of deep-seated disagreement or invite confounding analysis. People manage to go about their daily lives without too much trouble and consternation when they arrange to 'meet at the park' or 'buy a new vehicle'. Yet if we push a little further and seek more general answers or explore how particular meanings might be arrived at, we soon run into more perplexing and demanding problems. Indeed, efforts to address these and similar banal questions oblige us to confront a whole range of difficult issues and theoretical challenges about how people go about finding and fixing meaning in their lives and interactions.

In particular, when the questions *What is a park?* or *What is a vehicle?* are asked and sought to be answered in a legal setting, a sizable raft of puzzling topics about both the nature of language and the workings of law is soon brought to the surface. Like the proverbial iceberg, the seemingly small and visible part in view is dwarfed in comparison to the size and heft of what lies underneath the surface. In determining what it means to ask and answer *What is a park?* or *What is a vehicle?* lawyers of all kinds – students, practitioners, judges, academics, and others – are inevitably and inescapably drawn into some of the most recalcitrant problems on the jurisprudential agenda. Whether they choose to acknowledge or finesse these perennial puzzles, they remain pertinent and pressing – how is law different from (or the same as) other modes of inquiry in dealing with such problems? What is the relation between law and other modes of interpretation (e.g., politics, literature, or morality)? What tools are available to lawyers in handling such challenges? and What is involved in 'following the law'? Accordingly, as simple as the questions *What is a vehicle?* and *What is a park?* are, their resolution depends upon assuming or developing, often more implicitly than explicitly, some answers about or responses to these more profound and unsettling questions.

In this book, I want to get at some of these deeper issues on the jurisprudential agenda by exploring them in the context of such apparently routine enquiries as *What is a vehicle?* or *What is a park?* Indeed, I will concentrate on an old chestnut that is relied on by many jurists to explore and illuminate some of these larger and broader problems – how do and should lawyers go about interpreting and applying the rule of 'no vehicles in the park'?[1] To some, this may seem to be an unappealing and unedifying way of proceeding. However, I maintain (as do others) that it has much to recommend it. I will canvass some of the leading jurisprudential accounts on offer: they can all be understood and classified under the rubric of formalism. However, my task is not simply to demonstrate how these traditional approaches are found wanting as a way of thinking about and addressing both the bigger and smaller matters involved in confronting 'no vehicles in the park'. Instead, I will propose and present a more nuanced explanatory account of law and interpretation that can profitably be understood as an 'informal' intervention, neither formalist nor anti-formalist.

Looking for a Park

I will get the ball rolling by looking at two recent Canadian appellate decisions that had to deal with the very query of *What is a park?* The

[1] Apart from those theorists whose work I will directly deal with in this monograph, some of the more significant theorists who have tangled with this problem are Frederick Schauer, *Playing by the Rules: A Philosophical Examination of Rule-Based Decision-Making in Law and in Life* (1991); Steven L. Winter, *A Clearing in the Forest: Law, Life and Mind* (2001); Anthony D'Amato, Can Legislatures Constrain Judicial Interpretation of Statutes, 75 *Va. L. Rev.* 561 (1999); William N. Eskridge, Jr., The Circumstances of Politics and the Application of Statutes, 100 *Colum. L. Rev.* 558 (2000); Robert E. Keeton, Statutory Analogy, Purpose, and Policy in Legal Reasoning: Live Lobsters and a Tiger Cub in the Park, 52 *Md. L. Rev.* 1192 (1993); Andrei Marmor, No Easy Cases?, 3 *Can. J.L. & Jur.* 61 at 65–8 (1990); Pierre Schlag, No Vehicles in the Park, 3 *Seattle U.L. Rev.* 381 (1999); Frederick Schauer, A Critical Guide to Vehicles in the Park, 83 *N.Y.U.L. Rev.* 1109 (2008); Peter M. Tiersma, A Message in a Bottle: Text, Autonomy, and Statutory Interpretation, 76 *Tulane L. Rev.* 431 (2001); Paul Brest, The Misconceived Quest for the Original Understanding, 60 *B.U. L. Rev.* 204, 209–13 (1980); Kent Greenawalt, The Nature of Rules and the Meaning of Meaning, 72 *Notre Dame L. Rev.* 1449, 1460, 1463, 1474 (1997); Heidi M. Hurd, Sovereignty in Silence, 99 *Yale L.J.* 945, 984, 989–99 (1990); Michael S. Moore, A Natural Law Theory of Interpretation, 58 *S. Cal. L. Rev.* 277, 338–46 (1985); Samuel C. Rickless, A Synthetic Approach to Legal Adjudication, 42 *San Diego L. Rev.* 519, 520–3 (2005); and William N. Eskridge, Jr., No Frills Textualism, 119 *Harv. L. Rev.* 2041, 2041–3 (2006).

objective of my introductory discussion is to reveal how even the most prosaic business of legal activity draws upon and speaks to some basic and weightier jurisprudential queries. That said, it needs to be remembered that, no matter what some of its more imperialist practitioners claim, jurisprudential inquiry cannot offer any tried-and-true formula to arrive at a correct resolution, let alone provide a definitive set of answers to specific cases. What it does do is cultivate a working knowledge of theoretical debates that underlie and support lawyers' regular activities. In particular, it can unearth those common assumptions and controversial conventions that are taken for granted by lawyers in the act of ascertaining the law. Moreover, by grappling more seriously with the day-to-day workings of law and lawyering, jurisprudential study can reinvigorate itself and cast off its rather aloof and abstract posture. As such, my broader ambition throughout is to offer, by way of a primer, a rudimentary bridge between the worlds of legal practice and legal theory.

Under section 161(1)(a) of the *Canadian Criminal Code*,[2] a convicted pedophile can be prohibited from attending a variety of places where persons under the age of fourteen are or might be present. These places include a public park or public swimming area, a daycare centre, a school ground, a playground, or a community centre. The main purpose of this prohibition is obviously to protect young children and to put them out of a pedophile's way. However, this prohibition must be balanced against a person's freedom of movement because even pedophiles are entitled to lead a certain public life as long as they do not commit further crimes. In resolving this tension, it is important to be as clear as possible in determining to what places the prohibition does and does not apply. In a number of cases, the courts have been required to decide the meaning of 'public park' under section 161.

In *R. v. Lachapelle*,[3] a convicted pedophile who was subject to a prohibition order was apprehended at a carnival by two Royal Canadian Mounted Police officers who were aware of the order. He had attended the carnival with a ninety-two-year-old woman, Margaret Brown, who employed him as her daily help. They were there to have a hamburger and fries for dinner. The travelling carnival was set up on a vacant piece of private land in a large field. The carnival was busy and there were, as expected, many young children in attendance. At trial, Judge Milne held that the field in which the carnival was located was not a 'public park'

[2] R.S.C. 1985, c. C-5, s. 161(1)(a). 3. [3] [2008] B.C.J. No. 728 (S.C.).

and acquitted the accused. On the Crown's appeal, the British Columbia Supreme Court agreed and upheld the acquittal. In reaching his decision, Justice Butler preferred a limited view of what constituted a 'public park'. He decided that it did not include private land that was being used for recreational use, whether permanently or temporarily, and to which the public had access. Instead, he emphasized that, for property to constitute a 'public park' for the purposes of section 161 prohibition orders, it had to be set aside by some authority for use by the public. This meant more than simply being accessible to the public. Emphasizing the need for clarity and predictability, Justice Butler concluded:

> Prohibition orders issued under s. 161 are a significant limitation on the fundamental liberty of movement of convicted pedophiles. If the words of the section are given their ordinary meaning, the geographical ambit of the prohibition is clear and the offender will know with a high degree of certainty what locations must be avoided. The trial judge gave the words 'Public Park' . . . their ordinary meaning and read them appropriately in context. It was not the intention of Parliament to prevent a pedophile from attending at all events involving some element of recreation or play where children may be present. It is the specific location that determines whether or not the offence has been committed, not the nature of the activity occurring at the time. The fact that a travelling carnival with amusement rides is being held on a vacant, private field does not turn that field into a 'public park'.[4]

In the recent Ontario case of *R. v. Perron*,[5] another pedophile who was subject to a similar section 161 prohibition was arrested while working in a game booth at the Super Ex, a fair being held on the grounds of Lansdowne Park in Ottawa. The fair comprised the usual midway rides, game booths, concert areas, food courts, and a petting zoo. It was accessible to the public for a fee and attracted many young children. Lansdowne Park contains a football stadium, a civic centre with a hockey arena, and several other buildings. While there are trees and grassy areas around the fenced perimeter of the property, there is also an extensive paved area that serves as a parking lot for events. The fair was held on the paved area. At trial, Justice Lise Maisonneuve held that the fair was a 'public park' and convicted the accused.

On appeal, the issue was framed in terms of whether a 'public park' was exclusively a green space (e.g., lawns, trees, etc.) set aside for recreational use by the public or was primarily to be defined by its use alone

[4] Ibid. at para. 31. [5] (2010), 97 O.R. (3d) 538.

rather than by any of its landscaping features. In his judgment on behalf of the Court of Appeal for Ontario, Justice Stephen Goudge was again mindful of the need for care and clarity in circumscribing the accused person's freedom of movement. Nevertheless, he needed little persuading that the major identifying characteristic of a 'public park' was its recreational purpose, not the particular attributes of its physical geography. Accordingly, noting that the primary use of Lansdowne Park was recreational and that there was at least some greenery, albeit "peripheral," the fair was considered to be a 'public park' and the conviction was upheld. He concluded by noting:

> The appellant places significant reliance on *Lachapelle*, where the British Columbia Supreme Court determined that a prohibition order . . . did not extend to a vacant private field where a travelling carnival with amusement rides was being held. As I read the decision, the determining factor seems to be that the location was a vacant private field. If so, I agree with the result. If, however, the decision stands for the proposition that the nature of the activities taking place at the location is irrelevant, then respectfully, I disagree with it.[6]

In both of these cases, the judges said little about the more general interpretive method or jurisprudential route that they had relied upon to reach their decisions. There were small hints and casual asides, but there was nothing substantial or anything that suggested that they found their task to be particularly difficult or challenging. Indeed, it might well have been that the exploration of what a 'public park' means was a cover or consequence of incorporating a more purposive and substantive issue – the reason why the two pedophiles were there. It would seem that Lachapelle had a more deserving and compelling reason for why he was in a park (e.g., he did not go there of his own choice, but because it was an incidental aspect of his employment), whereas Perron could not offer such a justification (e.g., he chose to work there instead of elsewhere). In sum, what goes on offstage may be as important as what goes on onstage.

For the most part, however, the judges seemed to proceed on the understandable basis that *Lachapelle* and *Perron* were both rather run-of-the-mill exercises in adjudicative decision-making and legal interpretation that implied or raised no pressing jurisprudential concerns that made it stand out from any other case. Yet there is much to be found in

[6] Ibid. at para. 21.

and between the lines of these judgments that merits a much keener jurisprudential scrutiny and reflection. While this inquiry would likely not change the judges' decisions, it might give them, lawyers, and observers of the judicial process a more nuanced appreciation of how the most apparently prosaic of issues touches upon and resonates with more profound questions of law, language, politics, and interpretation. In determining *What is a park?* there is no escape from their unsettling terrain.

Finding Vehicles

Of course, in the same way that efforts to determine the answers to questions like *What is a park?* crop up throughout the law, there are also instances in which it has proved important to decide *What is a vehicle?* A leading example of such an occasion is the older American case of *McBoyle*.[7] While the judgments delivered offer a range of different arguments and come to a set of differing conclusions, the judges each go about the performance of their professional role in a plausible and legitimate way. Indeed, the judgments neatly illustrate how justification and disagreement go hand-in-hand in the world of judicial decision-making and legal interpretation. Indeed, cases like *McBoyle* tend to confirm, not do away with, the baffling indeterminacy of legal interpretation and judicial decision-making.

In *McBoyle*, the U.S. Supreme Court was tasked with deciding whether someone who had transported a stolen Waco aircraft across state lines from Illinois to Oklahoma was guilty of an offence under section 2 of the National Motor Vehicle Theft Act of 1919. That section of the Act provided that a motor vehicle included "an automobile, automobile truck, automobile wagon, motor cycle, or any other self-propelled vehicle not designed for running on rails". William McBoyle had been convicted at trial and given a prison sentence. This decision was affirmed by the Court of Appeals. Writing for the majority, Judge Phillips surveyed a number of general and legal dictionaries on the meaning of 'vehicle'. He came to the conclusion that:

> Both the derivation and the definition of the word 'vehicle' indicate that it is sufficiently broad to include any means or device by which persons or things are carried or transported, and it is not limited to instrumentalities

[7] *McBoyle v. United States*, 283 U.S. 25 (1931).

> used for traveling on land, although the latter may be the limited or special meaning of the word ... An airplane is self-propelled, by means of a gasoline motor. It is designed to carry passengers and freight from place to place. It runs partly on the ground but principally in the air. It furnishes a rapid means for transportation of persons and comparatively light articles of freight and express. It therefore serves the same general purpose as an automobile, automobile truck, or motorcycle. It is of the same general kind or class as the motor vehicles specifically enumerated in the statutory definition and, therefore, construing an airplane to come within the general term, 'any other self propelled vehicle', does not offend against the maxim of *eiusdem generis*.[8]

However, Judge Cotteral could not agree and dissented. He was prepared to concede that 'vehicle' might well include aircraft in some contexts. However, he did not believe that such an expansive reading of the term was warranted or intended in the National Motor Vehicle Theft Act; it was a penal statute and, as such, should be strictly construed. The force of the *eiusdem generis* rule of statutory interpretation (i.e., that general words following a particular designation are presumed to be restricted to things or persons of the same kind, class, or nature) recommended that 'vehicles' be limited to those that are of the automobile kind. Moreover, according to Judge Cotteral, the rationale for the Act was to address the proliferating incidence of automobile thefts across the United States in the late 1920s. Consequently, he came to the decision that:

> We may assume an airplane is a vehicle, in being a means of transportation. And it has its own motive power. But is an airplane classified generally with 'an automobile, automobile truck, automobile wagon, or motor cycle?' Are airplanes regarded as other types of automobiles and the like? A moment's reflection demonstrates the contrary. The discussions of the proposed measure are enlightening ... in showing that the theft of automobiles was so prevalent over the land as to call for punitive restraint, but airplanes were never even mentioned. It is familiar knowledge that the theft of automobiles had then become a public menace, but that airplanes had been rarely stolen if at all, and it is a most uncommon thing even at this date. The prevailing mischief sought to be corrected is an aid in the construction of a statute. I am constrained to hold that airplanes were not meant by the Act to be embraced in the designation of motor vehicles.[9]

On appeal, the Supreme Court was unanimous in allowing the appeal and acquitting McBoyle. Writing for the Court, Justice Holmes began by

[8] *McBoyle v. U.S.*, 43 F.2d 273 at 274 (1930). [9] Ibid. at 276.

conceding that he was equally open to the etymological notion that 'vehicle' might reasonably be used to signify a conveyance working on land, water or air. However, noting that other statutes had specifically referred to aircraft as being capable of inclusion in the class of 'vehicles', he insisted that its omission from the National Motor Vehicle Theft Act was significant. Accordingly, he held that 'vehicle' on this occasion did not include aircraft and that, therefore, McBoyle did not commit a criminal offence:

> in everyday speech, 'vehicle' calls up the picture of a thing moving on land. For, after including automobile truck, automobile wagon, and motor cycle, the words 'any other self-propelled vehicle not designed for running on rails' still indicate that a vehicle in the popular sense – that is, a vehicle running on land – is the theme. It is a vehicle that runs, not something, not commonly called a vehicle, that flies . . . It is impossible to read words that so carefully enumerate the different forms of motor vehicles and have no reference of any kind to aircraft, as including airplanes under a term that usage more and more precisely confines to a different class . . . When a rule of conduct is laid down in words that evoke in the common mind only the picture of vehicles moving on land, the statute should not be extended to aircraft simply because it may seem to us that a similar policy applies, or upon speculation that, if the legislature had thought of it, very likely broader words would have been used.[10]

As with the judicial efforts in *Lachapelle* and *Perron* to answer the query *What is a park?* the judges' opinions in *McBoyle* about *What is a vehicle?* leave as much unsaid as said. The major challenge is less about the actual decision made but more about the justifications offered for that decision. Each of the three judges works to convince their audience by a variety of interpretive strategies – legislative intention, ordinary meaning, purposive interpretation, and so on – that the outcome offered is more persuasive. None of them offers an excessively literalist response or denies that meaning might be contextually dependent. But each defends their chosen outcome and supporting rationale by reference to the substantive justness of the outcome. However, all judges come together in their efforts to demonstrate that the decision arrived at is not simply a function of each judge's individual political or moral sensibilities: the law has a real and objective meaning that stands outside and above the personal predilections of judges, even if those judges disagree about what that real or objective meaning is.

[10] Supra, note 7 at 26–7.

Nevertheless, the central challenge for judges and jurists is to persuade others that the law's meaning is stable and objective at the same time that it is also flexible and contextual. This task is difficult at the best of times, but it becomes doubly so when inquiries into *What is a park?* and *What is a vehicle?* are combined – 'no vehicles in the park'. The permutations and possibilities develop exponentially over and across time. Moreover, the seemingly workaday nature of the interpretive task belies the deeper and unsettling issues about finding and fixing meaning that underpin it. Behind the confident façade of the judicial opinions, there is a more anxious concern to hit upon an interpretive method that will do the heavy lifting. Mindful that judges are not supposed to be there to act without more on their own substantive opinions (whether they are commonplace or idiosyncratic) about formal meaning or substantive justice, they go to considerable lengths to demonstrate that their decisions are not only the expressions of individual judges' quirks and eccentricities. Instead, they strive to demonstrate that their decisions are the genuine product of a shared and distinctly legal technique. Without such a reliable and grounded mode of interpretation, the worry is that the performance of judicial decision-making will be dangerously open-ended and politically charged.

Of Judges and Jurists

Contemporary jurisprudence, especially its American brand, tends to be dominated by a certain pre-occupation with adjudication. The challenge of jurists has been to provide a convincing account of how judges judge and how they should judge in a constitutional democracy. This has led to a bewildering mix of offerings.[11] The basic division is between those 'formalists' who give priority to internal legal considerations in explaining and underwriting judicial decision-making and those 'anti-formalists' who look to external political factors as the motivating sources of judicial decision-making. There are almost no contemporary explanations that take an entirely extreme stance one way or the other. As much as no one any longer maintains that law can speak entirely for itself without judicial modulation or supplementation, so no one recommends that law has no role at all to play in moderating or constraining the ideological agendas of judicial decision-makers. Accordingly,

[11] *See* Brian Bix, Legal Philosophy in America, in *The Oxford Handbook of American Philosophy* 551 (Cheryl Misak ed. 2009), and Liam Murphy, *What Makes Law* (2014).

jurists join theoretical issue over the extent to which internal and external influences can and should combine to produce decisions and legal doctrine.

Accordingly, at the jurisprudential heart of both the formalist and anti-formalist accounts of adjudication is the juxtaposing of law and ideology. Each is characterized as a separate category that might influence but not fully be part of the other. On one side, there is 'law' as a substantive entity and professional activity. This is a collection of rules, principles, and doctrines that can be developed and applied in a technical manner to resolve a variety of disputes. The task of judges is to identify the appropriate legal norm and apply it to the facts of a case. On the other side, there is ideology. This is a set of ideas and beliefs that allow people to understand and evaluate social life and their own place in it. While broader than politics, an ideology comprises values (e.g., religion, ethics, etc.) that are partisan and in need of justification.[12] Whereas the strict formalist maintains that law should and can be applied by a judge without resort to his or her ideological preferences, the anti-formalist insists that any appreciation of adjudication begins and ends with the judge's ideological commitments.

So, in the context of *Lachapelle*, *Perron*, and *McBoyle*, the judges might be considered to go about their task by following a formalist or anti-formalist approach. Although each account has different nuances and important differences, they can be categorized into one of the two competing camps. The formalist will supposedly set aide his or her personal ideological leanings and decide by consulting what he or she considers to be the available and appropriate legal resources. Relying on a series of reasoning techniques that comprise the legal craft, the judge will arrive at a result that is in important ways the law's and not his or her own. On the other hand, the anti-formalist will consult his or her own ideological compass, choose a desired outcome, and rationalize it in terms of the existing legal doctrines and decisions. Of course, what counts as the best or least worst ideological outcome might well be obscure or elusive on the facts of cases like *Lachapelle*, *Perron*, and *McBoyle*. Nevertheless, although these cases do not involve large or controversial issues of political or moral significance, they are no less ideological for that. None of the judges can navigate the interpretive and legal maze without resort to some set of competing values and orientations.

[12] For a more sophisticated and critical account of ideology, see infra, Chapter 9.

Of course, there are few actual jurists (and certainly even fewer judges) who adopt such polarized and unalloyed stances. Almost all legal actors maintain that there is some seepage from one category to the other. The most common position is that, in so-called hard cases, judges will inevitably have to stray into the ideological fray and allow political values to inform their legal analysis. However, the traditional stance has been that such a resort to ideology is and should not be either personal or partisan. For such traditionalists, judges are not left entirely to their own devices and should not simply legislate their own political preferences. There are a variety of interpretive theories on hand – originalism, positivism, naturalism, purposivism, and so on – that claim to allow judges to bridge the gap between law and ideology in such a way that the law is applied and developed according to relatively neutral and objective criteria. These theories draw upon the society's general ideological resources and normative values but are not entirely beholden to the individual judges' own partisan and personal commitments. There exists a fine, but definable line between law and ideology. As such, contemporary jurists and judges can be grouped into formalist or anti-formalist camps without too much difficulty or controversy, even if this runs the slight risk of caricature.

For example, the formalist Joseph Raz contends that law is an authoritative set of rules that exists and is identifiable without regard to moral considerations. Although the content of law is factually given, its application will be interpretive and evaluative. By maintaining a strict distinction between the legal object to be interpreted and the act of legal interpretation, he claims to be able to preserve the vital distinction between law and ideology. Even though ideology plays a role in law's interpretation, it does not transgress the givenness or boundedness of law's content. On the other hand, the anti-formalist Richard Posner, both a judge and jurist, insists that the adjudicative act is value-laden. He is adamant that judicial decision-making cannot be performed without resort to a whole slew of political or what he prefers to term 'social science' desiderata (i.e., psychological insights into human behavior, moral values, economic logic, sociological patterns, etc.). However, even he concedes that the judge's reliance on such materials need not be idiosyncratic or personal; it can be objective to the extent that it grounds itself on empirical methods and scientific theory.[13]

[13] See infra, Chapters 7 and 8.

Although approaching things from opposite ends of the formalist spectrum, both Raz's and Posner's accounts work to preserve a distinction, albeit a little fuzzy and ill-defined, between law and ideology. As divided as they are in style and rhetoric, they end up in much the same place. Moreover, they rely on very thin and unconvincing accounts of what counts as both law and ideology. However, both the formalist Raz and the anti-formalist Posner do hint at, even if they fail to pursue, one of the most important, if unintended implications of their stances – that law and ideology are not separate spheres of influence; they are integral and mutually reinforcing features of judicial decision-making. Consequently, in contrast to both Raz and Posner, I recommend that, with a better understanding of both law and ideology, it will become apparent that they are not separate sources of influence in judicial decision-making. Instead, they combine to present legal interpretation as a law-and-ideology enterprise.

Conclusion

In contrast to these traditional and opposing approaches, I want to offer a more satisfying explanation of judicial decision-making that explains better the relationship between judges' ideological leanings and their attachment to law. To do that, I intend to take up the challenge thrown down by David Robertson. He complains that attempting to look at the world through the black-and-white lens of the law/politics dichotomy "is injurious ... because it is inadequately theorized".[14] I take this to mean that the either/or nature of the law/politics dichotomy (i.e., judges do law or they do politics) places an unnecessary straitjacket on jurisprudence; it not only misrepresents legal interpretation, but also does harm to efforts to understand it. Instead, by theorizing the relationship between law and ideology more thoroughly and more compellingly, I contend that I will be better able to develop an account of legal interpretation that sees law and ideology as both being integral parts of any reliable or adequate understanding of legal interpretation.

To accomplish this, I will take formalism to task in all its manifestations and reveal the frailty of its theoretical foundations and practical implementation. However, although resolutely opposed to formalism, I will not maintain or defend an anti-formalist stance. It is not my

[14] David Robertson, Appellate Courts in *The Oxford Handbook of Empirical Legal Studies* 592 (Peter Cane and Herbert Kritzer eds. 2010).

contention that, with formalism out of the way, lawyers will be released from the constraints and discipline that comprise the law and be entirely free to indulge their own political preferences and ideological leanings. Instead, I will work toward sketching an informal account of law and legal interpretation. Such an informal approach has no truck with either the claims of the formalists (i.e., that law is something separate from ideology) or those of the anti-formalists (i.e., that law is nothing other than ideological posturing). I reject such a dichotomy; it obscures more than it explains. When understood properly, legal interpretation is an applied exercise in law-and-ideology; it is both constrained and unconstrained in equal measure. This informalist account is particularly pertinent in regard to appellate decision-making. However, that said, I will be mindful of Arthur Leff's teasing caution that "to ask 'what really happened' of a reported case is something like trying to find the mood of a centre-fielder by reading a box score".[15]

[15] Arthur A. Leff, Law and, 87 *Yale L.J.* 989 at 1008 (1978).

2

Among the Formalist Ghosts

There are ghosts almost everywhere. People spend much of their time being haunted by some old wraiths or trying to escape their chilling effects. Of course, law and jurisprudence are no different. Indeed, they seem to deal with more than their fair share of chimeras and charismas – law's ghosts inhabit and spook lawyers' daily rites and professional rituals. Not surprisingly, much legal thought and work is done in thrall to a daunting series of spectral influences that holds great sway over both its ambitions and achievements. Indeed, in an important sense, jurisprudence – put simply, those efforts to step back from the actual practice and operation of law in order to make some general sense of it all – is where such ghostly tendencies are most frequently sighted, often invoked, and occasionally resisted.

In a manner of speaking, there is a spectre haunting contemporary law and judicial decision-making – *formalism*. Much academic work continues to operate within the cramping and pervasive spirit of this professional mind-set. The ghosts of formalism's jurisprudential ideas past not only prowl the corridors of the legal academic and practicing community, but also are welcome souls in their offices and classrooms. At its boldest, this intellectual tendency enables lawyers and jurists to present law and legal reasoning as an inward-looking and self-contained discipline that is largely separate from both the society within which it operates and the lawyers who work with it. This mysterious and, by some lights, almost mystical approach bestows an enormous authority on the law's adepts in determining what the law is and should be. Moreover, it allows lawyers to wield this power under an apparent stamp of institutional legitimacy. As such, a commitment to formalism enables lawyers and jurists to feign a professional humility and institutional subservience while, at the same time, imposing a contestable and partial ideology on the law's operation and thrust. This is a disheartening and disabling state of affairs that is in need of some serious and sustained ghost-busting.

A Ghostly Presence

There are various types of formalism – systemic, sociological, administrative, and so on – that occupy the attention of commentators and critics of law and the social sciences.[1] However, I want to eschew some of the fancier definitions of formalism and rely on a very simple and straightforward understanding of formalism: *that it is possible and desirable to do law without taking a personalized stance on the contested political and moral issues that law must grapple with and resolve.* Any approach that relies or insists upon such a premise is formalist. Although formalists come in many different guises and are deeply divided among themselves, they are all united in their adherence to the basic idea that there is a substantive and workable difference between doing law and doing ideology.

If formalism is the answer, then it is important to know what the question is. Of course, as Roscoe Pound cautioned, "our conception of the problem to which our discourse is addressed shapes both".[2] That said, the challenge for lawyers is perceived to be finding a way to do their work such that settling *what the law is* will not be dependent upon or reducible to only *who the judge or lawyer is* and what they would like it to be. Because law holds such a decisive role in social life, it is imperative that lawyers are able to demonstrate convincingly that law has a sufficient and available objectivity so that there is a real distance and space between what the law is claimed to be and what lawyers say that it is or want it to be. Law's authority depends on it having a meaning and force that is more than whatever lawyers think or do at any given time and on any given occasion: lawyers are expected and required to do their job in a way that goes beyond what their own and their clients' political, economic, or moral preferences dictate. While law and ideology might overlap, that is not by necessity or design, but by coincidence or chance.

Accordingly, formalism puts itself forward as an explanation and justification for the way that law works. It presents law as having an ingrained logic and lawyering as adopting a neutral and bounded method through which a just compromise of competing political, economic, or moral interests can be achieved. Its beauty is its insistence that the

[1] See Duncan Kennedy, Legal Formalism in *The Encyclopaedia of the Social and Behavioural Sciences* 8634 (2001).

[2] Roscoe Pound, Natural Natural Law and Positive Natural Law [1960], *Natural Law Forum* 70.

rational discourse of law is able to transcend the contested rhetoric of vulgar political, economic, or moral debate. In short, formalism presents itself as an approach that allows lawyers and especially judges to engage in and settle social debates in a distinctly legal and, therefore, legitimate way. Formalism encourages and underwrites a reliance on law as both a body of norms and an operational process that can be relied upon to give an objectivity or legitimacy to the resolution of a particular issue. It is a way for lawyers to say with conviction and justification that 'it's the law: not my opinion of what the law is or should be'. As is so often the case, Richard Posner captures this dimension of formalism when he states that it is "a belief that all legal issues can be resolved by logic, text, precedent, without a judge's personality, values, ideological leanings, background and culture, or real-world experience playing any role".[3]

It is important for me to note early that an alleged adherence to formalism will not in and of itself bring about dire implications for law's content or consequences. The results of formalist reasoning or interpretation may well turn out to be just in their substance or significance for the particular case. But that is more by serendipity than design. The claimed attractiveness of formalism is that it will be better, not worse, for society if lawyers are reined in and if the law, therefore, is defensibly separate from the judges who make it. Formalism is based upon the bedrock idea that it is possible to do law without confronting directly and head-on questions of substantive justice; law backs into them as a result of its preoccupation with formal methods of rule identification and rule application. The formal values of consistency, coherence, order, integrity, and the like are given a definite priority over the substantive and particularized qualities of the decisions reached and the rules formulated in terms of social justice.

In the formalist playbook, the content of law is derived from law's form or the formal character of legal reasoning. Legal interpretation cannot be judged only by the appeal or desirability of the outcome: the law's substance is distinctly second-best or subservient to its formal mode of elucidation. This is nicely illustrated by Herbert Wechsler's insistence that, whatever the substantive appeal of *Brown*'s condemnation of segregated schooling in 1954, it was a bad decision as it failed to take a neutral or principled stance on the tension between the freedom to associate and the freedom not to associate as part of a broader equality

[3] Richard Posner, *Reflections on Judging* 1 (2013).

doctrine. For him and other formalists, the mode of analysis was what counted, not the justness of the decision reached. If the method deployed was unconvincing or inappropriate, then the decision was wrong or illegitimate by formalist lights.[4]

As defended by the progressive constitutional scholar Lawrence Tribe, whatever else formalism might be, it stands squarely against an anything-goes or fully ideological approach:

> If the Constitution is law, and if we are trying to interpret that law, then the claim that a particular governmental practice, domestic or international, is efficacious, is consistent with democratic theory, and is in some popular or moral sense "legitimate" just doesn't cut much ice when the question before us is whether that practice is constitutional ... The enterprise of interpreting the Constitution of the United States ... is not always an easy one. Neither its precise ground rules nor its proper conclusions are likely ever to become matters of very broad consensus; indeed, if they do, I will be among the first to insist that something very peculiar indeed, and probably most unhealthy, has occurred. But, for all its difficulties, the enterprise of construing text and structure is a worthy one. Disciplined by basic notions of constitutional topology, the enterprise may be pursued with considerable rigor. And, at times, part of what it means to take that enterprise seriously is to protest in no uncertain terms when undertakings of a different sort altogether are put forth in its name.[5]

In this extract, Tribe hits all the high notes in the formalist register. He stresses the need for 'discipline' and 'rigor' in ascertaining the Constitution's distinctive meaning that is separate from 'popular' and 'moral' values or 'broad consensus'; it is the formalist's duty to defend this intellectual enterprise in the name of 'democratic theory'.

For example, how should judges decide on the meaning or import of a particular rule or legal doctrine? This question cannot be answered by simply stating that judges should be guided by their own political lights and moral values. A commitment to formalism demands that they must largely set aside their own preferences (and those of their clients) and seek to discern the appropriate legal position in a relatively neutral, objective, and impersonal manner. As such, formalism insists that the

[4] See *Brown v. Board of Education*, 347 U.S. 483 (1954), and Herbert Wechsler, Toward Neutral Principles of Constitutional Law, 73 *Harv. L. Rev.* 1 (1959).

[5] Lawrence Tribe, Taking Text and Structure Seriously: Reflections on Free-Form Method in Constitutional Interpretation, 108 Harv. L. Rev. *1221 (1995). See also Fred Schauer, Formalism, 97* Yale L.J. *509 (1988).*

effort be made to arrive at a legal opinion that is supported by the available legal materials and is not only dictated by or reflective of the preferences of the judges. The fact that the law takes a moral stance that does or does not align with the judge's is not cause for criticism or praise. Indeed, an expansive understanding of formalism recognizes that the substantive justice of a particular legal rule might well be relevant provided that the nature of that substantive justice is derived from or flows from the legal materials themselves. The justice relied on must be that of the law's, not that of the judge's.

This formalistic *modus operandi* applies whether the question at issue is the application of 'no vehicles in the park' or the constitutional legality of water-boarding as a permissible mode of enhanced interrogation by government agents. The fact that the latter raises more compelling political and moral concerns than the former does not mean that it is less amenable to formalist resolution. Indeed, it is exactly in those highly contested situations that formalism claims to display its practical and theoretical worth. By restricting the available materials to be consulted and insights to be gleaned to those of the law, a formalist approach claims to preserve the legitimacy of judicial decision-making as a privileged and authoritative mode of dispute resolution in a democracy. At its grandest, it offers itself as a get-out-of-jail card for judges and jurists who might otherwise succumb to the critique of being ideologues in judicial clothing.

Of course, judges might well differ over the correct or best legal answer to be given. At least in its more moderate renditions, formalism does not necessarily imply that there will always be one and only one correct answer to any particular controversy. Better and worse opinions will be offered, but they will be evaluated in terms of their professional craft and technical merits as much as by their substantive conclusions. This allows for considerable professional disagreement and practical leeway. Nevertheless, formalists maintain that there is a certain line between law and ideology that cannot be crossed. It is insisted that there are real limits that a good-faith engagement with the available legal materials places upon lawyers in their interpretive activities; creativity has its place, but it is a circumscribed and contained one. Legal opinions cannot be salvaged by their substantive attraction alone. Whether or not an opinion squares with moral sentiment is not the best or final evaluation of its quality or merit as a *legal* opinion.

A good example of this distinction is the heated debate over the 'torture memos'. Many lawyers and jurists insisted that that the supportive advice given by counsel to President George W. Bush on the legality of water-boarding was not only morally reprehensible, but also professionally invalid. Whatever its failings as in moral terms, it was not considered to pass muster as legal advice. However, this claim is not as solid or persuasive as many would like. As John Yoo, the main author of the 'torture memos', said, "there is certainly room for disagreement among reasonable people, acting in good faith, on these questions, but I still believe we gave the best answers we could on the basis of the legal matters available to us".[6] Consequently, the formalists have a difficult task in making the claim stick that the law, properly and even broadly understood, places some real constraint on what can be done and delivered in its name.

A Dubious Pedigree

Although it has many varieties, this notion of formalism has a long and distinguished heritage. Its origins can be traced back to the turn of the sixteenth and seventeenth century. Sir Edward Coke can be considered the godfather of legal formalism. He portrayed the common law as "the peculiar science of judges" which was centred on "the artificial perfection of reason" and could be attained only after "long, study, observation and experience".[7] This unabashedly elitist view tended to emphasize the reason and the science, but downplay the peculiarity and artificiality of law and legal reasoning. William Blackstone continued in this tradition when he cast jurisprudence as a "rational science of general and extensive principles" and portrayed the common law as being "fraught with the accumulated wisdom of the ages".[8] From these rather grand and over-wrought beginnings, formalism has gone through many iterations and incarnations. The formalist tradition is broad and evolving.

Despite the general disparagement of such a pinched and scientistic approach, formalism still casts a long shadow over the jurisprudential project throughout the twentieth century. Championed by Harvard's Christopher Langdell in the late nineteenth century, the formalist

[6] *Washington Post*, June 27, 2008. See also John Yoo, *Crisis and Command: A History of Executive Power from George Washington to George W. Bush* (2010). For a general discussion, see Bradley Wendell, *Lawyers and Fidelity to Law* 181–82 (2010), and Allan C. Hutchinson, *Fighting Fair: Legal Ethics in an Adversarial Age* 32–34 (2015).

[7] See Edward Coke, *Institutes of the Laws of England* I § 138 (19th ed., 1832).

[8] *Blackstone's Commentaries* I, 2 and II, 425 and IV, 435.

mind-set was given a pragmatic twist. Although there was still talk of taxonomic organization and geometric-like proofs, there was also the recognition that law did not apply itself. Relying on so-called Socratic dialogue and a select handful of leading cases, would-be lawyers were trained in the special techniques of legal reasoning so that they would be able to apply a relatively stable body of rules and principles to particular and different situations. In this way, law faculties began to be treated as the laboratories of jurisprudence where these professional skills could be cultivated and honed. Under the tutelage of this case-method pedagogy, young lawyers could become adept in Coke's 'peculiar science' and be active participants in the development of legal rules for a modern and changing world.

Although belief in such a pseudo-scientific understanding of law has fallen well out of fashion, the formalist mission remains very much at the heart of the lawyering process. Contemporary formalism is no longer about law's scientific or sterile logic. Indeed, many contemporary formalists are dismissive of the old-school approach; they distance themselves from any black-letter approach as being too limited, unduly isolated, and woefully inadequate as either a descriptive or prescriptive account of law and legal interpretation. It is now conceded not only that law arises in social and political circumstances, but that social values and political morality play a vital role in the operation of the law. Accordingly, modern and old-school formalists maintain that there are certain facts of the matter, be they legal or moral, that transcend and discipline the beliefs of its participants about what the legal enterprise does and does not entail. It is the source of these facts that distinguish formalists. So, suitably educated and experienced in those facts of the matter and the designated methods for identifying them, lawyers will be able to go about their work confident in the belief that they are doing the right and professional thing.

As such, modern formalists not only concede, but also insist that legal reasoning does rightly concern itself with political standards and moral values. The substantive justice of the decisions reached is inside, not outside the purview of lawyers. However, they so insist in a suitably formalistic manner by adopting an expansive view of the available legal resources. Rather than focus only on law's rules, they look to the values and purposes that inhere within law itself and animate those rules: the law has its own set of ideological commitments. The judgments in *Lachapelle*, *Perron*, and *McBoyle* testify to that. Consequently, a formalist approach grapples with political and moral values, but does so in a very particular and bounded way. Most importantly, it looks to law's own values and purposes, not those of the judges or anyone else. Such ingenuity allows lawyers to have their formalist cake and to eat it too – they work with values as well as rules, but through a constrained and professional method of engagement.

This separation of law (even when expansively understood) from open-ended ideology is a move that keeps faith with the spirit, if not the letter of Coke and Langdell's formalism. Accommodating both positivist and naturalist accounts of law and lawyering, it functions as a hedge against an anything-goes approach to law and legal reasoning. By insisting that there is something about 'law' that places a constraint on lawyers' and judges' efforts to construe what it is, a buffer is put between their own ideological preferences and their account of what the law is. Going well beyond the discredited old-school vision of law as mechanical algorithm, modern formalism attempts to colonize a middle ground between a naive faith in the dispositive power of law and an unsettling fear that untethered judges will become ideologues at large: "judges are not just politicians in robes, although that is part of what they are ... owing to the indeterminate character of many cases to legalist analysis".[9] However, so capacious is that middle ground that it can render the difference between a formalist and a non-formalist account so small and inconsequential that there is nothing to distinguish them. A black-letter mentality has been abandoned, but only to be replaced with a black-spirit one.

A Ghost of Many Different Kinds

Of course, formalism is not one large monolithic theory of law and legal interpretation. It comes in many different varieties that compete against one another in the competition to seize and don what they claim to be the true mantle of legal formalism. Moreover, as with many similar *contretemps* across academe, the ferocity of this internecine debate is nasty and unrelenting: formalists reserve as much (and, occasionally, more) animosity for their formalist kin as they do their out-and-out anti-formalist or informalist opponents. Consequently, it is important to deal with the leading modes of contemporary formalism separately so as to highlight their relative failings and successes. In so doing, it

[9] Lee Epstein, William Landes, and Richard Posner, *The Behaviour of Federal Judges* 385 (2014).

becomes possible to expose better the general infirmity of the theoretical and practical foundations on which they rest and by which they claim to be supported.

I will concentrate on the four most popular and distinguishable kinds of legal formalist approaches. Each of these captures something important about the operation of law and lawyering, but each also manages to put a very different spin on the requirements and implications of the formalist project:

- *Positivists* of a traditional character are formalistic (in the way that I construe it) by insisting that there is a thereness or brute factness to law that must be respected. When this body of rules is ignored or misconstrued by some recalcitrant judges, the resulting interpretation is invalid for that fact alone. This applies no matter how attractive or desirable in prescriptive terms such an interpretation may be. Although there might be rare occasions or 'hard cases' when judges will have to branch out into unregulated and perilous ideological terrain, judicial decision-making in general can be performed in a detached and impartial manner.
- *Naturalists* of different shapes and sensibilities are formalistic in that they resist the positivists' minimalist claims. They seek to reaffirm the importance and necessity of moral and political inquiry to the main business of lawyers and judicial decision-making. For them, law contains its own political morality such that inquiries into *what the law is* are intimately connected to *what the law ought to be*. In this naturalist incarnation, a formalist rendition of judicial decision-making becomes a thoroughly value-drenched, but contained enterprise.
- *Originalists* strive to situate themselves between the positivists and the naturalists. They look to the circumstances and context within which a contested set of rules were enacted and strive to ground a more determinate meaning based on the prevailing views and values at that earlier moment in time. For them, the substantive justice of any decisions reached is beyond the purview or responsibility of the judge. If people do not like what the rules originally mean and the decisions that they give rise to today, they can and should change the legal rules in question.
- *Hard positivists* are of a more modern and uncompromising stature than their softer colleagues. They are adamant that law inhabits the realm of philosophical necessity, not that of contested moral and political judgments. As such, the role of judges is seen to be entirely

objective and detached in their capacity to fix and apply the extant rules of law. There is no mandate or need for judges to stray into the realm of ideological contestation. To do so is to undermine the legitimacy of the whole legal enterprise.

- *Incrementalists* take a traditional common law approach to legal interpretation. drawing on a range of techniques, they maintain that the law can be applied in an incremental fashion to new problems and that it can be developed in a low-key manner to changing social circumstances. As craftspersons, they rely upon the law's own internal dynamics to allow it to evolve in measured and modest ways.

Despite its continued prestige within legal circles, there is no shortage of efforts at ghost-busting when it comes to formalism. There has always been and remains strong and varied lines of critique that combine in the belief that, for all its huff and puff, formalism is a faux account of law and legal interpretation. Largely drawing their inspiration from the American legal realists of the 1920s and 1930s, they insist that there is no method or legal approach that can save the law and lawyers from their ideological selves. When it comes down to it, the emperor has no clothes on at all. Those who see the emperor adorned in elegant and more fashionable outfits are simply deluded by virtue of their naivety, complicity, or lack of insight. This critique began as an easy demolition of the scientific strain of formalism, but it has not lagged as the going has gotten tougher. The outfits may have changed and the justifications may become ever more sophisticated, but there is the same failure to convince critics that there is a sufficiently distinctive mode of legal reasoning or interpretation that can be usefully or plausibly contrasted with ideological advocacy. The style might not be the same, but everything else is – law is ideology dressed in other garb.

The realist Fred Rodell was perhaps the most uncompromising critic in the assault on formalism. He rejected out of hand the idea that it was possible to regard the American Constitution as a reliable source of explicit guidelines that were capable of direct elucidation, application and implementation by a professional legal community. He maintained that a fair-minded study of constitutional law supported the view that its "alleged logic … is equally amorphous, equally unconvincing, equally silly whether the decisions the court is handing down are 'bad', 'progressive' or 'reactionary', 'liberal' or 'unliberal'".[10] For him and like-minded

[10] Fred Rodell, *Woe unto You, Lawyers* 31 (1939). See also infra, Chapter 8.

critics, formalism was simply a convenient mode of professional denial that allowed lawyers to say one thing and do another. For them, lawyering is not so much a rational enterprise as a vast exercise in rationalization. Law is never simply there; it is always political in the sense that what counts as the law has to be argued for and defended politically at every turn. As such, the law is riddled with ideology that chops and changes with the identities of its privileged personnel. As one critic bluntly put it, "the law is . . . and always will be *ad hoc* and *ad hominem* to a fault".[11]

An Informalist Opening

Although I dismiss formalism out of hand, I also contend that an anti-formalist approach fails to take the legal enterprise seriously. While the unbuttoned anti-formalist critique is bracing and revealing, it is more beholden to formalism than it realizes. It slips too easily into being simply the flip-side of the same methodological coin: formalists and many anti-formalists are the yin and yang of legal thought. Each relies on the other to make its case. On the one hand, formalism (i.e., it's all law) relies on the bogeyman of anti-formalism (i.e., it's all ideology) to bolster its appeal – "if not this, then the abyss". On the other hand, in its eagerness to raze formalism to the metaphorical ground, anti-formalism denies that law has almost any existence or influence at all – "it is ideology all the way down". Neither formalism nor anti-formalism works as a cogent account of law and legal interpretation. While each has something important to say about law and lawyering, they both overstate and exaggerate their claims.

Lawyers and judges are both more and less constrained by the law's constitutive rules than both the formalists and anti-formalists allow and pretend. They are more constrained in the sense that they cannot get completely outside rules and exercise an entirely free political choice. Unless they are acting entirely in bad faith, judges are committed to working with the rules and routines of the legal process; the law influences their ideology as much as their ideology impacts upon the law and their decision-making. But they are less constrained in the sense that they are not obliged to reach any particular decision as the result of the professional commitment to resolve disputes through resort to those rules and routines. Law is a special kind of activity or game that is

[11] Grant Gilmore, Products Liability: A Commentary, 38 *U. Chi. L. Rev.* 103 at 108 (1970).

defined by rules and roles, one where the nature and effect of those rules and roles are always in play. When properly understood, the critical claim is not that 'anything goes', but that 'anything might go'.[12]

From a formalist perspective, the fear is that, without the possibility of a workable theory of legal interpretation, the Rule of Law will be subverted; democratic governance will succumb to the tyranny of special-interest groups and/or become a 'judocracy'. For all their internal bickering, positivists, naturalists, and other formalists come together in their agreement that the preservation of the Rule of Law "has the value of promising to make politics safe, of preventing Leviathan from becoming Frankenstein's monster, . . . [of imposing] real restraints on arbitrariness or despotic conduct".[13] Yet it is the formalists themselves that fuel the very fears that they then claim to assuage: they insist that, without adequate determinacy in legal discourse, judicial arbitrariness will become the order of the day and adjudication will collapse into a series of *ad hoc* and unprincipled encounters; 'muddling through' will be all that is left. As an informalist account of legal interpretation and judicial decision-making seeks to explain, this fear and its formalist appeasement is misplaced and exaggerated.

No theory of legal interpretation, be it formalism or any other, can provide a method or means that will relieve lawyers and judges from the responsibility and challenge of constantly arguing and rearguing what should and should not be done in particular contexts at particular times. It is not so much that rules do not exist, but that they do not exist as canonical directives whose meaning is available without interpretation and which can impersonally dispose of cases. Judicial decision-making – the fixing of the pertinent rule, the ascertainment of its meaning, and its application to disputed facts – is incapable of being done in any technical or non-ideological way. In short, law never simply is; it is something to be argued for or with, not something to be argued from. As conventional and social matters, acts of judicial decision-making are contextual and, therefore, open: the fear of an entirely rule-free choice is as contrived as faith in rule-bound choice. Any claim that judges are being held back from a frenzy of arbitrariness only by rules' restraining power not only is unrealistic but does scant credit to the integrity and efforts of most judges. An informalist account of legal interpretation can accommodate

12 See Allan C. Hutchinson, *All in the Game: A Non-Foundationalist Account of Law and Adjudication* (2000).

13 Neil MacCormick, The Ethics of Legalism, 2 *Ratio Juris* 184 at 188 (1989).

both the idea that judges do rely on legal considerations and the idea that they are driven by ideological influences.

As a human enterprise, judicial decision-making is a thoroughly messy, complicated, and continuing enterprise; it is folly to try and explain it by reference to some simple and one-dimensional causal algorithm. Law does not stand aside from politics or fulfill a moderating check on ideological decision-making. Nor does ideology operate independently of or outside of extant law's materials and tools; they are part and parcel of the same intellectual venture. This informalist conclusion strongly recommends that the focus of any jurisprudential inquiry should not be about whether law or ideology is more or less important in judicial decision-making. Instead, recognizing that both play an indispensable role to varying degrees at varying times, the emphasis must be upon charting and explaining how ideological preferences can be more effectively dealt with in the adjudicative forum. As I will show, this is a historical and critical undertaking, not an empirical or theoretical one.

Conclusion

Accordingly, stories about law and legal scholarship, like all tales, "are haunted by the ghosts of the stories they might have been".[14] Indeed, law remains thoroughly spooked by the jurisprudential phantoms of what it perhaps could, but maybe should never be. A more appropriate response to such jurisprudential fantasizing is not awe-induced toleration, but a defiant and decisive act of ghost-busting. The time has come to break free of as many ghosts as possible. That said, there is no bargain, Faustian or otherwise, that can get society out of the continuing present to some redemptive future or forgiving past. The present is all that there is or will be and it is everyone's responsibility to make it the best that it can be. Consequently, an informal account of legal interpretation does not offer itself as a privileged source of methodological insight or so-called right answers. After all, if it did, it would become simply one more formalist theory. Instead, by at least clearing away much of the intellectual debris and theoretical fog that continues to interfere with efforts to understand properly the practice of legal interpretation and judicial decision-making, an informalist can contribute to a more informed and authentic account of that practice.

[14] S. Rushdie, *Shame* 116 (1995).

3

Walking Softly

The Positivist Contribution

Insofar as practicing lawyers ever stop to think about what they are doing in a broader or deeper way, they tend to be attracted to a relatively straightforward and workaday account of law. For them, lawyering is a prosaic art in which their task is to isolate and apply the extant rules to resolve disputes and establish reasonable policies for social regulation. Not quite the black-letter lawyers of old, they still remain squarely in the Blackstonian-inspired formalist fold, albeit with a more greyish and less elevated self-image. Contemporary lawyers and judges defend the notion that law is a settled body of rules, that it can be applied by resort to a range of recognized legal techniques, and that the result can be justified by reference to a series of argumentative reasons. However, they tend to recognize that their professional commitments and craft do not hold all the answers to life's moral mysteries and political challenges. In this regard, a modest and understated positivism has served the legal community well; it works as a jurisprudential fanfare for the ordinary lawyer.

Championed by Herbert Hart in his acclaimed mid-twentieth-century book *The Concept of Law*, this positivist project places analytical emphasis on rules, regularity, reasonableness, and common sense. As such, it offers itself as a theoretical reassurance to mainstream lawyers so that they can continue with their professional work without too many qualms about its legitimacy or efficacy in the grander scheme of things. None of this is surprising. Hart's avowed aim was to provide an essay in 'descriptive sociology' in that he sought to make more coherent and compelling sense of lawyers' daily routines; it was a commentary rather than an exposé.[1] While this scholarship has understandably garnered strong approval among lawyers, it has done little to convince formalist critics. Hart's ideas run out of steam at the very point that they are most needed – Hartian

[1] H.L.A. Hart, *The Concept of Law* vii (3rd ed. 1994). The editor of this third edition, Leslie Green, has described it as "the most influential book in legal philosophy ever written in English." Ibid. at xl.

positivism has little to say about the resolution of so-called hard cases where rules are unclear or where they clash. For them, Hart's response that judges have a discretion and responsibility to do the best that they can simply does not cut the jurisprudential mustard. When the crunch comes, the positivists' apparent humility belies both a certain anxiety about the firmness of the jurisprudential ground on which they claim to stand and a certain hubris about their privileged role in resolving some of the more profound issues on the social and political agenda.

In the Middle of the Road

From his positivist standpoint, Hart views law as a social fact that can be understood and analysed on its own terms as something different from morality, social values, economic logic, and the like. It is a central article of positivist faith that debate about *what law is* must be kept separate from debates about *what law ought to be*. This means that it is important that inquiries into the substantive merit of a legal rule be distinguished from those into its formal status as a legal rule. To ground his thesis, Hart understood that it was necessary to demonstrate that there is a certain 'thereness' to law so that its existence is not always reducible to someone's opinion or personal whim. Of course, the extent to which law is kept separate and apart from other social norms varies from one positivist's account to another's. Hart was very much of a softer variety in that he maintained that there are no necessary connections between law and morality; he did not take the harder line that there are necessarily no connections between law and morality.[2]

Within these positivistic parameters, Hart settled upon the idea that law is a functional and sophisticated system of rules. There are the obligation-imposing primary rules that comprise the bulk of substantive legal doctrine, like criminal and contract law. But there are also the authority-conferring secondary rules that distribute institutional power and jurisdiction, between legislatures and courts for example, over the creation and enforcement of those primary rules. Being a good lawyer, therefore, entails both a grasp of the extant rules and the skill to apply them in an appropriately professional manner; moral sensibility is to be encouraged, but is not essential to good lawyering. In so many ways, therefore, the Hartian positivists are arch-formalists as a result of their defining insistence that there is a brute factness to law that can

[2] For an inquiry into 'hard positivism' and its implications for legal interpretation, see infra, Chapter 7.

and must be observed: respect for the law's formal attributes trump concern with its substantive merits in the practicing lawyer's almanac.

Against this analytical backdrop, Hart went on to develop a reasoned and reasonable account of modern lawyers as rule-mongers. Because the law consisted largely of a body of settled rules, lawyers could go about their daily work by relying on those rules as a source of official guidance for themselves and their clients. While there might well be fuzzy edges or gaps in the law, lawyers could proceed confidently in the knowledge and understanding that their work can and should be done in a relatively detached and impersonal manner. The tools of the positivist lawyers' trade were designed to achieve descriptive accuracy as much as give rise to prescriptive appeal. Lawyers were primarily in the business of serving the law, not creating it. In particular, with a settled body of rules available, judges could go about their task safe in the knowledge that they were doing something different from their legislative colleagues. If policy was created by lawyers, it was an unavoidable consequence of their rule-focused activities.

Of course, without there being a critical mass of settled rules, the legitimacy of the lawyering craft would become suspect as the primary distinction between the law as-it-is and the law as-it-ought-to-be would be lost. Too much discretion or fuzziness would compromise the lawyers' claims to be acting in a positivist and professional manner. So, with characteristic even-handedness, Hart went about developing an account of legal reasoning that could inhabit a middle ground of justificatory rule-based reasoning. His goal was to situate it between the excesses of both an overly formalistic and anti-formalistic approach; he craved the best of both worlds and the worst of neither. For Hart, legal judgment was to be more than the exercise of personal choice, but less than a demonstration of scientific proof. As such, he continued the neo-formalist tradition of setting apart law as a normative world that largely, if not entirely, marched to the self-generated beat of its own normative drum. Of course, the effort to show that "discretion occupies an intermediate place between choices dictated by purely personal or momentary whim and those which are made to give effect to clear methods of reaching clear aims or to conform to rules whose application to the particular case is obvious" is hardly novel or enlightening in its own right.[3] But, because it fit both the formalist and positivist bill, Hart proceeded to colonize and map that place in a distinctive fashion.

[3] H.L.A. Hart, Discretion, 127 *Harv. L. Rev.* 652 at 658 (2013). This is a previously undiscovered and unpublished essay from 1958. For a critical and more general response

Hart gets started by explaining how the exercise of judicial discretion is an inevitable feature of any legal system: it cannot be done away with entirely. For him, there exists the double indeterminacy of facts and aims that makes discretion both a necessary and desirable evil. So, eschewing the effort to come up with some formulaic or algorithmic way to settle hard cases, he embraces the indeterminacy of language and introduces an all-important distinction between the core and penumbra of a rule. The core comprises those standard or settled instances "in which no doubts are felt about its application".[4] In contrast, the penumbral area of a rule houses those instances that make the application of the rule sufficiently contestable; its resolution will demand a certain exercise of evaluative judgment because the situation will "have some features in common with the standard case [but] will lack others or be accompanied by features not present in the standard case".[5] In other words, whereas the law will be certain and given in the core instances, it will be up for grabs and in need of clarification in the penumbra's fuzzy edges: "the hard core of settled meaning is law in some centrally important sense and . . . even if there are borderlines, there must first be lines".[6]

If the judicial task in easy cases (i.e., where the facts fall within the rule's core meaning) is straightforward, Hart did not mean to portray the resolution of hard cases (i.e., where the facts fall outside the rule's core meaning) as being entirely open-ended and discretionary. While he recognized that "the criterion which makes a decision sound in such cases is some concept of what the law ought to be" and that "in the penumbral situation judges must necessarily legislate", judges should be concerned with "adapting their decisions to the growing needs of society" by looking to the law's own "aims, purposes and policies". He cavilled at treating the extension of old rules to new cases as judicial legislation, because doing so failed to appreciate the obvious difference between a deliberate act of law-making and the incremental development of a rule so as to advance the rule's "continuing and identical purpose, hitherto less specifically apprehended".[7]

The upshot of all this is that, for Hart, the loss of complete certainty and predictability is the worthwhile price that has to be paid for the law

to the posthumous publication of this essay, see Allan Hutchinson, Chewing Cud: Revisiting Hart and Jurisprudence, 5 *Juris.* 29 (2014).

[4] H.L.A. Hart, Positivism and the Separation of Law and Morals, 71 *Harv. L. Rev.* 593 at 607 (1958).

[5] Ibid. [6] Ibid. at 614 [7] Ibid. at 608, 609, 609, 614, and 627.

being flexible enough to handle unanticipated cases in a fair and just manner. The challenge, therefore, is to strike an appropriate and manageable balance between the rule application of clear cases and the rule production of hard cases. Moreover, this must be done in such a way that systemic certainty is not sacrificed entirely to particularized flexibility. On this issue, Hart was adamant that, if clear cases do not comprise the bulk of adjudicated decisions, "we should not attach significance and value to them or think of such decisions as reached through a rational process".[8] For Hart, therefore, the existence of such clear cases was crucial not only to his account of lawyering, but also to the basic validity of his entire jurisprudence as a theory of law.

Accordingly, Hart's reliance on the core/penumbra distinction is intended to preserve the vital positivist quality of law as something that can be identified and utilized as a matter of fact rather than by resort to value-laden evaluation. Without this distinction (and the existence of a large body of settled rules), Hart's whole account begins to collapse in on itself. In short, unless Hart and his followers can defend his claim that his proposed rule application will work "smoothly . . . over the great mass of ordinary cases", he will have pulled the rug of his rule-based account of law out from under himself.[9] As I will show, that is exactly what he has done. Hart is unable to contain the radical implications of his defence of how the exercise of judicial discretion works. While he has made a strong case against the *arbitrary* or *capricious* exercise of choice, he has not made one against its political open-endedness. As is generally revealed by the discussion of 'no vehicles in the park', the judicial efforts in *Lachapelle* and *Perron* provide more grist for this particular mill.

Taking a Ride

In grappling with the interpretive challenges of 'no vehicles in the park', Hart ran through several permutations of possible facts and their likely judicial outcomes. He stated that "plainly this [rule] forbids an automobile, but what about bicycles, roller skates, toy automobiles?" Much of his time was devoted to explaining how we might apply the rule to "bicycles, roller skates, [and] toy automobiles" which are "uncontrolled by linguistic conventions." Yet Hart did little to defend his blunt conclusion that

[8] H.L.A. Hart, Problems of the Philosophy of Law in H.L.A. Hart, ed., *Essays in Jurisprudence and Philosophy* 108 (1983).
[9] Hart, *Concept*, supra, note 1 at 127–8.

the rule "plainly . . . forbids" "automobile[s]".[10] He simply asserted that automobiles are vehicles as a matter of fact; they are part of the core's meaning and comprise one of the rule's settled meanings. At bottom, his claim seemed to be that 'vehicle' simply does include automobiles and to deny that would be absurd or perverse. But what is this plain meaning? Where and how does it come by its plainness? And why should this plain meaning exert such authority over lawyers and others?

Throughout his considerable *oeuvre*, Hart was not clear about the deeper nature of these theoretical claims about 'automobiles' plainly being 'vehicles' or the philosophical status of what is meant by something being a matter of fact. Nevertheless, whatever his general stance on such issues, he was in something of an interpretive bind on the practical front. If he claimed that the use of 'vehicle' is always and plainly inclusive of 'automobiles', he would have run into the brute historical reality that 'vehicle' was a word long before automobiles were in existence; it presumably had some different core and settled meaning at that time. As such, it is simply nonsensical to claim that a word has a plain and core meaning outside of its immediate or pertinent historical context. However, if Hart conceded the relevance of history, he would have been confronted by the equally brute reality that words receive and change their meaning in light of the particular social conventions and linguistic customs in place; meanings (even 'core' ones) are not fixed, but shift and change with their informing social context.[11]

As such, it can be seen that the meaning of 'vehicle' or 'park' has little to do with the words themselves, but with the tentatively accepted and continually shifting routines and practices of meaning-giving in play. Legal interpretation is an organic and dynamic practice. In short, there is no Context of contexts to fix authoritatively a word's plain meaning at any particular point in time or place. There will always be simply more or less agreement about the proper context of any word and, therefore, its present plain meaning. Accordingly, the plainness of any meaning is the contextual result of prior agreement, not the fixed foundation for debate about the extent of that agreement. The meaning of 'vehicles' and 'park' will be open to change as the interests in play and the consequences of

[10] Hart, *Separation*, supra, note 4 at 607 and 611.

[11] Another interpretive manoeuvre put forward is to distinguish between "a former vehicle, or a quasi-vehicle, or even a vehicle-in-progress" and "a real vehicle". This seems even more far-fetched. See Frederick Schauer, A Critical Guide to Vehicles in the Park, 83 *N.Y.U.L. Rev.* 1109 at 1116–17 (2008).

one outcome over another slip and slide. What today is settled and 'plain' will tomorrow be unsettled and opaque. In such a world, the nature of what counts as a fact will itself be evolving and evanescent.

It takes little effort or imagination to illustrate this contingent and shifting relation between the core and penumbral meaning of 'vehicle' or 'park'.[12] At any particular time in any particular place for any particular purpose for any particular community, the delineation of their core and penumbra may accurately track the prevailing consensus or fracture as the consensus begins to fray at the edges. However, it is difficult to sustain and defend Hart's precise division as an enduring account of the meaning of 'vehicle' or 'park'. Even within a particularized context, there will be debate and disagreement over not only whether penumbral cases sufficiently resemble core instances to warrant inclusion as vehicles or parks, but also where the line between core and penumbra is to be drawn – does a motor car include a police car, ambulance, fire truck, or maintenance vehicle? Does a vehicle encompass a child's toy, a wheelchair, a child's stroller, a skateboard, a lawn mower, or a statue of a motor car? Does a park include an industrial park, a marine park, an amusement park, or a provincial/state park? Does it include a car park? And, of course, when the two questions are part of the same effort to apply the rule of 'no vehicles in the park', does one inquiry affect the other?

In the Canadian challenge of determining the meaning and application of 'public park' for the purposes of a section 161 prohibition order, a Hart-inspired judge would presumably first isolate the settled or plain meaning of 'public park' and then ascertain whether the facts of either *Lachapelle* or *Perron* did or did not fall within it. If they did, the case would be disposed of without more. If not, the judge would engage in a more creative, but still constrained exercise of legal reasoning that canvassed the possible purposes, aims, and policies of the statutory rule; the fact that involved a criminal rather administrative prohibition might be considered relevant. Having completed such an inquiry, a decision would, presumably, be reached by the judge that best reflected a reasonable balancing of those indicators. This is what the judges in *Lachapelle* and *Perron* claimed to do. Whether this approach meets the standards of a formalist decision is open to debate.

[12] Hart, *Concept*, supra, note 1 at 126. For an extended historical example about how the core and penumbra of words shift and reconfigure, see Allan C. Hutchinson, *All in the Game: A Non-Foundationalist Account of Law and Adjudication* 78–80 (2000).

In *Lachapelle*, Justice Butler saw the judge's task as being that of giving the words 'public park' "their ordinary meaning" and reading them "appropriately in context". In line with this approach (and without much apparent difficulty or reflection), he decided that a 'public park' was "an area that is set aside or designated as a park by some authority". Moreover, he went on to add that applying this "ordinary usage" would "normally be uncontroversial".[13] Similarly, in *Perron*, Justice Goudge accepted that his role was to ascertain the "grammatical and ordinary sense" of the words 'public park' (as well as harmonizing that sense "with the scheme of the Act, the object of the Act, and the intention of Parliament") and apply it to the facts at hand.[14] Nevertheless, although Justices Butler and Goudge found it easy to state their allotted task of building on and being constrained by the words' plain meaning, they found it much more difficult to follow through with the task in any uncontroversial or simple way – how do you locate the ordinary meaning? What if the plain meaning is itself contested? And what is so plain and ordinary about a word's plain and ordinary meaning?

Of course, the problem with this plain and Hart-sanctioned approach is that it seems to beg the whole question that it is intended to answer – it demands some way in which to identify a core instance from a penumbral problem that itself does not confound or implicate the positivist fact/value distinction that the core/penumbra distinction is intended to finesse or obviate. Indeed, in *Perron*, and to a lesser extent in *Lachapelle*, the exchange between the court and the accused's counsel was explicitly centred on determining the ordinary meaning of 'public park' "in its regular everyday use".[15] However, even though Justices Butler and Goudge were very similarly situated, they chose to employ a different criterion as to what characterized a 'park'. Whereas Justice Butler thought the plain meaning pivoted around its official designation, Justice Goudge preferred a definition that emphasized its usage. Such a sharp difference does not auger well for the identification of its 'plain meaning' in any plain or uncontroversial sense.

Much the same can be said about the courts' efforts to define 'vehicle' in *McBoyle*. Justice Holmes builds his whole judgment on the ground of "everyday speech" and "popular sense". Despite his assertion that "when a rule of conduct is laid down in words that evoke in the common mind only the picture of vehicles moving on

[13] *Lachapelle* [2008] B.C.J. No. 728 (S.C.) at paras. 31, 28, 28, and 26.
[14] *Perron* (2010), 97 O.R. (3d) 538 at para. 12. [15] Ibid. at para. 9.

land",[16] he offers no other explanation of why such 'popular' or 'common' meanings are to be ascertained and, more pertinently, why they should govern judicial decision-making. Moreover, reliance on such popular or common meanings begs the important questions of when and why such meanings should be set because its application would lead to an unjust or silly outcome. The common law is strewn with examples of this occurrence where exceptions are grafted onto rules and viewed as part of the rule itself.[17] Indeed, it is less that popular or common meanings rule, but that they do so as long as they lead in directions and to destinations that are consistent (or, at least, not inconsistent) with the judges' own personal and substantive intimations of justice. The mere fact that it takes an appellate court of professional experts to resolve debate over what counts as a word's popular or common meaning is ironic evidence enough that the search for meaning is more difficult and less straightforward than many pretend or propose.

As this short judicial excursus shows, if Hart's core/penumbra distinction does not have a certain built-in operational efficacy, it will be of little use to the judge or jurist. Put another way, unless there is a core meaning to 'core', the task of affixing plain meaning will be highly elusive. The judge will have no place from which to enter or break the circle of interpretive and evaluative choice; he or she will be engaged in a transparently boot-strapping argument. Consequently, like it or not, there is no plain and ordinary meaning that is plainly and ordinarily there and available for judicial use without there being some contestable act of discretionary choice; it is all penumbra, or, to put it another way, core and penumbra will themselves be interchangeable. Moreover, this elusiveness of 'plain meaning' spells big trouble for Hart's more ambitious theoretical claims about the nature of law. If there are only a few settled rules that lend themselves to easy application, then the formalist gambit (i.e., that law has a factual thereness independent of its moral or political reconstruction) will have failed; law will be an inescapable and inseparable mix of fact and value.

A Good Night's Sleep

Hart sought to avoid both the anti-formalist nightmare in which "judges always make and never find the law" and the formalist dream that

[16] *McBoyle v. United States*, 283 U.S. 25 at 27 (1931).

[17] Hart, supra, note 1 at 136.

"they never make it".[18] By so doing, he wanted to ensure that legal theory would abandon some of its more disturbing nocturnal imaginings, both reassuring and frightening, so that legal practice would be able to get on with its day job in a refreshed and undistracted way. As such, Hart's patented jurisprudential formula for a legal good night's sleep is prosaic and pragmatic – indeterminacy may be an inescapable feature of the exercising of judicial discretion, but it is always relative, marginal, and not to be exaggerated. Nevertheless, in taking this stance, Hart himself seems to be in a bit of daydream more than anything else. His proposed solution manages to have any persuasive force only for those who have already drunk the formalist Kool-Aid. Those who have not done so or are immune to its intoxicating charms remain suitably unimpressed and unpersuaded. Like common sense itself, the positivist reliance on plain meaning is unconvincing as meaning is never beyond disputation; it is a site for contestation, not a hedge or guarantee against it.

First, there is the problem of rule formation. When there is an applicable statute, as with section 161 of the *Criminal Code* in *Lachapelle* and *Perron* or section 3 of the National Motor Vehicle Theft Act in *McBoyle*, the identification of the pertinent rule can be uncontroversial. Even then, there may be competing rules or gaps in the statutory scheme; a statutory rule is never unencumbered. However, in a common law system, much of the law is embedded in the various decisions and precedents of the courts. Although there are "a vast number of determinate rules" and this exercise will be productive of "very little doubt", Hart concedes that "any honest description" will recognize considerable leeway for judicial involvement in identifying exactly what the rule is.[19] Consequently, even at this early stage of legal interpretation, indeterminacy is a characteristic feature of the adjudicative process – there is no one correct or authoritative method for determining the relevant precedent from among the many competing lines of cases, identifying the rule for which a particular precedent stands, isolating the precise verbal formulation of that rule, or enumerating possible exceptions to that rule. Indeed, this process of rule formation is often done with an eye on what this will mean for its

[18] See Hart, American Jurisprudence through English Eyes: The Nightmare and the Noble Dream, 11 *Geo. L. Rev.* 969 at 989 (1977).

[19] Hart, *Concept*, supra, note 1 at 131–2. It is worth emphasizing that Hart uses *rules* to encompass all the norms and standards that judges call in aid when determining the law and its application. For him, the difference between "all-or-nothing rules and non-conclusive principles . . . is a matter of degree." Ibid. at 262. See also Allan C. Hutchinson, *Evolution and the Common Law* (2005).

application toward an outcome in a particular case. Rule formation and rule application are never entirely separate activities.

Second, there is the problem of exactly what happens in the area of penumbral choice. Hart's advice was that this power to decide 'hard cases' is not to be performed in a vacuum or done in an arbitrary or ideological way. When legal rules fail or run out, judges are not somehow out on their own, but are subject to "a wide variety of individual and social interests, social and political aims, and standards of morality and justice" that are encompassed in the working norms of legal doctrine. Indeed, it is the development and refinement of these "criteria of relevance and closeness of resemblance ... [that] characterize whatever is specific or peculiar in legal reasoning." While there is no uniquely correct result, judicial choice is a rational and constrained process in which "many decisions can be clearly ruled out as incorrect"[20] and in which the failure to ensure real or idealized unanimity among judges is not fatal. It seems to follow, therefore, that while Hart contends that "a margin of uncertainty should be tolerated and indeed welcomed",[21] he is also confirming that, for the positivist claims to hold true, there must be a high degree of operational certainty. In this talk of 'peculiar reasoning', the ghost of Lord Coke seems to be in very close attendance.

Yet these concessions to the realities of exercising judicial discretion, along with the need for rule identification, manage to undermine the whole Hartian enterprise. Although there is much appeal to Hart's fanfare for the ordinary lawyer and his depiction of lawyering as a pragmatic craft, he glosses over more than he explains; he assumes too much that is itself in need of explanation. While it is true that the law is very much an exercise in professional argumentation, its available resources are so capacious and its crafted techniques are so adaptable that it can easily be made to justify a range of plausible and contradictory substantive results. This is nowhere more evident than in the operation of judicial discretion. Indeed, although his later and more established scholarship shifts from this emphasis, the early Hart of *Discretion* does tend to capture nicely much of law's irresistibly protean quality. He explains the exercise of discretion as a mode of justification in that judges "have to weigh and choose between competing interests".[22] Yet unless there is some agreed-upon or common set of social scales for such weighing (which Hart declares that there is not), this seems a very tall

[20] Ibid. at 107, 124, and 107–8. [21] Ibid. at 251–2.

[22] Hart, *Discretion*, supra, note 3 at 663.

order for the formalist. Rather than standing on solid ground, formalists will find themselves slipping and sliding on marshy terrain.

Despite Hart downplaying its significance, the weighing of competing interests is surely at the heart of political and ideological wrangling: the identification and balancing of such interests do not lend themselves to simple or uncontroversial performance. Indeed, it is in the 'weighing' and 'choosing' among 'competing interests' that law occurs as much as in the outcome of that measuring activity. As Hart framed it, in 'weighing' and 'choosing' between 'competing interests', there are "no clear principles or rules determining the relative importance of ... constituent values or, where they conflict, how compromise should be made between them".[23] Whether or not he subsequently subscribed to such a view, the Hart of *Discretion* hints at, even if he does not fully appreciate or pursue it, the critical insight that law is more an open-ended process than a closed one. As he goes on to observe, "arguments in favour of one decision or another may be rational without being conclusive".[24] Yet there is no special or distinctive rationality that law possesses. The exercise of discretion occupies that area of human judgment "where reasonable and honest men may differ" and where there are "no clear principles or rules determining how compromise should be made between [competing interests]".[25] This Hartian concession is corrosive of the ambitions and commitments of a formalist approach.

Put more directly, the factual thereness of law runs out at the very point when it is most required (i.e., when opinions differ and agreement runs out). Law is always in a deep state of becoming, not being, and legal interpretation is its cultivating medium. Although this elusive quality of law helps Hart and his positivist associates to accommodate and explain legal change, it does so at the considerable expense of revealing law as being little more than the stylized product of ideological preference. Hart seems to acknowledge this, but does not follow through on its more radical and anti-formalist implications. Even more pointedly, when this account of the resolution of hard cases by way of judicial discretion is combined with the instability of the core/penumbra division on which the distinction of hard and easy cases is based, the fragility and implausibility of a Hartian positivism as a cogent account of law and legal interpretation is exposed; this is especially so for judicial decision-making. In contrast to the received chorus of jurisprudential approval

[23] Ibid. at 660. [24] Ibid. at 665. [25] Ibid. at 664 and 660.

that it tends to receive, Hart's account of legal interpretation is more accurately understood as less of a fanfare for the ordinary lawyer and more of a lament.

Conclusion

Hart is truly worth commending for his efforts to stay true to Jeremy Bentham's commitment to "pluck the mask of Mystery from the face of Jurisprudence".[26] All his work is an instructive endeavor in such plucking: he offers a clear and accessible jurisprudential view of the legal process. But to the extent that he has been successful, he has managed only to pluck it away in order to replace it with his own lightly theorized veil of analytical common sense. In a manner of speaking, the main strength of Hartian positivism is also its greatest weakness – it offers very much a surface view; it fails to plumb the deeper and icier waters that flow strongly under the thin ice of conventional understandings and common sense. For all the continuing hoopla that surrounds Hart's *The Concept of Law* and the positivist tradition to which it gave rise, it leaves more questions unanswered than answered. It speaks to the already converted, not to the yet-to-be-persuaded unbeliever. The response to this perceived failing has been the diversification of jurisprudence into four different streams – a naturalist uprising (Chapter 4), a purposivist awakening, (Chapter 5), an incrementalist revival (Chapter 6) and a positivist retrenchment (Chapter 7).

[26] Jeremy Bentham, *A Comment on the Commentaries and a Fragment on Government* 410 (J.H. Burns and H.L.A. Hart eds. 1977).

4

Walking with Purpose

A Naturalist Turn

The main thrust of Hart's account of legal interpretation was that lawyers could get on with most of their professional business without worrying too much about perplexing moral or contested political issues. There would be difficult circumstances or 'hard cases' that might demand some limited incursion into such fraught territory, but these were relatively few and far between. Of course, Hart was not recommending that lawyers should be inured to the immorality of certain rules or political results. There was nothing in his positivist approach that prevented lawyers from working toward challenging and changing rules that were unjust in themselves or their application; he was a leading advocate for change in the law's substance.[1] But this was outside their strictly professional brief: lawyers can (and should) concern themselves with the law's morality, but that itself was a personal choice, not a professional inevitability. This bifurcated stance did not persuade everyone. Others took a very different view.

In many ways, Hart was distancing himself from a naturalist approach to law and legal interpretation that tied law's nature and substance to an entrenched set of moral directives. Stretching back to the Middle Ages and before, this often-theological commitment insisted not only that should law reflect and promote certain moral standards, but also that the very nature of law was bound up with this moral responsibility. At their most uncompromising, these naturalist scholars maintained that law was denied its status as law if it did not comply with or contain these moral values.[2] Although this particular jurisprudential tendency had been understated and under-represented in the first half of the twentieth century, it experienced a mid-century uprising. Jurists such as Lon Fuller and Ronald Dworkin began to resist positivism's minimalist claims and sought to reaffirm the importance and necessity of moral inquiry to lawyers and legal study. In positivist terms, the moral 'ought' was not

1 See, for example, H.L.A. Hart, *Law, Liberty, and Morality* (1963).
2 See John Finnis, *Natural Law and Natural Rights* (1980).

separate from law's 'is', but an essential part of it. Legal interpretation was inevitably and happily involved in the business of morality and politics.

A Fuller Account

The celebrated debate that took place between Herbert Hart and Lon Fuller at Harvard Law School on the occasion of Hart's Holmes Lectures in 1957 was about much more than legal interpretation. Still operating in the institutional shadow and moral stench of the Nazi era, the two antagonists were more heatedly engaged about the general relation between law and morality. In particular, they joined issue over whether a legal rule or body of rules might lose its designation and force as 'law' because its origins, format, or substance made it so morally offensive as to cease to be law and to obviate citizen's obedience to it. Fuller resisted Hart's positivist claims and maintained that law had its own inner morality that underpinned it and had to be respected. Moreover, for Fuller, it was not possible to do law without taking into account some moral norms. Although not a natural lawyer in the grand tradition, Fuller mounted a vigorous assault of what he believed was the ethical barrenness of positivist legal theorising.[3] He insisted that lawyers as lawyers simply were and must be involved in the morality of law.

Fuller was as clear, if as opposite as Hart in his jurisprudential ground zero – it is neither possible nor desirable to keep the domains of law and morality separate. For Fuller, any legal theory worth its intellectual and political salt must commit itself to ensuring that law and morality do not part company; the Nazi experience should be warning enough about the dangers of allowing such a schism. Notwithstanding that, most contemporary commentators tended to dismiss Fuller's naturalist position and declare Hart to be the winner in this defining positivism-versus-naturalism debate. Whatever the moral basis of Fuller's claim, it is seen to be simply unconvincing and untenable as an analytical account of law's status as law. As the history of racist and sexist laws show, bad law is no less law for its badness in form or substance. However, although still a minority tendency, Fuller's naturalist ideas have experienced something

[3] See Lon Fuller, *The Morality of Law* (1964). For a fascinating and more personalised contextual account of this debate, see Nicola Lacey, *A Life of H.L.A. Hart: The Nightmare and the Noble Dream* (2004).

of a revival with the fiftieth anniversary of the Harvard debate, at least as they relate to legal interpretation.[4]

In locking jurisprudential horns over the foundational issue of the law/morality divide, Hart and Fuller ventured into territory that brought into question the theoretical basis and practical dynamics of legal interpretation. In particular, they traced out the basic implications of their respective positivist and naturalist stances for the less fraught, but no less heated matters of interpretive method and adjudicative role in the modern democratic state. This involved a spirited exchange over how to go about determining the meaning and application of mundane rules. In particular, they joined issue over how to go about interpreting the rule that there are to be 'no vehicles in the park'. While the larger issues remained in the background, there was much about the spirited engagement over legal interpretation that addressed indirectly, but crucially, the efficacy and, therefore, validity of the law/morality separation. Fuller was much more successful and acclaimed for his part in this encounter over legal interpretation.

Fuller began his proposed demolition of Hart's approach to rule application with a reminder about how essential a straightforward account of 'plain meaning' is for Hart's positivist defence of law as being ascertainable as an as-it-is as opposed to an as-it-ought-to-be entity. He rejected Hart's claims about the interpretive 'thereness' of law and its meaning. Fuller believed that it was so much errant nonsense to pretend that "in applying the word to its 'standard instance', no creative role is assumed by the judge ... [and] he is simply applying the law 'as it is'".[5] For Fuller, it is not the case that the rule or its constituent words – 'vehicles', 'in', and 'park' – have a fixed meaning. Instead, it is simply the case that, in a particular context, any extant social agreement about what those words mean singly or collectively is sufficiently broad and accepted that no one is presently prepared to argue that the rule or words might carry a different meaning. In saying this, Fuller was not denying that words have meaning. Rather, he was contending that words do not underwrite agreed meanings. On the contrary, it is social agreements that fix and unfix the meaning attributed to words. As contexts shift and

[4] See, for example, *The Hart–Fuller Debate in the Twenty-First Century* (Paul Cane ed., 2010).

[5] Lon Fuller, Positivism and Fidelity to Law – A Reply to Professor Hart, 71 *Harv. L. Rev.* 630 at 662 (1958).

change across time, geography, and social communities, so the meaning given to words will itself shift and change. As Fuller put it:

> [i]f in some cases we seem to be able to apply the rule without asking what its purpose is, this is not because we can treat a directive arrangement as if it had no purpose. It is rather because, for example, whether the rule be intended to preserve quiet in the park, or to save carefree strollers from injury, we know, "without thinking", that a noisy automobile must be excluded.[6]

As Fuller rightly points out, it is this 'without thinking' that hides, rather than does away with, the deeper value commitments and choices in play. Fuller is insistent that there is no plain and ordinary meaning that is plainly and ordinarily there. Nor is such plain meaning available for judicial use without some contestable act of discretionary choice. While this act of discretionary choice might be invisible or unappreciated, it is no less real or significant by that fact alone. Moreover, so exposed, Hart is left in a considerable dilemma. He needs some solid ground to launch his positivist project. Without it, the judge will have no place from which to enter or break the circle of interpretive or evaluative choice; he or she will be engaged in a transparently boot-strapping argument. In short, Fuller contends that Hart's formalist gambit will have failed.

For Fuller, all meaning is context specific, and its fixing involves the attribution of purpose. In regard to 'no vehicles in the park', he took the stand that the legislator's intentions or policy aims not only worked to give meaning to the rule, but also placed limits on the meaning that could be attributed to it in future acts of rule application. As such, any legal interpreter is tasked with being "sufficiently capable of putting [themselves] in the position of those who drafted the rule to know what they thought 'ought to be' ... [and it] is in the light of this 'ought' that we must decide what the rule is".[7] However, this purposivist approach has more than its own fair share of problems. If what-the-law-is is always influenced by what-the-law-ought-to-be, how is it possible to complete the formalist project? In effect, Fuller called Hart's semantic bluff, but managed only to let the political cat out of the judicial bag. As I will now explain, there is no way of getting that particular unruly animal back in,

[6] Ibid. at 662–3.

[7] Ibid. at 666. Others who have more recently followed Fuller's purposivist lead include Stephen Breyer, Our Democratic Constitution, 77 *N.Y.U. L. Rev.* 245, 266 (2002), and Peter L. Strauss, The Courts and the Congress: Should Judges Disdain Political History?, 98 *Colum. L. Rev.* 242, 252–3 (1998).

once it is out. 'Purpose' turns out to be as elusive and as unreliable a constraint on judicial discretion as Hart's criticised 'plain meaning'. Ironically, Fuller's own formalist ambitions fall foul of the same anti-formalist criticism as those of Hart.

A Sense of Purpose

The short judgments in *Lachapelle* and *Perron* provide strong evidence of the wisdom of Fuller's stance toward Hart. The judgments confirm that there is no straightforward or incontestable way to distinguish a Hartian core from a penumbra. Despite the judges' declared reliance on the supposedly plain and ordinary meaning of 'public park', they had no way to establish that meaning in an exclusively factual as opposed to evaluative way; it was a mix-and-match process. For example, in *Perron*, Justice Goudge consulted the Canadian Oxford Dictionary; it offers eight definitions of 'park'. He concluded summarily that "six are of relevance . . . all are specified locations characterized by what goes on there . . . [and], for most of the six, it is some form of recreational activity".[8] It is unclear how Justice Goudge's conclusion explains the inclusion of 'industrial park' in his privileged list of six.

However, in *Lachapelle*, Justice Butler seems to have arrived at a different conclusion about the plain meaning of 'public park'; he emphasised designation over usage. In light of what Justice Goudge said in *Perron*, it is a stretch to conclude that "any member of the public"[9] would know that all "areas set aside for indolence and rest of the body and soul" – "Stanley Park, including the aquarium and the zoo area[,] . . . the endowment lands at the University of British Columbia[,] . . . the Sky Train greenbelt[,] . . . the marine parks in the province, waterfront parks [,] . . . and all beaches, lakes and rivers in Canada capable of being used by people for bathing"[10] – were included in the definition of 'public park'. As Fuller noted, the evaluative work is being done off-stage and "without thinking",[11] but it is still being done. As Fuller would have noted, Justice Butler bolsters his reliance on plain meaning by calling in aid "the intention of Parliament".[12]

[8] *Perron*, (2010), 97 O.R. (3d) 538 at para. 15.

[9] *Lachapelle*, [2008] B.C.J. No. 728 (S.C.) at para. 28.

[10] Ibid. at para. 27., Butler J. citing Maughan P.C.J. in *R. v. Graf* (1988), 42 C.R.R. 146 at para. 150 (B.C. Prov. Ct.).

[11] Fuller, supra, note 5 at 663.

[12] *Lachapelle*, supra, note 9 at para. 31.

So what does Fuller recommend? And is it any more plausible and persuasive than Hart's intervention? For Fuller, the best way to control meaning as well as respect the institutional role of judges in democratic societies is to seek the general purpose of the rule to be interpreted and applied. This involves inquiries into legislative intent, but it also extends to analysing the broader purposes of the rule-makers; legislators are assumed to be a group of reasonable politicians who act and enact in reasonable ways and for reasonable purposes – "what can this rule be for? What evil does it seek to avert? And what good is it intended to promote?"[13] While these are pertinent and helpful questions, they hardly seem capable of easy or uncontroversial answers. While Fuller is surely right to reject Hart's simplistic reliance on a core of plain meanings, his own confidence in purposive meaning seems misplaced. Indeed, the ground of 'imputed purpose' seems no more solid than 'plain meaning'.

As both a philosophical and practical matter, there is little to suggest that it is possible to identify a particular legislative intent or purpose that is capable of grounding and authorising statutory interpretation over time. As a practical matter, even if courts were correct in their assumption that an application of legislative intent would best fulfill their democratic mandate, it is difficult to know how it would be possible to locate such intent. The initial step of distinguishing intention from aspiration, expectation, and the like is probably insurmountable. There is no reason to assume that everything that legislators say is what they mean or intend. Further, the attempt to generate a finding of what a large group of legislators would have wanted over time, after circumstances have changed, and in unanticipated disputes, seems destined to be frustrated; the identification of past intentions or aims, particularly of collective entities, remains doggedly resistant to present or determinate interpretation.[14] Legislators rarely have a specific or exact intention in mind across a range of potential future disputes, so this prompts the most speculative of 'what if' investigations: if legislators had thought

[13] Ibid. at 665. See Henry M. Hart, Jr., and Albert M. Sacks, *The Legal Process: Basic Problems in the Making and Application of Law* (William N. Eskridge, Jr., and Philip P. Frickey eds., 1994).

[14] For an excellent account of the difficulty of determining the meaning of "no vehicles in the park" by reference to legislative intent, see Paul Brest, The Misconceived Quest for the Original Understanding, 60 *B.U.L. Rev.* 204 at 209–13 (1980). For a punishing critique of the mistaken turn toward intentionalism in statutory interpretation, see Neil Brooks, The Appropriate Role of Courts in Interpreting GST Legislation: Reflections on the Canadian Experience, 6 *Aust. G.S.T. J.* 1 at 7–11 (2006).

about or anticipated a problem (which they did not), how would they most likely have answered it?

If it is not naive to believe that legislatures are filled with reasonable politicians who are engaged in pursuing reasonable goals reasonably and candidly, it is most definitely wishful to think that they agree on what 'reasonable' means in general or specific settings. As both Justices Butler and Goudge's judgments in *Lachapelle* and *Perron* clearly show, the fixing of general intent over why certain convicted child-offenders might be banished from 'public parks' might be relatively easy (i.e., to protect children from pedophiles), but its application to specific situations is far from straightforward. Consequently, the idea that legislative intent or imputed purpose can act as a curb on judicial interpretive freedom is unconvincing; it simply replaces one problematic context with another. And if this is so of legislative intent or aims in the short term, it is doubly difficult after the elapse of several decades or more.

This criticism applies equally to judicial efforts to interpret 'vehicles'. In *McBoyle*, the judges' opinions make it hard to determine the difference between what the rule demands as an objective matter and what a particular judge thinks would be the best reading of it in terms of the substantive outcome. Mindful that all three judges concede that 'vehicle' can be legitimately interpreted to include both aircraft and boats as well as automobiles, their challenge is to isolate an interpretive strategy that enables them to claim that they are drawing their decisional conclusions from the rule, not the other way round. Although Justice Holmes insisted that judges should not 'speculate' about the policy or purpose behind the Act, the dissenting Judge Cotteral placed considerable weight on the fact that "the prevailing mischief sought to be corrected" by the Act was the theft of automobiles, not aircraft.[15] However, as Holmes noted, "the statute should not be extended to aircraft simply because it may seem to us that a similar policy applies, or upon speculation that, if the legislature had thought of it, very likely broader words would have been used".[16] Consequently, the search for the legislative purpose is far from determinative in fixing the meaning of any particular rule; not only is there often more than one purpose in play, but also, even if there is a single purpose, it may be read at different levels of generality (e.g., to penalize the theft of automobiles or all vehicles, including, but not limited to automobiles). Consequently, there is a circle of interpretation that is

[15] *McBoyle v. U.S.*, 43 F.2d 273 at 276 (1930).
[16] *McBoyle v. United States*, 283 U.S. 25 at 26–7 (1931).

hard to break or resolve by reference to some objective or given purposive reasoning: discretionary choice seems to be unavoidable.

For both Hart and Fuller, therefore, there is an insufficient acknowledgment of the corrosive effect of time and place on the effort to fix words with plain meaning. The shifting contexts of meaning-creation and meaning-application (and, of course, their bewildering combination across time) defy any uncontroversial judicial method of deciding cases that relieves judges of the considerable burden of choice. While the definition of 'public park' for section 161 purposes of the *Criminal Code* or of 'vehicle' for section 3 purposes of the National Motor Vehicle Theft Act may not be particularly weighty, it takes little imagination to see how the stakes can be quickly and sizably raised on more pressing and wide-ranging occasions. As Fuller himself noted, "the matter assumes a very different aspect, however, if our interest lies in the ideal of fidelity to law, for then it may become a matter of capital importance what position is assigned to the judiciary in the general frame of government".[17] If the territory of 'purpose' is soft and mushy in statutory contexts, how much more fickle is the search for solid ground in constitutional cases?

Importantly, however, Fuller was not subscribing to an anything-goes approach to the execution of judicial responsibility in applying rules. As Hart did in recommending how judges should cope with their role in penumbral areas, Fuller acknowledged that judges are not free everywhere and always to interpret rules or their purposes as they wish. He called attention to the law's "structural integrity" or "fabric of thought" that judges must strive to detect and follow in their interpretive exertions.[18] So disciplined, it is the task and responsibility of lawyers and judges to identify and work with the law's overall purposive enterprise "so that we may know truly what it is, but it is also something that we inevitably help to create as we strive (in accordance with our obligation of fidelity to law) to make the [law] a coherent, workable whole".[19] As such, the judge's duty to observe and respect a "fidelity to law not only permits but demands a creative role from the judge, but beyond that structure it does not permit him to go".[20]

Accordingly, the crucial difference between Hart and Fuller is that, whereas Hart treats such creative reasoning as exceptional and occasional, Fuller maintains that it goes to the very heart of the regular

[17] Fuller, supra, note 5 at 634. [18] Ibid. at 670 and 667. [19] Ibid. at 667.
[20] Ibid. at 670.

judicial task. And, of course, too much penumbra and too little core, let alone no core at all, would be fatal for Hart's positivist insistence on the analytical separation of law and morality. Yet without some agreement about the thrust and content of this 'structural integrity', Fuller is left in much the same place – the moral basis for law's integrity is insufficiently settled or specific to fulfill its controlling and disciplining function. However, Fuller's achievement was to get the naturalist ball rolling again; it was for others to push it further along. The most prominent jurist to work up these claims about law's integrity into a full-blown account of adjudicative interpretation is, of course, Ronald Dworkin. It is to his work that I now turn.

Looking for Integrity

Critics and defenders alike have retained Hartian positivism's central article of faith – namely, that rules are the basic currency of legal transactions and that their core meaning is sufficient to allow people to resolve most situations. Even the most anti-positivist of jurists seems to accept that there are frequent occasions on which the straightforward application of a rule will need little or no justification. However, although they concede that Hart was accurate in observing that rules were open-textured and that their application did not exhaust the judicial function, neo-naturalist jurists have contended that he failed to appreciate the extent to which the law consists of more than rules. Behind and within the rules is a political morality that should guide and constrain legal interpreters when the application of the rules is unclear or even undesirable. For the naturalist, therefore, the primary task of theorists and judges is to detect and cultivate the moral-political principles that breathe life into the dry bones of legal rules. While united in that task, neo-naturalists have differed over the nature and content of the principles and policies at work in the law. Whereas some have detected a 'wealth maximization' principle that animates legal doctrines, others have unearthed a more philosophical thread that emphasises 'corrective justice'.[21]

But it is the work of Ronald Dworkin that has captured the modern allegiance of most naturalist jurists and lawyers. Throughout his extensive body of work, he was a leading advocate for a moral reading of law.

21 See Richard Posner, *Law and Economics* (1983), and Ernest Weinrib, *The Idea of Private Law* (1995).

For him, such an approach was both inescapable and desirable; an account of what-law-is was inseparable from a debate about what-law-ought-to-be. Nevertheless, like Fuller (and unlike old-school naturalists), he did not insist that law's rules comply with some external standard or body of moral norms. Understood properly, law contained its own moral map and compass. However, in contrast to Fuller, Dworkin took the more expansive view that this moral component and practice represented a more substantive, not merely procedural set of moral commitments. As such, Dworkin presented an account of law and interpretation that was both naturalistic and formalistic – resort to the law enabled interpreters to offer both a just resolution of hard cases and one that was grounded in something other than their own untethered ideological preferences. He defended the position that "law . . . is deeply and thoroughly political, . . . [b]ut not a matter of personal or partisan politics".[22] In sweep and style, Dworkin continued within as he reworked the grand formalist tradition of Coke and Blackstone.

To ensure that there is no misunderstanding about his jurisprudential ambitions, Dworkin reminds critics and fellow-travellers alike that he remains fully committed to the idea that "justice plays a role in fixing what the law is". Moreover, he insisted that "moral considerations figure among the truth conditions of propositions of law" and that "a proposition of law is true if it flows from principles of personal and political morality that provide the best interpretation of the other propositions generally treated as true in contemporary legal practice".[23] Having confirmed his formalist credentials, he proceeds to elaborate what he thinks is involved in this distinctly moral and constructive interpretation of law. Whereas the positivists insist that there is a thereness or factness to law, Dworkin built on this and expanded that thereness to include law's moral facts. He maintains that the moral claims that he makes are not simply based on personal moral preferences on his part, but are predicated upon 'moral facts' whose status is as fixed and objective as the law's own social factness. For him, some moral positions are "plain wrong, not wrong only because people think it".[24] Accordingly, Dworkin insists not only that there is an indispensable moral dimension to law, but that

[22] Ronald Dworkin, *A Matter of Principle* 146 (1985).
[23] Ronald Dworkin, *Justices in Robes* 35, 5, and 14 (2006).
[24] Dworkin, Objectivity and Truth: You'd Better Believe It, 25 *Phil. & Public Affairs* 87 at 98 (1996).

such a dimension has a solid factual basis and can be included in "the brute facts of legal history".[25]

For Dworkin, judges are political actors whose power is limited by a legal system's history and liberal character; they must interpret the extant legal materials in their best light as a theory of political morality. The judge breathes political vitality into the lifeless words of legal texts by applying the twin tests of 'formal fit' and 'substantive justice'. Any interpretation must be able to demonstrate some plausible connection with society's legal history and advance its vision of social justice. While this task can be only provisionally and partially performed, the conscious striving for such a perfected theory is the hallmark of naturalist interpretation. For Dworkin, there are right answers to legal controversies, even if we disagree about what they are.[26] In pursuing and operationalising these ideas, Dworkin uses the instructional device of the chain novel. He recommends that judges and lawyers think of themselves as being part of an enterprise in which their task is to pick up where the last judge left off and develop the novel of the law along lines that not only continue the narrative thread, but also make it into the best novel that it can be. For Dworkin, the beauty of this is that it can help explain both continuity and change in the progress of the law as well as account for the different political, but constrained judgment of individual lawyers.

Elevating legal conversation to a privileged and principled form of democratic discourse, he casts the courts as the central constitutional institution through which the citizenry can debate, articulate, and implement its collective standards for social justice. Even rank-and-file lawyers are not left to their own devices because they must be instructed by and work in the service of the overarching "principle of integrity"; this is a "more dynamic and radical standard than it first seemed, because it encourages [lawyers] to be wide-ranging and imaginative in [their] search for coherence with fundamental principle".[27] In this way, Dworkin claims to have gone beyond the limitations and naivety of Hart's positivistic reliance on 'plain language'. In its place, he offers a value-drenched account of law and legal interpretation. This conjures up the possibility that lawyers will be able to fulfill their interpretive duties

[25] Ronald Dworkin, *Law's Empire* 255 (1986).
[26] Dworkin never abandoned the one-right-answer thesis, although he did modify it considerably. See Dworkin, supra, note 22 at 382, fn.1.
[27] Dworkin, supra, note 22 at 400 and 220.

in a way that it is both professional and political – the holy grail of formalist jurisprudence.

Accordingly, Dworkin has obliged and allowed most legal scholars to concede that law is about political-moral values as much as legal rules. He has expanded lawyers' horizons by insisting that, in resolving disputes, they concentrate not only on the rules in play, but also on the overall moral integrity of the law's body of rules at large. In short, he has made it purportedly safe for traditional scholars to talk about values and remain squarely with the formalist framework with which they are familiar. However, notwithstanding some of his more extravagant philosophical claims, Dworkin has been far from convincing in persuading both jurists and lawyers that the performance of the interpretive task can be both value infused and non-ideological. Despite his insistence to the contrary, law remains highly political in the sense that it inevitably amounts to the accumulated product of lawyers' values and ideological preferences; lawyers will interpret as they do because of, not in spite of, their personal values and political assumptions. As such, the law will remain "a body of practices observed and ideas received over time by a caste of lawyers" with all that this entails.[28] The fact that many lawyers share the same values does not mean that those values are any less ideological in source or partiality.

Lost in the Park

So, confronted with a rule like 'no vehicles in the park', what would a Dworkinian approach (or Dworkin's imaginary judicial alter ego, Hercules) recommend? The first thing to establish would be whether this was the kind of rule that "applies itself."[29] However, this is no small or easy matter. Apart from falling into all the traps that ensnared Hart's positivist reliance on 'plain meaning', it manages to back Dworkin into a very tight corner from which there seems little escape. Presumably, a rule might well have a reasonably settled or simple meaning, but its application to particular facts might lead to injustice. For example, an ambulance is a vehicle, but its prohibition from the park might well be considered undesirable and counterproductive in many instances. This means that even rules that 'apply themselves' might well demand a more

[28] A.W.B. Simpson, The Common Law and Legal Theory in *Legal Theory and Common Law* 20 (W. Twining ed. 1986).

[29] Dworkin, supra, note 22 at 353 and 351.

elaborate and principled resolution. In effect, every easy or straightforward application of a rule would dispense with a case only where its outcome was just or fair; the rule would not be 'applying itself'.

For example, although it might be that a car is thought to be obviously a 'vehicle', it does not follow that this is an 'easy case' in the sense of the rule 'applying itself'. Treating the plain meaning of vehicle as including a car results from the fact that, so doing, does not lead to an unjust result. If it did, then it would be a hard case in which the rule does not 'apply itself'. Similarly, although it might be that a public recreational space might be thought of as being within the core meaning of 'park', its apparently plain meaning would 'apply itself' only if it gave rise to a result in the particular case that was suitably just or, at least, not unjust. Consequently, the plain meaning of rules is not so plain at all. Nor is it dispositive of the case at hand. Plainness of meaning is the end result of a deeper and more involved, if implicit, inquiry; it is not the initial and inquiry-dispensing premise for a case's resolution.

The upshot of this insight is that Dworkin must treat all cases as 'hard cases'. However, if he does so, not only will his claim that some rules manage to 'apply themselves' be scuttled, but also his whole account of law will be in grave peril. Without some set of fixed and apply-by-themselves rules, his principled and coherentist approach to hard cases will have nothing substantial on which to work; the demand for system-wide 'integrity' will be empty and unattainable. If all cases are potentially hard cases and, therefore, in need of principled resolution, there will no longer be a set of 'brute facts' from which to generate the set or scheme of moral principles that underpin the law and inform the resolution of particular cases. The brute facts of history either will be missing in action or, more likely, will simply turn out to be a function of the deciding lawyer's own moral commitments or ideological preferences.

There is also another general problem with Dworkin's formalist exposition. In a characteristically naturalist gambit, he insists that legal doctrine contains an implicit structure or latent ideal whose incomplete development is to be brought to institutional consciousness. However, in a hallmark move, he then proceeds to put that ideal to work as the basis for criticizing and reforming the recalcitrant portions of legal practice. The challenge here is to ensure that the balance between the ideal-oriented doctrine and its anomalous segments is maintained. Once the latter begins to compete with the former as a matter of descriptive accounting, Dworkin's claims to be discovering the law's order rather than creating it will be confounded; it will begin to become obvious that Dworkin's own normative ideals are driving the whole process of formalist explanation. Moreover, what began as a reassuring promise of incremental reform will be compromised by the opportunistic threat of wholesale transformation. In this fragile exercise of naturalist jurisprudence, "deviations and contradictions become intellectual and political threats rather than intellectual and political opportunities".[30] Accordingly, the naturalists are obliged by their own lights to tread an impossibly thin line between a valid practice of internal illumination and an invalid exercise in external projection.

Such a treading is fraught with all kind of obstacles and blockades. Contrary to what most naturalists insist, any reasonable inquiry into law's deep structure and plot will have to concede that many competing and often contradictory rivals for moral priority will present themselves. Indeed, it is difficult to see how an internal-to-law and objective evaluation can be made that will give controlling pride of place to one scheme over another. The resources and materials of law are so voluminous and so variable (as well as being generated over a long stretch of time by a large cast of judicial actors) that legal inquirers tend to see and prioritize what they want to see and prioritize. Dworkin's account of law-as-integrity is particularly susceptible to such a challenge. While there is an ample threshold of doctrinal support for his own brand of enlightened liberalism, there is also much doctrinal material that can be easily justified by reference to a more conservative (or even radical) philosophy than Dworkin's own ideological preferences.

Dworkin's response to these dilemmas is both unpersuasive and telling. It seems excessively audacious to assert, as he does, that "we have no difficulty in identifying collectively the practices that count as legal practices in our own culture" and that they are "treated as given in day-to-day reflection and argument". As an empirical matter, this sounds unconvincing. As I have argued, the appearance of easiness or plainness is a result of not the rules being settled but the social agreements behind them. Indeed, Dworkin seems to confound himself when he concludes that "law cannot flourish as an interpretive enterprise in any community unless there is enough initial agreement about what practices are legal practices so that lawyers argue about the best interpretation of roughly the same data".[31] That might well be, but this means that Dworkin will

[30] R. Unger, *What Should Legal Analysis Become?* 40 (1996).
[31] Dworkin, supra, note 22 at 91, 66, and 90.

have little to say on those occasions when a viable theory of legal interpretation is most needed – those occasions (or 'hard cases') where the initial agreement begins to facture, where 'the brute facts of history' are less brutish, and where the 'data' become unsettled. And, as I have argued, this is the situation in all cases because rules can never 'apply themselves'; they are in need of principled or, as I prefer to call it, ideological resolution.

Mindful that Dworkin has been developing and refining a moral theory in tandem with his legal theory, there exists a very suspicious relationship between the two. In particular, it strains credulity for him to arrive always at the same conclusion that the 'best justification' of the law as-it-is is almost perfectly congruent with his own moral account of the law as-it-should-be. Time after time, Dworkin's assessment of whether any important legal decision is defensible or not is measured entirely by its conformity with what he maintains is the substantively best decision according to his own preferred moral theory or ideological stance. This congruence is simply too politically convenient to be theoretically convincing. Whether the subject is abortion or school segregation, Dworkin's best reading of the American Constitution always turns out to be the one that reflects and favors his own moral theory.[32] Accordingly, even though Dworkin maintains that "anyone who accepts law as integrity must accept that the actual political history of his community will sometimes check his other political convictions in his overall interpretive judgment",[33] this 'sometimes' never seems to happen when it comes to Dworkin's own critique of law or 'political convictions'. This troubling state of affairs casts considerable doubt on the capacity of Dworkin's naturalist account to achieve its primary formalist ambition – to allow lawyers to be political but non-ideological.

In proposing his moral reading of the law, Dworkin's gamble is not only that judges will be capable of utilising the appropriate philosophical method, but that they will get it right in the sense of settling upon a 'best justification' of the law's facts that takes the law in a more, not less just direction (at least according to Dworkin's own set of moral commitments). In some circumstances, what amounts to the 'best justification' will be elusive. For example, in *Lachapelle* and *Perron*,[34] any number of outcomes might fit the bill; there is no one principle of criminological

[32] See, for example, Ronald Dworkin, *Freedom's Law* (1996).
[33] Dworkin, supra, note 22 at 255. [34] Supra, notes 8 and 9.

commitment (e.g., rehabilitation, retribution, and deterrence) that can claim structural priority in interpreting the relevant section of the *Criminal Code* and its surrounding jurisprudence. It is a long stretch to maintain, as Dworkin does, that there is one right answer and that that answer is the one that best lines up with his own preferred view. Different judges might reach entirely opposite, but legitimate conclusions in relying on Dworkin's proposed methodology. The same applies to 'no vehicles in the park'. Again, there are different candidates for principled recourse (e.g., lower noise levels, less air pollution, and less traffic) that might equally assert authoritative pull.

Yet, setting aside any theoretical concerns, the historical record of courts is far from encouraging; 'the brute facts of legal history' are not so reassuring. For example, even a cursory glimpse at the historical sweep of American or Canadian constitutional law strongly suggests that the political performance of the courts has been mixed at best. It seems indulgent on Dworkin's part to point out that the 'bad' decisions were also legally invalid. Even if they were, Dworkin's own method suggests that a good-faith interpreter would be obliged over time to incorporate those bad decisions into any coherentist or integrity-based development of the law. This would result in the deep morality of the law taking on a different substance as the 'deviations' and 'contradictions' eclipsed the earlier order, integrity, and substantive thrust of the law. In this sense, Dworkin has hitched his wagon to governing ideas (i.e., integrity and coherence) that can equally deliver not only differing decisions, but also just and unjust ones. And, as legal history shows, it frequently does. Despite his formalist ambitions, Dworkin has provided more grist for the anti-formalist and informalist mill.

Conclusion

The challenge for these naturalist jurists, like Fuller and Dworkin, was twofold: to integrate a moral dimension into legal interpretation, but still keep faith with the demands of the formalist tradition, and to demonstrate that law's moral dimension was not simply a slightly detached distillation of their own moral commitments. Their success in this endeavor has been decidedly mixed. They have managed to put moral inquiry and reflection back on the jurisprudential agenda: it is difficult to dispute that legal interpretation involves and implicates moral and political values. However, they have been taken to task for their failure to explain this phenomenon in a way that satisfies those jurists of a more formalist persuasion. They have let the political cat out of the legal bag, but they have not been able to contain or tether it in a convincing or disciplined manner. Yet the naturalist revival has been sufficiently effective that it has obliged positivists and others to rethink the validity and worth of their own efforts. It is to three of those interventions – originalism (Chapter 5), incrementalism (Chapter 6) and hard positivism (Chapter 7) – that I now turn.

5

Back to the Future

An Originalist Gambit

The urgent need for a reliable and effective method of interpretation is palpable among contemporary judges. Without one, it is thought that they will be unable to claim any special authority or force for their legal decisions; they will be revealed as merely applying their own ideological preferences under the cover of some transparent jurisprudential device. Of course, what that professional method is and, as important, whether *any* approach is up to the task asked of it is a matter of heated academic dispute; it is at the centre of this book's analytical challenge. However, in recent years, one method in particular has stepped forward and garnered a serious amount of judicial and professional support: originalism. It has become the *théorie du jour*. In response to the growing chorus of complaints about naturalism and positivism, this mode of formalism seeks to regain the objective ground and redeem the formalist project. Although it is most often associated with constitutional law and interpretation, it also claims to be the best and only method that can confer legitimacy on the judicial process. So successful has it been that American judges and jurists at least are almost required to explain and defend their approach to decision-making in terms of their allegiance or animosity to originalism; this is no small achievement.[1]

While it has managed to make the tension within interpretive debate more focussed, the rise of originalism has also raised the argumentative temperature without generating any real jurisprudential progress. It is in many ways, for good and bad, an amalgam of positivist and naturalist ideas. By claiming to work with found meanings and settled purposes, it represents itself as the true heir to the formalist tradition. Again, at the heart of this contretemps is the fundamental disagreement over whether the best forms of originalism are genuine and defensible modes of legal interpretation or whether they are simply political ideologies masquerading as methods of legal interpretation. Not surprisingly, I want to argue

[1] For an excellent survey of the rich and varied theories on offer, see Thomas E. Baker, Constitutional Theory in a Nutshell, 13 *Wm. & Mary Bill Rts. J.* 57 (2004).

that, as with all other modes of formalistic theorizing, the originalists' sin is to preach legal theory but to practice political ideology; it functions as a cover for, not a substitute for ideological decision-making. However, I also want to show that, although originalism (like any other kind of interpretive proposal) is never entirely innocent of political affiliation, the precise cut of that political orientation will vary with the changing historical context of its deployment.

Let's Get Originalist

When it comes to interpretation, constitutional law and adjudication are where the theoretical rubber hits the concrete road. Because the jurisprudential stakes are so high (i.e., unelected bureaucrats set aside the legislated policies of elected representatives or invalidate the actions of the executive branch of government), there is the felt and urgent judicial need to adopt some method or technique that will enable them to maintain a genuine distinction between their own views and those of the law or the Constitution itself. In recommending what judges should and should not be doing, jurists might be forgiven for simply putting out there their vision of what the Constitution should mean as a matter of political morality. The text, be it constitutional or statutory, is considered to be neither unimportant nor determinative in its authority. More tacitly accepted than openly proclaimed, the idea was that the Constitution is a site for reasoned and considered debate about what the political direction and moral commitments of society are to be. Of course, the difficulty with this idea of a living or organic Constitution was that not only did it threaten to expose the democratic (il)legitimacy of constitutional adjudication, but it gave jurists no special or privileged authority as jurists; they were simply cast as another cadre of ideological warriors, albeit outfitted in respectable garb and speaking in measured tones.

Some jurists decided that this was no way to proceed: it devalued their academic standing as much as it failed to win the constitutional war. The perceived path forward was first to resist the received wisdom that the Constitution was not a stable set of political commitments, but a site for political debate about the kind of society Americans wanted. Having accomplished that, they would insist that it was possible and desirable to establish a mode of interpreting that set of constitutional provisions that could claim a theoretical authority. This method would be validated not simply by the extent of prevailing ideological support for its substantive recommendations, but by its validity and virtue as 'theory'. And this is exactly what the originalists have sought to do over the past few decades. Rather than simply put forward a proposal for what would be the most appealing and just way to think about the Constitution, the originalists offer a full-blown theory of constitutional interpretation. They seek to claim the high ground of truth and objectivity in the struggle to capture the lower turf of constitutional politics.

The justification for this approach is largely obvious and initially attractive. Their key move is, of course, to claim that originalism is not "a political ideology, [but] . . . a constitutional theory".[2] They work on the assumption that, if you can convince people that your recommended way of proceeding is a theory, then your approach will be seen to trump all competing initiatives, especially the 'living Constitution' one, as a matter of practical fact and theoretical authority. 'Theory' (or, at least, a successful one) is seen as something that is unsullied by politics or partiality; it gains its political traction from the fact that it offers an accurate, objective, detached, and reliable account of a particular phenomenon. By shifting the debate to the theoretical plane, the originalists can claim to be speaking in the authoritative accent of truth and impartiality, not in the debased argot of ideological and partisan engagement. As such, originalism is presented as a quasi-scientific approach that transcends or, at least, distances itself from run-of-the-mill constitutional politics. Viewed in this light, originalism is a concerted effort to make good on the formalist mission.

Like most theoretical affiliates, the originalists are a rag-tag bunch. They spend as much time in-fighting as they do in a focused confrontation with their non-originalist or organicist opponents. However, their unifying credo is the belief that the Constitution did have a meaning when it was introduced and that such a meaning should still govern judicial review today. But that is where the consensus ends.[3] Originalists are seriously and heatedly divided about how to go about fixing what that meaning is and what to do about the plethora of competing precedents (and amendments) that have developed since the Constitution's enactment.

[2] Robert W. Bennett and Lawrence B. Solum, *Constitutional Originalism: A Debate* 65 (2011).

[3] See Dennis J. Goldford, *The American Constitution and the Debate over Originalism* (2005); *Originalism: A Quarter-Century of Debate* (Steven G. Calabresi ed., 2007); and Johnathan O'Neill, *Originalism in American Law and Politics: A Constitutional History* (2005). For a helpful typology of originalism, see Mitchell N. Berman, Originalism Is Bunk, 84 *N.Y.U. L. Rev.* 1 (2009).

There are many varieties of originalism, but most originalist-oriented theories can be divided into two broad categories: those more traditional approaches that seek the original intention behind the Constitution and those more recent interventions that attempt to determine the original public understanding of the Constitution's text. Whereas the former looks to the intentions of the Constitution's Founding Fathers in giving some substantive and practical bite to the text's sweeping and abstract declarations, the latter choose to place its interpretive money not on what the Founders intended but on what those declarations were understood to mean in that society at that time. As an originalist approach has begun to find broader favor in recent decades, it is the newer mode of this interpretive strategy that has begun to claim pre-eminence among originalist fellow-travellers.[4]

Eschewing the effort to identify and substantiate the elusive intentions of the Constitution's drafters, these neo-originalists put their energies and faith in what they consider to be a more achievable goal – "what I look for in the Constitution is precisely what I look for in a statute: the original meaning of the text, not what the original draftsmen intended".[5] As summarized by one of its more sophisticated exponents, this originalist commitment is built upon four inter-related precepts:

(1) that each provision of the Constitution has a fixed meaning
(2) that the task is to unearth the original public meaning of each provision to be retrieved
(3) that such an original public meaning has the force of law
(4) that there is a vital distinction between constitutional interpretation and constitutional construction[6]

The basic claim is that such neo-originalism possesses the necessary objectivity and stability that can offer a solid and dependable theoretical foundation on which to base a viable practice of constitutional adjudication in a democracy with a written constitution. In line with this, it is argued that, when judges do depart from the original meaning of the Constitution, they are acting improperly by working against the formalist

[4] Leading neo-originalists include Gary Lawson, On Reading Recipes . . . and Constitutions, *85 Geo. L.J.* 1823 (1997), and Michael Paulsen, How to Interpret the Constitution (and How Not To), 115 *Yale L.J.* 2037 (2006). Older intention-based originalists include Robert Bork, *The Tempting of America* (1990), and Raul Berger, *Government by Judiciary* (1977).
[5] A. Scalia, *A Matter of Interpretation* 38 (1998).
[6] Bennett and Solum, supra, note 2 at 64–5.

constraints of constitutional law. The role of judges is to apply the Constitution. If people do not like the results of that, then the neo-originalist solution is clear – it is not for judges to remedy the situation by ever-more-creative interpretations but for politicians to amend the Constitution. In the statutory context, this is exactly what Justice Holmes sought to do in *McBoyle* with his reliance on "popular" and "everyday speech" at the time of the statute's enactment in order to resolve the meaning of 'vehicle'.[7]

Accordingly, the Constitution's original meaning is posited to work as both a solid basis for decision-making and as a realistic hedge against ideological unruliness. However, at their more modest and less dogmatic, neo-originalists do not recommend that this entails a formulaic or rote application of the Constitution's 'original public meaning' to contemporary issues. If the original meaning is clear, it will apply directly to the resolution of controversies before today's courts; if it is not, then it will be necessary to ascertain what the text would mean at the time of its adoption in regard to such contested issues. In such matters, a crucial distinction is made between interpretation (i.e., fixing a constitutional provision's public meaning) and construction (i.e., applying that interpretation to the facts at hand). Originalists insist that judges and lawyers should be able to agree on the broad limits of the interpretively defined construction space. However, with echoes of Hart's core/penumbra strategy, it is conceded that there will be room for variation and disagreement within it.[8]

In its relatively short life, neo-originalism has begun to hold considerable sway over both the bench and academe. This is no mean feat. But its success has as much to do with its ideological appeal as its intellectual validity. There are two main and general objections to the new originalism that seem particularly devastating. The first is that it is an open question whether it is possible to make reliance on it operational in a practical and sufficiently precise sense. The second is that, even if that question could be answered convincingly, neo-originalism has not made a sufficient case in support of its foundational claim to offer the kind of legitimating justification for relying on the Constitution's public meaning that is craved by the formalists themselves. As I will demonstrate,

[7] *McBoyle v. United States*, 283 U.S. 25 at 26 (1931). Some originalists claim Holmes to be one of their own. See Antonin Scalia and Bryan Garner, *Reading Law: The Interpreation of Legal Texts* 200 (2012).

[8] Supra, Chapter 3, and Bennett and Solum, supra, note 2 at 26.

despite the ingenuity and doggedness of its adherents, originalism fails on both counts. Confirming that two wrongs do not make a right, the originalists manage to combine the failings of both Hartian positivism and Fullerian naturalism as well as add a few of their own for good measure.[9]

Shoveling Smoke

The irrepressible jurist Oliver Wendel Holmes, Jr. would have had the number of the originalists. In their efforts to bring their abstract originalist commitments down to earth, they are confirmation that "lawyers spend their professional careers shoveling smoke".[10] Despite their claims to offer a viable escape from the tendency for judges (and jurists) to turn constitutional interpretation into a vehicle for ideological advocacy, the neo-originalists hide more than they reveal; there is a whiff of the mystical and mysterious about their craft. Ironically, this group includes Holmes himself in his judicial role in *McBoyle*. They struggle to demonstrate how the pivotal task of locating the public meaning of constitutional provisions at their enactment can be completed without committing what they consider to be the same and unruly ideological error. In short, they cannot reach the higher non-ideological ground that they need to reach if they are to succeed in their formalist mission. Once all the rhetorical smoke and 'good' intentions are set aside, it is ideology almost all the way up and down.

Although the originalists claim to take history seriously, they play fast and loose with historical materials to suit their own purposes. As such, originalism is not only 'history light', but bad history. The vaunted neo-originalist shift from focusing on the Founders' intentions to the constitutional provisions' original public meaning changes only the venue, not the enormity of the task. As one critic nicely frames it, originalism is more akin to divination than interpretation because of its reliance on "materials almost as enigmatic as the dreams Joseph was called upon to interpret for Pharaoh".[11] Contrary to what the originalists suppose, the

[9] See supra, Chapters 3 and 4.

[10] Holmes, attributed in Edward Knappman, *Watergate and the White House*, vols. 1–2, 100 (1973).

[11] See Bennett and Solum, supra, note 2 at 125 (quoting *Youngstown Sheet & Tube Co. v. Sawyer*, 343 U.S. 579, 634 per Jackson J. (1952)). The classic critique of originalism remains Paul Brest, The Misconceived Quest for the Original Understanding, 60 *B.U. L. Rev.* 204 (1980).

world, past and present, is not as black and white as they would wish or need it to be; there is simply too much semantic and normative indeterminacy to underwrite the degree of certainty and clarity that the originalist project demands and asserts. While it might be possible to make a little headway on establishing some generalities about the eighteenth-century meaning of some words and phrases, all lawyers know that the hermeneutical devil is very much in the contextual details.

Historians disagree about a great deal, but there is considerable disciplinary agreement that the search for one unified and reliable meaning in the American Constitution's provisions is a sleeveless errand. Historians are not merely cataloguers who assign facts their proper place in the grander scheme of artifactual things as if by rote. Theirs is a more active role because there is a continuing interaction between both historians and the facts they generate and between the present and the past. Of course, events occur at different times and places and their basic reporting can be right or wrong, but determining their larger significance and meaning is a much more ambitious and fluid affair. At their more provocative, historiographers suggest that there is a moral and political dimension to history-writing that can be fudged and hidden, but never completely done away with. Reality is not the unadorned certainty that most people imagine or crave: "the facts speak only when the historian calls on them: it is he who decides to which facts to give the floor, and in what order or context". Put simply, there is no that's-the-way-it-is; the historical story shifts in significance and meaning as "the angle of vision" changes.[12] Historical truth is a slippery bar of soap that cannot, even if grasped, wash away the moral ambivalence that cakes lived history. The interpreter and that to be interpreted are neither separate nor collapsible into each other. Being in a dialectical and contextual relationship, there is no one Context of contexts to stabilize or give exclusive validation to any particular interpretation.

These caveats and admonitions are especially pertinent to efforts to interpret sweeping and generally phrased documents such as the American Constitution. However, it also applies to relatively modest instances of statutory interpretation as in *McBoyle*. While the historical distance between the Act's enactment in 1919 and its interpretation in 1931 is short (although the incidence of aircraft theft might well have increased substantially in those intervening years), there is no attempt by

[12] E.H. Carr, *What Is History?* 11 and 86 (1961).

Holmes to go back: his efforts to locate the "ordinary" or "everyday" meaning of 'vehicle' is intuitive and immediate. Indeed, it is something of a question-begging argument. Holmes offers no arguments or justifications for his restriction of the statutory meaning of 'motor vehicle' to automobiles. Indeed, in so doing, he makes no sustained attempt to counter Judge Phillips's claim that "both the derivation and the definition of the word 'vehicle' indicate that it is sufficiently broad to include any means or device by which persons or things are carried or transported, and it is not limited to instrumentalities used for travelling on land".[13] It is more about assertion and assumption, not analysis and persuasion. Although there is good reason to define 'vehicle' in the Act as being limited to automobiles, that is as much about it chiming with Holmes and Phillips's different sense of substantive justice (i.e., should an aircraft thief be treated the same as a car thief?) than anything else.

While the neo-originalists make some valiant efforts at this 'hiding' exercise, they are unable to contain the ideological infiltration that occurs throughout the interpretive enterprise. Like most founding processes and documents, the American Constitution was born of political compromise; politicians and citizens were as divided, albeit in different ways, about the appropriate resolution of contested political issues as not only later generations, but also today's generation. This political and substantive ambivalence runs throughout the constitutional text; the resulting compromises animate the continuing efforts to interpret it. Indeed, in an ironic twist, there is ample historical evidence to conclude that the Founders – neither democratic demigods nor elitist demons – would have been much more comfortable with a non-originalist and dynamic approach to the interpretation and application of the Constitution than an originalist one.[14]

Falling Short

Throughout history, therefore, originalism has promised much, but delivered both too little and too much. The fact that there has been a failure to pin down a needed stable meaning to ground the interpretive enterprise (too little) has also meant that there has been a range of equally plausible, but conflicting meanings on offer (too much). While

[13] *McBoyle v. U.S.*, 43 F.2d 273 at 274 (1930).

[14] Gordon S. Wood, *The Idea of America: Reflections on the Birth of the United States* (2011).

this diversity and range of possible interpretations is a challenge for all would-be formalist interpreters, it is especially debilitating for originalists. If originalism is to make its theoretical case, it must be able to identify a certain and broad consensus on what the 'original meaning' is. Without that, the idea of an independent and detached constraint on judges' own ideological leanings would be rendered fanciful. So, although neo-originalists place their faith in a historical reading of the Constitution, it is history itself that lets them down; there is no reading that can transcend the context of both the text's enactment and its future reading. Ironically, the originalist is a certain kind of organicist in methodological clothing.

Furthermore, the historical record on the influence of originalism on the work of the courts is far from reassuring for its supporters. As times change and challenges vary, judges have made only selective and opportunistic resort to originalism. When they have done so, there is a tendency for it to be put to ideological ends and uses; it has been deployed as a convenient and pseudo-validating support for judges' own ideological preferences rather than a check upon them.[15] It is noticeable that in neither *Lachapelle* nor *Perron* did the judges engage in such an attempted retrieval in their efforts to give meaning to 'public park'.[16] Moreover, if they had done so, it is difficult to imagine that any confusion or indeterminacy could have been dispelled by so doing. The public meaning of 'park' in the 1990s, even if different, was no less clear or suggestive twenty years later. However, it is more instructive to look at two recent constitutional examples that give practical substance to these general criticisms. Taken together, these two decisions show that originalist interpretation hides as much as it reveals.

In the Supreme Court's recent Second Amendment decision in *District of Columbia v. Heller*, the majority and the principal dissent drew upon the supposed interpretive authority of originalism. In the 1870s, the courts, politicians, and citizens all conceded that the Second Amendment protects an individual right against government encroachment on carrying firearms, but they could not agree on the extent of that right or the scope of government regulation. The only thing that has changed today over two centuries later is that the nature of that disagreement has shifted. There is still no consensus on the meaning of the Second Amendment; the relevant actors all disagree, but along slightly different

15 See Frank Cross, *The Failed Promise of Originalism* (2013).
16 [2008] B.C.J. No. 728 (S.C.) and (2010), 97 O.R. (3d) 538.

lines. In reaching diametrically different views of the original public meaning of "the right of the people to keep and bear arms," Justices Antonin Scalia and John Paul Stevens each offered a rigorous examination of the constitutional text and its public context.[17] Both make a persuasive claim to have met the threshold of plausible validity as a historical thesis about the Constitution. As such, it can only be concluded that the historical record is sufficiently ample and indecisive to warrant both outcomes. It is the politics of the particular 'originalist' that wins the day.

A similar pattern is illustrated in the Citizens United case in 2010. Justice Stevens' dissent (joined by Justices Ruth Bader Ginsburg, Stephen Breyer, and Sonia Sotomayor) took the line that any decision striking down campaign-financing restrictions on corporations as unconstitutional could not be defended on originalist grounds: the Framers "had little trouble distinguishing corporations from human beings, and when they constitutionalized the right to free speech in the First Amendment, it was the free speech of individual Americans that they had in mind". The concurring opinion by Justice Scalia (joined by Justice Samuel Alito and, in part, by Justice Clarence Thomas) insisted that the majority's result was faithful to originalism in that there was no historical evidence that the Framers contemplated that the government could restrict the political speech of business corporations.[18] Again, each judgment can be assumed to be a bona-fide attempt on the part of the dueling judges to elucidate original meaning. Similarly, it can be concluded that the tie-breaker was not interpretive authenticity but ideological resonance.

In resisting the claim that there is a sufficiently stable and precise public meaning for those words and phrases used in the Constitution, I am not running the silly argument that there is no workable or available meaning to words. As the more modest neo-originalists insist, while there is linguistic under-determinacy, it does not result in there being no determinacy at all. Relying on Hart's distinction between enduring cores and shifting penumbras,[19] they make the mistake of thinking that

[17] See *District of Columbia v. Heller*, 128 S. Ct. 2783, 2790, 2790 n. 6 (2008) (Scalia, J.) (examining text of Constitution and "other founding-era documents" to determine scope of Second Amendment right) and ibid. at 2831–6 (Stevens, J., dissenting) (reviewing text and constitutional drafting history of Second Amendment).

[18] *Citizens United v. FEC*, 558 U.S. 310 (2010). See Leo E. Strine, Jr., and Nicholas Walter, Originalist or Original: The Difficulties of Reconciling *Citizens United* with Corporate Law History (February 2015).

[19] Bennett and Solum, supra, note 2 at 21–2, and supra, Chapter 3.

this core is itself fixed and stable. The fact is that, while words do have a core meaning, that core meaning is itself buffeted and changed by the historical currents of social practice; meaning is always temporary, provisional, and contextual. It is not so much that the linguistic core grounds meaning or that meaning is always unfixable, but that there is no fixed meaning that is beyond further interpretive contestation and revision: today's core can become tomorrow's penumbra . Consequently, the originalist effort to stabilize constitutional interpretation on the shifting ground of public meaning is profoundly unconvincing. This is so for both 'parks' and 'vehicles' as it is for more abstract and important constitutional provisions.

Alternatively, drawing upon the interpretation/construction distinction, it has been conceded that judges have considerable leeway in their efforts to complete and refine the core meaning when applying it to modern situations and/or unanticipated circumstances. Again, while this has some appeal, it defeats the main *raison d'être* of the originalist method if it is modern sensibilities that govern, not historical understandings. By shunting the bulk of the hermeneutical work into the construction phase, neo-originalists give the whole interpretive game away. In effect, they begin to look and act more like organicists than originalists. The decisions in both *Lachapelle*, *Perron*, and *McBoyle* recommend and support this conclusion. No matter how inconvenient or frustrating this conclusion might be for formalist jurists generally, it is simply the interpretive fact of the constitutional matter. Originalism, whether neo- or otherwise, works only as a thinly veiled exercise of political ideology, not as a compelling constitutional theory.

This critical conclusion is confirmed by a leading neo-originalist treatment of what counts as a 'vehicle' for the purposes of the 'no vehicles in the park' rule. Writing in a scholarly capacity, Scalia begins his analysis by insisting that an ordinary interpretation of 'vehicle' does include an ambulance; any other result would be perverse. Moreover, the problematic consequences that follow from such an interpretation are the responsibility of legislators, not the judges; it is for rule-makers to make exceptions, not judges.[20] However, Scalia abandons or softens his strict formalist stance when the going gets really tough. He calls in aid certain common-law doctrines that are used to provide a contextual constraint or supplement to the originalist-controlled reading of certain texts.

[20] Scalia and Garner, supra, note 7 at 36–9.

So, although an ambulance is a 'vehicle', its entry into the park does not contravene the rule because there are exceptions based upon 'necessity' that circumscribe the rule's application.[21] In short, for all his huff and puff, Scalia does not have the interpretive courage of his own originalist convictions; he puts interpretation in the service of greater substantive justice concerns (and his own at that). Originalism rules, unless its dictates are considered unpalatable. As such, it is less an interpretive methodology than a convenient tool for advancing a partial political agenda.

Going Public

Even if it were possible to identify with any confidence the public meaning of the Constitution's text at its enactment, there is no compelling argument for the insistence that such a meaning should govern today and in the future in all constitutional matters. It is, of course, reasonable to assert that the actual text of the Constitution should carry significant weight in constitutional law and decision-making. After all, it would be bizarre to ignore the text and for judges or jurists to make it up as they go along. However, there is no reason to think that (1) what has happened since the text's enactment (e.g., the precedent corpus) carries no weight at all, (2) that the commitment to public meaning should be fixed in time and at that particular time, and (3) that the enactors themselves intended to give exclusive priority to their own local understandings of the abstract and universal directives that they put in place. Although originalists assert that their interpretive method has the considerable virtue of prioritizing the institutional values of stability and predictability by way of the Rule of Law, that is something that needs to be justified; it is itself an argument of contestable ideological preference, not an interpretive fact.

For example, while it is only 'cruel and unusual' punishments that are to be prohibited under the American Constitution, what counts as 'cruel' or 'unusual' is open to interpretation; it is not beholden to its public meaning in the late eighteenth century. The history of punishments imposed has changed in the last two centuries. To put it another way, there needs to be more and more focused arguments as to why the public meaning of the drafters' generation (e.g., corporal punishment) should be given priority over those of any later generations, including the present

[21] Ibid. at 300.

day. If the judges want to change the textual content of the Constitution, they cannot. But if they want to change the meaning of the existing textual context, then they can. In terms of fidelity to law, it is hard to understand why an old public meaning should always trump a newer one. The Constitution belongs to no generation exclusively. The dead hand of the past can claim no greater legitimacy than any other living hand (and perhaps less) without resort to some independent ideological account. In short, the neo-originalists turn out to be much more 'lively' than they can or are willing to concede.

Apart from the unconvincing force of the interpretation–construction distinction, one prominent exponent admits that there are occasions of 'extraordinariness' (e.g., 'an emergency' or 'horrendous evil') where the courts are entitled and sometimes obliged to abandon or deviate from the accepted original meaning of a constitutional provision; *Brown* (and its abolition of segregated schooling) is offered as the example *par excellence* of such a situation.[22] However, this manoeuvre seems too transparent by far and leaves any originalist attachment hanging by a thin thread. Rather than let originalist meaning take them wherever it will, its defenders lose their constitutionalist faith when it takes them to places that they really do not want to go. They turn out to be fair-weather originalists, who stick with originalism when its results chime with (or do not offend) an accepted sense of substantive justice, but abandon it when it does not. Although they might be prepared to take a non-originalist approach only in exceptional circumstances, it hints at the crucial fact that it is the substantive political cut of decisions that neo-originalism generally delivers that is the main consideration in legal interpretation, not its formal originalist pedigree.

It is by no means accepted by all philosophers that 'theory' provides an authoritative epistemological warrant for truth and knowledge. All interpretive theories are contingent and social because they always arise from and within, directly or indirectly, their sustaining historical and political context; no theory is innocent of historical or political significance. As such, the traditional enterprise of constitutional theorizing can be more usefully apprehended as part of a political tradition which privileges certain values and interests over others. The virtues of an originalist approach are not as self-evident nor as insulated from political values as originalists suggest: its methodological strictures are not immune from

[22] See Bennett and Solum, supra, note 2 at 35 and 48. *Brown v. Board of Education*, 347 U.S. 483 (1954).

the push-and-pull of the various social, economic, institutional, ideological, and cultural currents in play. Consequently, what has managed to get itself accepted in the community of constitutional theorizing will be attributable to something other than the simple force of a 'good idea'. The epistemological dimension (i.e., what is the correct methodology to access the true meaning of the Constitution?) is intertwined with the ideological dimension (i.e., what political interests and values are promoted by such a methodology?).

Consequently, despite protestations that neo-originalism is not 'a political ideology', an originalist approach to constitutional adjudication seems to line up with a particular political ideology in terms of both its own modern roots and the 'original' constitutional era that it invokes and valorizes.[23] It is undisputed that the turn to modern originalism occurred in the 1970s and was an attempted conservative hedge against the liberal-leaning decisions of the Warren Court; it became the jurisprudential stalking-horse for a right-wing agenda that saw the Supreme Court as a significant institutional barrier to such a revival.[24] This originalist approach has since been championed by those who make no bones about their own ideological leanings; its most prominent judicial exponents are the proudly conservative American justices William Rehnquist, Antonin Scalia, and Clarence Thomas. Interestingly, the originalist approach has generated little enthusiasm or support elsewhere.

Whatever the modern context of the originalist upsurge, its reference back to the era of the American Revolution and the founding generation is likely, at a minimum, to engender a preference for certain conservative values. While there is no monolithic ideology that can be attributed to late eighteenth-century American society, it is reasonable to conclude that the general thrust of the interests represented and the values upheld might be less progressive than those of the liberal 1960s and 1970s. It could be said that this is a self-conscious combination of interpretive theory and political ideology. These values are right wing by contemporary lights. Its adherents tend to be more against increasing immigration,

[23] Some American scholars claim that originalism can be used to defend a more progressive political vision of substantive justice. See, for example, Jack M. Balkin, *Living Originalism* (2011). This further illustrates that an originalist approach is more politically open-ended than its most of defenders recommend.

[24] Edwin *Meese* III, Speech Before the American Bar Association (July 9, 1985), reprinted in *The Great Debate: Interpreting Our Written Constitution* 9 (Paul Cassel ed., 1986). See also Reva B. Siegel, Dead or Alive: Originalism as Popular Constitutionalism in Heller, 122 *Harv. L. Rev.* 191, 241 (2008).

taxation, gay rights, and abortion, and more in favor of the death penalty, torture, balanced budgets, and military detention.[25] All of this is to suggest that, although the originalist approach is framed in terms of respect for the constitutional text, its driving force is the ideological preference for those general values that are thought to be crystallized by that text.

The follies and foibles of originalism are neatly illustrated by the Canadian situation. In one of the most celebrated Canadian cases, the courts had to decide in the late 1920s whether a woman could be a "qualified person" to sit in the Senate. While a contemporary reading would most likely include women, the accepted meaning of "person" in 1867 at the time of the country's founding enactment would likely have not. While the Supreme Court of Canada stayed with the earlier meaning, the Privy Council held that it was not 'original meaning' that held interpretive sway. Lord Sankey laid out an alternative approach that became and remains the hallmark of Canadian constitutional adjudication:

> The *British North America Act* planted in Canada a living tree capable of growth and expansion within its natural limits . . . Their Lordships do not conceive it to be the duty of this Board – it is certainly not their desire – to cut down the provisions of the Act by a narrow and technical construction, but rather to give it a large and liberal interpretation so that the Dominion to a great extent, but within certain fixed limits, may be mistress in her own house.[26]

The dilemma in the Persons case for originalists is obvious; it puts them between a rock and a hard place – if the original meaning of a constitutional provision is sufficiently clear (as it was here), then originalists are compelled to either go with it, even if it takes them to the most politically unpalatable of contemporary places, or abandon it and allow contemporary meaning to trump original meaning in the name of substantive justice. Accordingly, in such hard cases, the originalist faith is put under severe and, some might say, fatal strain; its adherents would face a crisis of legal conscience. If originalists compromise themselves or soft-pedal in

[25] Jamal Greene, Nathaniel Persily, and Stephen Ansolabehere, Profiling Originalism, 111 *Colum. L. Rev.* 356, 373 (2011) ("They are more likely to express morally traditionalist, hierarchical and libertarian cultural values"). Indeed, it is the recuperation of those values and ideas that has fuelled the platform of the Tea Party. See Adam Liptak, Tea-ing Up the Constitution, *N.Y. Times*, March 13, 2010.

[26] *Edwards v. Canada (Attorney General)*, [1930] AC 124 at 136 (PC).

the most important of constitutional encounters to avoid gross injustice or 'extraordinariness' (e.g., gender equality in democratic opportunities), then they seem to place political pragmatism above theoretical principle. As such, they begin to look very much like their interpretive enemy, the disparaged and wishy-washy organicists. In Scalia's terms, they incorporate the "glaring defect" that "there is no agreement, and no chance of agreement, upon what is to be the guiding principle of the [Constitution's] evolution".[27]

These difficulties are confounded by what would be an originalist approach to the Canadian Charter of Rights and Freedom. Because it was enacted in 1982, any resort to originalism by Canadian judges would result in a much more liberal reading of the Charter; the general tenor of the times was relatively much more liberal and progressive in Ottawa in the early 1980s than in Philadelphia in the mid-1780s. Indeed, somewhat ironically, it was precisely because of the more liberal and progressive politics of the late 1970s and early 1980s that the American originalist movement arose and took off. To be a modern Canadian originalist for constitutional purposes might well be to be more of an advocate for liberal, not conservative judicial interpretations and decisions. As such, Canadian-based neo-originalists would be left in a very tight spot – remain true to the concrete (and liberal) ideological implications of originalism as presently practiced or to the abstract theoretical integrity of the originalist methodology. Of course, they could come out at the same conservative place as in the United States by pushing all the important interpretive work into the construction zone. However, this would serve only to expose their originalist approach for what it is – a convenient cover for a substantive conservative ideology.[28]

The upshot of all this is that neo-originalism is revealed as simply another political ideology flying under the false colors of a constitutional/interpretive theory. Once neo-originalism abandons its exclusive gold standard of original meaning, the difference between a non-originalist or 'living tree' approach is shaved so thin as to be non-existent. To put it another way, the only difference is one not of jurisprudential orientation but of ideological alignment. Neo-originalism simply becomes one

[27] Scalia, supra, note 5, at 44–5.

[28] There has been a couple of high-profile judicial appointments of self-described originalists by the past conservative government as a push-back to the perceived liberal drift of the Supreme Court of Canada. See Tories Appoint Two Conservative Law Professors as Judges, *Globe and Mail*, December 17, 2014.

more futile theory on the scrap-heap of constitutional law and legal interpretation. However, this exposure does have the clear advantage of returning the jurisprudential and interpretive debate squarely where it has and should have been all along – on the contested terrain of ideological politics.

Conclusion

There are many lessons to be drawn from the false promise of originalism. A pertinent one is that, in legal interpretation generally and constitutional interpretation particularly, more progress might be made if all parties were to recognize that the main action and central bone of contention is not about abstract theory but about constitutional politics – what are the political values and ideological commitments that animate and drive judicial decision-making? American originalists (and non-originalists) glimpse but choose to ignore it or lose their critical nerve at the crucial moment; they treat the challenge of constitutional or textual interpretation as being a universal theoretical conundrum, not simply a parochial puzzle that has its own ideological valence. As such, they preach legal theory but practice political ideology. A more open recognition of that fact might actually invigorate the vital *political* discourse that surrounds constitutions and that their application is intended to stimulate. As one long-forgotten enthusiast put it, "the difficulty has been not so much with the instrument as with ourselves".[29]

[29] Florence E. Allen, *This Constitution of Ours* 7 (1940).

6

In a Common Cause

An Incremental Approach

As the ambitious efforts of the naturalist and originalists have run into severe criticism on several fronts, there has been a certain retrenchment in the efforts to salvage the formalist project. A more modest mode of intervention is recommended. Such an approach is suggested by the pragmatic methodology of the common law approach to judicial decision-making and doctrinal development. The central idea is that the contested ground of ideological politics can be avoided or finessed by adopting the celebrated virtues of incremental and evolutionary development of legal doctrine from case to case. In both constitutional law and statutory interpretation, judges and jurists are supposed to stake out a minimalist and centrist ground between the implausible (and conservative) textualist claims of the originalists and the grander (and more liberal) tendencies of contemporary naturalists. In important ways, these incrementalists or 'common lawyers' valorize rather than lament the common law tradition of legal craft and 'muddling through'. In law and life's race, they are self-proclaimed and proud tortoises, not hares.

As an informalist, I am not unsympathetic to what they are trying to do in insisting that theory is a way of coping locally, not a universal panacea. But (and it is a large 'but') they are mistaken to maintain that this can be done in a formalist and non-ideological fashion. Emphasizing that 'moderation in all things' is the best policy, these incrementalists maintain that the best way to get things done in law, legal interpretation, and jurisprudence is to be slow, but steady. While it is a tantalizing prospect, this approach is no less ideological than any other formalist-inspired intervention. After outlining the incrementalists' strategy, I will show how it is found wanting as a viable hedge against 'law as ideology' – their account of the dynamics of judicial decision-making is empty and unedifying, and their prescription for constitutional interpretation is hostage to a Burkean conservative ideology. As pragmatic as they claim to be, the incrementalists remain under the misguided spell of a formalist mind-set.

A Traditional Approach

The common law tradition is still very much part of the ethos and mindset of modern lawyers and jurists. As well as referring to a rich body of rules and principles accumulated and refined over the centuries, this tradition also has a crucial methodological dimension that exhibits "a profound reverence for the wisdom of our ancestors".[1] For common lawyers, therefore, the legal past is not simply a store of rules and rulings but an obligatory source of value and guidance; past decisions possess a moral prestige and accumulated wisdom that have normative priority over present understandings and uninhibited ratiocination. As such, judicial decision-making is an institutional practice that treats its own traditions seriously. Because of its own insecurities, jurisprudence jumped on the Darwinian bandwagon of the nineteenth century more quickly and more zealously than most other disciplines. Indeed, from the pioneering work of Henry Maine, O.W. Holmes, Jr., J.H. Wigmore, and Arthur Corbin through to more recent technical efforts, the evolutionary motif has always loomed large over jurisprudential efforts to explicate the nature and content of the common law.[2]

When this conserving and conservative quality is added to the fact that judges have independent institutional justifications for steering clear of open-ended and creative decision-making, the claims of tradition are very strong in defining the appropriate approach and limits to adjudication and legal interpretation. By viewing themselves as custodians rather than creators of tradition, judges can fulfill their controversial roles with seriousness and safety; they can resist or, at least, hold at bay the anti-formalist challenge that law is simply politics in different garb. Nevertheless, although operating within an official culture of institutional conservatism, all judges and jurists not only acknowledge that the law does indeed respond and change to new circumstances and fresh challenges, but they also celebrate and champion the law's capacity to do so. As Beverly McLachlin, now the Chief Justice of Canada, succinctly framed it, "over time, the law in any given area may change; but the process of change is a slow and incremental one based on the mechanism

[1] Conciliation with America in *Writings and Speeches of Edmund Burke*, vol. 3, p. 139 (P. Langford ed. 1981).

[2] For a brief history, see E. Donald Elliot, The Evolutionary Tradition in Jurisprudence, 85 *Colum. L. Rev.* 38 (1985); and Alan Watson, *The Evolution of Law* (1985). Modern naturalists, like Dworkin, also incorporate such an evolutionary attitude of 'fit'. See supra, Chapter 4.

of extending an existing principle to new circumstances ... [and] major revisions of the law are best left to the legislature".[3] As such, the common law tradition is a case-by-case, evolutionary, and modest mode of formalism.

In order to achieve a mix of stability and flexibility, judges and jurists have developed a more nuanced and organic attitude toward its own and society's traditions. For them, the common law mentality treats the existing traditions of law, in both substance and method, not so much as a fixed or ossified process, but as a living resource that allows for and incorporates change. Over time, it has recommended slow growth, principled extension, institutional deference, professional competence, political neutrality, cautious revision, and, most important, progressive development. It has operationalized this by relying on a series of doctrinal manoeuvres that can loosen or lessen the force of existing precedents (e.g., inventive gap-filling, extensive exceptionalism, subtle distinction-drawing). So enabled, judges and jurists work on the assumption that there can be some satisfactory, principled, and long-term trade-off between stability and change. On this view, the common law is a firmly grounded, finely balanced, ethically defensible, institutionally justified, politically legitimate, and self-improving enterprise. As Benjamin Cardozo famously put it, in times of conflict or crisis within law and society, "history or custom or social utility or some compelling sentiment of justice or sometimes perhaps a semi-intuitive apprehension of the pervading spirit of our law, must come to the rescue".[4] In this way, law's traditions can keep pace with society's own changing traditions and demands.

For some, the common law's development proceeds by way of an internal, mysterious, and fixed logic.[5] But contemporary exponents take a more pragmatic and clear-eyed approach. For instance, Melvin Eisenberg offers a 'generative' concept of the common law in which a combination of doctrinal principles and social propositions is effected and governed by a series of institutional rules that bind judges in the performance of their adjudicative responsibilities. These institutional principles are intended to ensure legitimacy in a democratic society – *objectivity* (i.e., impartial judges applying universal rules), *support* (i.e., these universal rules applied are supported by general standards of society), *replicability*

[3] *Watkins v. Olafson* [1989] 2 S.C.R. 750 at 760–1 per McLachlin J.
[4] Benjamin N. Cardozo, *The Nature of the Judicial Process* 40–3 (1921).
[5] See, for example, David J. Ibbetson, Natural Law and Common Law, [2001] *Edinburgh L. Rev.* 4.

(i.e., they are generated by a consistent methodology that allows reliance and predictability), and *responsiveness* (i.e., which methodology attends to professional corrective discourse about the law and its shortcomings). Viewing the common law as an activity as much as a body of rules, Eisenberg claims to explain how the common law achieves both certainty through the existence of overriding doctrinal principles and flexibility through the incorporation of social propositions. The institutional principles are claimed to be able to reconcile the tensions that arise out of law's need to utilize the past to resolve disputes and to contribute to the future by enriching the supply of legal rules.

In identifying such social propositions, Eisenberg concedes that this resort to social morality will not be an empirical or value-free exercise: judges are to draw upon those norms that they believe would likely obtain social support and favor by all. Within such a scheme, "the landmark cases of the common law do not involve an attempt by the courts to change existing social standards, but a decision by the courts to bring legal rules into congruence with existing social standards".[6] As such, Eisenberg offers an account of common law development that claims to tie what the law is to what it should be, but in a way that is intended to be sufficiently disciplined and controlled to satisfy the formalist demands of mainstream jurisprudence. Indeed, in making this claim and concession, he joins a chorus of contemporary jurists who insist that, although there is no grand theory or master narrative that can capture this measured development, it proceeds on the jurisprudential basis that "determinations of legal meaning must rely in part on distinctively legal norms ... [that] are necessarily internal to legal practice and require interpreters to exercise a form of legally constrained judgment or choice".[7] The identification and articulation of these norms and judgments will be vital to the legitimacy of the incrementalists' formalist project, especially insofar as this common law approach is intended to apply to statutory and constitutional interpretation.

Of Statutes and Constitutions

The appeal of this common law approach has much to recommend it, notwithstanding some of the extravagant claims made about its

[6] Melvin Eisenberg, *The Nature of the Common Law* 19 (1988).

[7] Richard Fallon, Jr., The Meaning of Legal "Meaning" and Its Implications for Theories of Legal Interpretation, 82 *U. Chi. L. Rev.* 1235 at 1241 and 1243 (2015).

jurisprudential cogency and completeness. The emphasis is on small and tentative steps forward so as to avoid large or controversial shifts in the law's direction and outlook. However, contemporary theorists have begun to rely on this evolutionary method in the interpretation of statutes and constitutions. Their central insight is that the effort to fix meaning by reference to a particular theory or formula is misguided and destined to fail. To varying degrees, these common lawyers or incrementalists have insisted not only that judges are ill-equipped and ill-suited to act in a deeply theoretical way, but that there is no upside to doing so as there is no single or superior approach to interpretation that is warranted by the idea of interpretation itself. There are multiple sources and techniques that recommend themselves for judicial uptake, but none can assert an exclusive or dominant authority. Aided by jurists, judges must look to a battery of possible resources – history, structure, purpose, intent, precedent, moral values, and social consequences – to reach reasonable and practical results.

On the statutory front, the incrementalists do not ignore the text. Instead, they recognize that its meaning will never be self-evident and that it can (and will) change over time: a strict textualism has little to offer when the going gets more controversial and divided. The text is the starting point for the interpretive search (and will be important for that fact), but will not alone be determinative of the final destination. Different approaches will suggest themselves on different occasions, but there is no meta-theoretical calculus that can inform that important choice or the weighting between the different sources on specific occasions. That said, incrementalists insist that this does not give judges *carte blanche* to do as they see fit in applying statutory imperatives; there is a distinctively legal as opposed to ideological way of proceeding. Again, the judicial mind-set will focus on modest and incremental moves that respect legislative reasonableness and sidestep more contested ideological terrain. This will be especially so in dealing with statutory frameworks in the administrative context; practical workability will and should trump artificial textualism.[8]

So, when it comes to 'no vehicles in the park', the incrementalists accept that there is no canonical meaning or theoretically sanctioned route to it. The idea that there is or could be a 'right answer' is much more jurisprudential trouble than it is worth. Instead, they recommend

[8] Cass Sunstein, Interpreting Statutes in the Regulatory State, 103 *Harv. L. Rev.* 405 (1989).

that the judges should employ an approach that looks to all available resources (e.g., intent, purpose, precedent, consequences) and craft a result that is as measured as it is modest. So, in *Perron* and *Lachapelle*, the judges' efforts to work with the pulls and pushes of the different sources were genuine and balanced; the fact that they came to different outcomes is not considered be a cause for concern. Similarly, in *McBoyle*, each judge relies upon an established approach to statutory interpretation. Again, their disagreement about the appropriate outcome is not troubling because, without there being any one right answer, it is their relative capacities to persuade that is in issue. As such, legal interpretation gains its institutional legitimacy and normative traction by virtue of the judges' willingness to pursue their craft through techniques that are professional and practical.

In constitutional matters, the interpretive challenge is, of course, even greater. It is one thing to take a pluralistic approach to the meaning and effect of particular legislative schemes or sections, but it another thing entirely to strike down such schemes and sections in the name of constitutional justice. However, it is because the stakes are higher and the political heat is more intensive that judges should take an incremental and cautious approach. Drawing upon the common law tradition, it is advocated that judges inhabit the less demanding foothills than strive to reach the rarified heights of the constitutional peaks. Consequently, the incrementalists have no truck with the fundamentalist and abstract assertions of positivist, naturalist, or originalist theories about the proper source and ground of constitutional meaning. Instead, they opt for shallowness over depth in theorizing and narrowness for width in rulings; humility, not hubris, is their stock-in-trade. For them, constitutional law demands a principled balance or dynamic middle ground between deference and transformation in seeking to arrive at responsible and constrained decisions: "the enterprise of constitutional justification requires consistent application of fair standards of valid argument".[9]

In an extended account of constitutional decision-making, Cass Sunstein argues that the most appropriate and efficacious way for

[9] See also Richard H. Fallon, Jr., How to Choose a Constitutional Theory, 87 *Cal. L. Rev.* 535 at 579 (1999). See also Richard H. Fallon, Jr., A Constructivist Coherence Theory of Constitutional Interpretation, 100 *Harv. L. Rev.* 1189 (1987); David Strauss, Foreword: Does the Constitution Mean What It Says?, 129 *Harv. L. Rev.* 1 (2015); and David A. Strauss, Common Law Constitutional Interpretation, 63 *U. Chi. L. Rev.* 877 (1996).

judges to proceed is to "speak softly and carry a small stick". Insisting that there is no one, sure-fire way to elicit constitutional meaning, he contends that the best interpretive approach depends on "what will make the constitutional system better than worse". In the American context, this means that judges and jurists must defend their interpretive preferences and decisions in terms of fulfilling both the institutional and substantive demands on judges in a republican system of constitutional democracy. For him, the incrementalists' belief that "small steps are often the right steps" is the safest and surest way forward as it avoids dangerous leaps in the dark. As such, he celebrates the "integrity and coherence" of both legal and social traditions as revealed in the history of American constitutional thought. However, while he is traditional on institutional matters (e.g., separation of powers and national security), he is more intrusive when it comes to individual rights (e.g., race, sex, disability, etc.) because there are more compelling reasons for "traditions to be held to account".[10] But even when judges challenge traditions (as part of the constitutional tradition itself), they must do so in a minimalist way such that legal precedent and social traditions are destabilized as little as possible. As such, the constitutional minimalist calls upon the tradition of incrementalism in matters of and law and social change.

Consequently, the hope of these 'common lawyers' is that, by lowering the theoretical and political heat, there will be less contestation and division; judicial decision-making will be able to proceed on a more modest and pragmatic basis. There might well be a little bit of conservatism here and a little bit of progressivism there, but the resulting mix will be the product of a professional craft that will be based on an approach that will finesse the trap of 'doing ideology' under the guise of 'doing law'. But in striving to be almost all things to almost all people, these scholars deliver much less than they promise. While the incrementalist approach has some legitimacy outside of statutory and constitutional matters (as there is some prospect of legislative intervention and correction), it faces an almost impossible burden in those other areas of legal interpretation. Indeed, this formalist-inspired account of law and judicial decision-making fails as both a descriptive project and as a prescriptive proposal in such matters.

[10] Cass Sunstein, *Constitutional Personae* 17, 44, xvi, 70, and 107 (2015).

A Great Tradition

Judges often declare that "judges can and should alter the common law to reflect [social, moral and economic] needs as they change over time".[11] That judges 'should' strive to do this is neither surprising nor controversial. But it is the 'can' that has proved more controversial. Obviously, judges can do whatever they want; they can augment, amend, abandon, or ignore legal doctrines as they see fit. However in seeking to 'alter the common law to reflect needs as they change over time', judges are caught in a debilitating double-bind. First, they require some politically neutral device by which to calculate and calibrate the changing needs of society: this seems to be an unavoidably political and contested task. Second, having elucidated such needs, the judges must alter the common law to 'reflect' such needs. Apart from the difficulty of ascertaining which rules best satisfy certain needs, they must alter the law in a way that best respects the common law's own evolutionary expectations about itself – the legitimacy of adjudication is seen to reside in the fact that judges keep in check their partisan political preferences by resort to the formal discipline of principled argumentation. However, this seems an especially difficult and challenging task.

For instance, while Eisenberg's attempt to integrate legal rules and social values is ingenious, it manages to refute, not confirm, his traditional hypothesis that law is not political in any deep or partisan way. At a crucial juncture, he notes that "using the norms of the general community in fashioning common law rules [works only] so long as the community is not exceptionally pluralistic and the norms claim to be rooted in aspirations for the community as a whole".[12] But in conflicted and class-ridden societies such as the United States and the United Kingdom, this means that Eisenberg has nothing to contribute by way of explanatory justification. His theory runs out at the very point where it is most needed in the resolution of most disputed matters. He has little legal advice to offer judges in disputed matters of law. As if this was not enough, Eisenberg compounds the problem by stating that, in monitoring the interplay between social and doctrinal propositions, judges must balance social congruence, systemic consistency, and doctrinal stability. However, this does not so much resolve the traditional problem of setting

[11] *R.W.D.S.U., Local 558 v. Pepsi-Cola Canada Beverages (West) Ltd.*, [2002] 1 SCR 156 at para 17 per McLachlin J.

[12] Eisenberg, supra, note 6 at 21. These ideas are developed more in Allan C. Hutchinson, *Evolution and the Common Law* (2005).

off substantive justice against formal reliance as restate it. He concludes that precedents should be followed if there is substantial social congruence, "even though another rule would be marginally better".[13]

But these concessions are tantamount to admitting that what drives the common law is political evaluation rather than legal analysis. Or, to put it another way, this reduces legal analysis to little more than political debate. And this, of course, is exactly what Eisenberg and other traditional defenders of the common law approach are supposed to be flatly against. To state, as Eisenberg does, that judges should do what they think is politically reasonable whether it involves applying, extending, distinguishing, exceptionalizing, reformulating, or overruling existing rules is to give the whole jurisprudential game away. It shows that the resort to the past is no more legitimating than any other legal manoeuvre because there is no one past to be identified, no one way of applying that past to the present, and no one way of knowing whether the present utilization of the past will be relevant to the problems of the future. Furthermore, even a rudimentary grasp of the common law's history reveals that the law's own leading cases are often the product of abrupt change, not the slow development that incrementalists recommend. Contrary to Holmes's opinion that "great cases, like hard cases, make bad law",[14] an informalist insists that that they are truly emblematic of the common law's ideological character and best capture its dynamic and almost radical spirit.

'Great cases' are those decisions – *Hadley*, *Donoghue*, *Hedley Byrne*, and their ilk in English tort law and *Brown*, *Griswold*, *Miranda*, and their kind in American constitutional law – that are regarded by almost all lawyers as landmarks of the common law tradition. While their precise import and reach are continuously contested, any credible account of the common law has to be grounded upon such decisions.[15] However, their very existence and the circumstances of their origin confound the legitimacy of the process that they allegedly anchor and from which they purportedly arise. Great cases are less a continuation of legal tradition and more of a break with existing traditions; they tend to exemplify a deviation from existing commitments, not a derivation from them. Accordingly, while great cases represent the common law's impressive

[13] Ibid. at 75.

[14] *Northern Securities Co. v. United States*, 193 US 197 at 400 (1904) (Holmes dissenting).

[15] See Allan C. Hutchinson, *Is Eating People Wrong?: Great Legal Cases and How They Shaped The World* (2010) and *Is Killing People Right?: More Great Legal Cases and How They Shaped the World* (2016).

pragmatic capacity to adapt to fresh challenges and new conditions, they also present jurists with their most pressing jurisprudential challenge. Insofar as great cases are the heart and soul of the common law, it must be explained why that common law tradition is considered to extol all the virtues of restraint and caution that the very creation and acceptance of great cases so gloriously flout. As such, the common law tradition is most ably and adequately represented by the work of so-called "bold spirits," not "timorous souls".[16] If great cases are the crowning glory of the common law tradition, they are the Achilles heel of its jurisprudential apologists.

To make their case, the incrementalists must show that incremental adaptation is not simply a cover for radical realignment and, as important, that the balance between stability and change is neither ad hoc nor unpredictable: the balance must itself be explained by something other than ideological preference. However, like the social past that it draws upon, the law's traditions are rich, multiple, and competing: they are notoriously difficult to pin down with any specificity or precision. The only real choice for tradition-committed judges is not whether to follow the past but to determine which aspects of that past they intend to emphasize or treat as dominant. In other words, there is no way that judges can simply follow the past in a mechanical or legal way without taking some critical and political stance about the particular past they intend to follow, its present meaning, and its implications for future activity. The choice to uphold the status quo or traditional values is no less political than the decision to rupture or reinterpret them: "preservation is as much a freely chosen action as are revolution and renewal".[17] Consequently, the claim to be preserving uncritically a particular tradition is unconvincing as the common law tradition itself is so capacious, nuanced, multi-textured, motile, diffuse, and irrepressible that there is no one simple given tradition to be preserved.

It should come as no surprise, therefore, that the reliance upon tradition is not a move away from politics. It is more properly understood as a particular kind of ideological commitment and a Burkean reactionary one at that.[18] Although tradition is not a determinative or

[16] *Candler v. Crane, Christmas & Co.*, [1951] 2 KB 164 at 178 per Lord Denning M.R.

[17] Hans-Georg Gadamer, *Truth and Method* 281–2 (J. Wei and D. Marshall trans. 2nd ed. 1989).

[18] See supra, note 1, and Edmund Burke, *Reflections on the Revolution in France* 58–9, 84 (J.M. Dent & Sons 1940) (1790).

irrebuttable source in the incrementalist account, it does operate as a baseline or strong thumb on the adjudicative scales; there is a presumption against rocking the boat. The basic idea is that courts should not be getting too far ahead or too far behind social consensus. But, put forward as a response to the 'what makes the constitutional system better than worse?', it is squarely ideological and partisan. The steps may be small, but they still have to be going somewhere. Being moderate and gradual in one's actions is no less ideological than any other political stance; it is about style, not substance. It is simply not possible to be an incrementalist *tout court*. This has enormous subversive potential that can eat away at the whole enterprise of statutory and constitutional interpretation as understood from a formalistic perspective. Although put forward as a way of making decisions in less or non-ideological ways, it is itself hostage to a particular judge's ideological orientation.

In an important sense, the incrementalists are hoist by their own petard. A major building block of its adherents is that no interpretive theory can do sufficient work to relieve the interpreter's personal responsibility for identifying and justifying any particular result. While the choice of interpretive theory will be significant in elucidating those interpretive factors that are important (e.g., the text or framers' intentions) and even the relative weight given to them (e.g., past over present value), that choice will not be decisive: the same interpretive theory can be used to warrant very different results. Accordingly, if no interpretive theory can deliver, it has to be the ideological framework within which the interpretive theory is deployed that will point to, if not dictate, the outcome reached or desired. This is not to suggest that the interpretive approach used will have no impact on the range of decisions reached; interpretive under-determinacy is not the same as there being no direction or tilt at all. However, an interpretive approach decisively cuts one way or another only when it is connected to and driven by a particular set of ideological preferences. While it might well initially orient the judicial task in one direction, it will not lead it to any particular destination without more. It is the interpreter's ideological stance that backstops any theory of statutory or constitutional interpretation and that is the real explanation for the actual decisions reached by judges.

The Obergefell Outing

From a formalist perspective, constitutional judges and jurists must be able to explain why something is good constitutional law, but not only because it is good politics. Once the difference between good law and good politics is no longer maintained, there is no reason to treat legal decisions as any more neutral, objective, or non-ideological and, therefore, authoritative than political opinion. So, for example, the central dilemma in constitutional law is to demonstrate that *Brown* is not only politically appealing and that *Plessy* is politically deplorable, but that *Brown* is good constitutional law and *Plessy* is bad constitutional law.[19] Although the task of reconciling constitutional law and partisan politics is difficult in a single case, it become positively Sisyphean when one throws in all the other contested great or almost-great cases. How is it possible to demonstrate conclusively that some permutation of *Brown*, *Roe*, and *Bowers* is or is not good constitutional law in a way that is somehow different from the general debate over what is and is not good politics? This challenge is particularly acute for the incrementalists.

These observations can be neatly illustrated by the recent decision in *Obergefell*, one of the most anticipated rulings in recent years.[20] Against a mixed legislative and popular background (i.e., thirty-six states and the District of Columbia allowed gay couples to marry and the rest did not), it determined that the right to marry was a fundamental right inherent in the liberty of the person. Under the Due Process and Equal Protection Clauses of the Fourteenth Amendment, therefore, same-sex couples had the same right to marry as heterosexual couples. As many predicted, the Supreme Court divided along ideological lines in a 5-4 decision; the four opinions of the Court were heated and polarized in their divisiveness. In short, the *Obergefell* decision was a classic constitutional decision. If the minimalists' ideas are to have any jurisprudential traction, they must be applicable and illuminating in exactly such a great case. While they do to a small extent, they do not to a much larger extent.

The majority opinion was given by Justice Kennedy; it was joined by Justices Ginsburg, Breyer, Sottomayor, and Kagan. Although often conservative leaning, he was bold and broad in his reasoning on this occasion: he reached a progressive result. In recognizing that "history and tradition guide and discipline this inquiry but do not set its outer boundaries", he resisted the temptation to "proceed with caution". Arguing that to deny same-sex couples the right to marry would create "substantial and continuing harm", he saw no reason why deference to

[19] *Brown v. Board of Education*, 347 U.S. 483 (1954), and *Plessy v. Ferguson*, 163 US 537 (1896).
[20] *Obergefell v. Hodges*, 576 U.S. 1 (2015).

the democratic process was appropriate if it resulted in a negation of people's protected liberties: "fundamental rights may not be submitted to a vote; they depend on the outcome of no elections". If the right to marry was a fundamental right, then its exercise could not be denied to all couples, regardless of their sexual orientation or identity. While he prepared to demand that governments respect a broad vision of fundamental rights that places strict constitutional limits on their democratic actions, he also defers to a gathering popular momentum of support for same-sex marriage as part of changing attitudes that "are characteristic of a Nation where new dimensions of freedom become apparent to new generations" and where "new insights and societal understandings can reveal unjustified inequality within our most fundamental institutions that once passed unnoticed and unchallenged".[21]

Chief Justice Roberts delivered a stinging dissent. Emphasizing that "judges have power to say what the law is, not what it should be", he strongly cautioned his colleagues not "to confuse our own preferences with the requirements of the law". So, he determined that, "although the policy arguments for extending marriage to same-sex couples may be compelling, the legal arguments for requiring [the extension of marriage to same-sex couples] are not", and, therefore, "the majority's position is indefensible as a matter of constitutional law". Moreover, by improperly removing the issue of same-sex marriage from the democratic realm, Roberts warned that the Court was "making a dramatic social change that much more difficult to accept". In so deciding, he eschews any grand statements about constitutional rights and counsels a very cautious approach that is framed as respectful of popular governance.[22]

The dissents of Justices Scalia, Thomas, and Alito were even more unequivocal and vehement. Justice Scalia took high dudgeon with the majority's opinion. He lambasted it for "the hubris reflected in today's judicial Putsch" and considered that it was "couched in a style that is as pretentious as its content is egotistic". However, behind the fiery rhetoric, he placed great originalist weight on the view that "until the courts put a stop to it, the public debate over same sex marriage displayed American democracy at its best".[23] In a similar vein, Justice Thomas complained that the majority's opinion "distorts the principles on which this Nation

[21] Ibid. at 11, 23, 28–9, 24, 7, and 20.

[22] Ibid. at 3, 2, 10, and 2. If a more sophisticated and broader view of what counts as ideological is taken, Roberts is equally ideological. See infra, Chapter 9.

[23] Ibid. at 6, 7, and 2.

was founded". Emphasizing that "in the American legal tradition, liberty has long been understood as individual freedom from governmental action, not as a right to a particular governmental entitlement", he concluded that the decision "will have inestimable consequences for our Constitution and our society".[24] Along similar lines, Justice Alito predicted that constitutional chaos would reign as a result of the majority's failure to uphold the Rule of Law and hasten "the deep and perhaps irremediable corruption of our legal culture's conception of constitutional interpretation".[25]

The dissenters offer a robust challenge to the majority's approach. They adopt a deferential posture to an unfolding democratic and political drama. However, they do so in the name of a conservative ideology. The difference from the majority is not simply between doing law and doing ideology, but between opposing ideologies. On this occasion, the dissenters stand up for popular sovereignty. But, like the majority, they are willing to strike down governmental intervention on, for example, health care or gun control, as a matter of constitutional correctness when it offends what they consider to be the Constitution's fundamental values. As such, it is not so much the interpretive theory of the dissenters (e.g., originalist or deferentialist), but the deep cut of their ideological commitments. The gap between the *Obergefell* decision being good or bad constitutional law and good or bad politics is non-existent; each feeds off the other.

So how would the incrementalists recommend deciding *Obergefell*? Their self-imposed challenge is to identify a mode of proceeding that relies on no one interpretive approach (as none is dispositive of the issue in and of itself); that respects precedent, tradition, and principle; and that does this in a modest, minimalist, and slow-moving way. This is a very tall order. Not surprisingly, it is beyond their capacity to meet it. Indeed, their efforts to explain what was good and bad about the judicial approaches in *Obergefell* do more to compound the situation than resolve it.

The basic problem is that it is not possible to be a minimalist or incrementalist *tout court* – you need to have something to be minimalist about or some direction to make incremental progress toward. It seems highly unhelpful to claim that some "build incrementally in a liberal direction, whereas others build incrementally to the right".[26] As regards

[24] Ibid. at 7 and 18. [25] Ibid. at 7–8. [26] Sunstein, supra, note 10 at 39–40.

Obergefell, there is a reasonable case to be made that both the majority and the dissenters acted incrementally; one gave constitutional consolidation to the political momentum of the validating states and the other deferred to the unfolding dynamic of that political shift. Indeed, David Strauss praised both majority and dissenters in *Obergefell* as adopting a common law approach, even if they arrived at diametrically opposed outcomes: "so even in the dissent, the recognized sources of law were precedent, tradition, and general principles derived from those sources ... [and], faced with precedent that left it room to manoeuver, the Court chose the course that seemed to it to be morally preferable".[27] On such a view, 'moral preferability' rules, not law. And the right 'moral preferability' is nothing more than that favored by five out of nine judges.

Tackling *Obergefell* directly, Sunstein celebrates the decision and the majority's opinion as doing the right thing because it "pays attention to an actual or emerging moral consensus, certainly with respect to fundamental rights". He identifies this reference to social trends and practices as being the lifeblood of judicial decision-making in constitutional matters: "if the arc of history is clearly on one side, then judges are likely to pay respectful attention". Such decisions become part of "our national fabric" and are worthy of respect for that fact alone. This is a very Burkean stance; tradition grounds rights, not the rationalist scrutiny of them. On such an analysis, Sunstein would be in something of a pickle if 'the arc of history' or the unfolding 'national fabric' were travelling in a more conservative or even homophobic direction. Unless, of course, Sunstein went only with 'social consensus' on individual rights when it suited him as an ideological preference. It might simply be said that Sunstein, like the majority and the dissenters in *Obergefell*, would tailor his interpretive means to suit his ideological ends. Indeed, his conclusion that "the meaning of our founding document, as we live it, is a product of social movements and struggles"[28] suggests exactly that – it is politics, not law that wins the day.

Accordingly, if an incrementalist can go left or right, then what is the point of their intervention? Although put forward as a formalist way of differentiating law and ideology (i.e., there exists "legally constrained

[27] Strauss, supra, note 9 at 6–7, 8, and 7 (2015). Both Sunstein and Strauss explicitly build on a Burkean tradition.

[28] Cass Sunstein, Gay Marriage Shows Court at Best, *Bloomberg Views* (June 6, 2015), www.bloombergview.com/articles/2015-06-26/gay-marriage-shows-court-at-its-best.

judgment"[29]), it fails because it is itself held hostage to a particular judge's ideological orientation. Being moderate and gradual in developing the law is no less ideological than any other jurisprudential rendition of formalism. Such a common law approach can neither explain the past nor do much to assist in constraining future decisions. As the history of great cases reveals, the common law approach is as much about transformation and politics as it is about stability and law. At the end of the day, constitutional theorists, such as Sunstein, Strauss, and Fallon, do little more than make a very middle-of-the-road plea for the courts not to get too far ahead and not to get too far behind social consensus. But that appeal is squarely ideological in thrust and justification. Moreover, as their comments on *Obergefell* display, the judges are free to do almost whatever they want and still be able to claim that they are acting in accordance with law and its professional methodology – 'no vehicles in the park' can mean whatever judges and jurists want it to mean. This is no methodology at all.

Conclusion

The minimalists are little like the tortoise in *Aesop's Fables.*[30] Tired of listening to the hare brag about how fast he was, the tortoise challenged him to a race. The hare ran ahead of the much slower tortoise and taunted him on how slow he was. So confident was the hare of victory that he decided to take a short nap. However, the tortoise carried on at his slow and steady pace. He managed to cross the finish line while the hare was still asleep. Of course, the moral of that oft-told tale is that the steady, if slow, win life's race over the fast and flash. But there is another lesson to be taken from it (as well as the lesson about resolve over complacency). The pace of travel is not the measure of all things; it is the certainty of getting to the destination. In the minimalists' case, this can be taken as suggesting that they are no different from the more ambitious and heroic naturalists; they are on much the same track and heading in much the same direction. It is all about strategy and style, not commitment and destination: the more modest and moderate can achieve more than the boastful and bold. This is no bad message. But the incrementalists' insistence that it will be enough to "speak softly and carry a small stick" falls well short of salvaging the formalist project.[31]

29 Fallon, supra, note 7 at 1243.
30 *Aesop's Fables* no. 237 (Laura Gibbs ed. 2002).
31 Sunstein, supra, note 10 at 17.

7

A Hard Line

Further Positivist Efforts

If Hart was the poster boy of twentieth-century positivism, Joseph Raz has become its twenty-first-century face. His extensive and sophisticated work represents the high-water mark of analytical jurisprudence. It amounts to a philosophical theory of law that is as rigorous and demanding as it is provocative and controversial. In traversing law's terrain, he is adamant that, whatever the purposes and methods of other disciplines (e.g., sociology, history, anthropology), any philosophical analysis worth its name must concern itself with delivering insights and understanding about law that are of universal significance. While general conclusions about local laws and systems are important and helpful, they will have no philosophical value unless they can say something general and enduring about law as an institutional phenomenon. A corollary of this is that legal philosophy must insulate itself from contingent moral and political influences that will compromise or contaminate its project of making statements about law's nature and operation that are not only universally valid, but also locally accurate. As Raz himself puts it, "where necessity reigns, considerations of moral and political desirability have no role to play".[1]

I will challenge Raz's hard-line variety of positivism – and, therefore, much contemporary work in legal philosophy – by concentrating on his crucial methodological distinction between the local and contingent and the universal and necessary. It will be my contention that, as there are no places where 'moral and political desirability' do not play a role, 'necessity' has no reign. Accordingly, I will argue that the hard positivist version of legal philosophy cannot live up to its own methodological expectations and standards of validation. For all its impressive erudition and sophistication, therefore, Raz's work is better understood as a manifesto of 'local enthusiasms' that, while instructive and useful in themselves, can lay no claim to reveal the necessary features of law's

[1] Joseph Raz, *Between Authority and Interpretation: On the Theory of Law and Practical Reason* 265 (2009).

existence or of its interpretive practices. Blinded by the philosophical light, there is more formal brilliance than substantive bottom-line to Raz's jurisprudential interventions. While his account of law as a body of authoritative rules holds much intuitive appeal, the devilish genius is in the contestable details of his exposition of the relationship between law and political morality in offering an flawed account of legal interpretation.[2]

No Ordinary Joe

Hart's failure to maintain the definitive positivist distinction between law and morality was seized upon by the naturalists and the purposivists as a welcome opportunity to drive home the inseparable link between law and morality. In their different ways, they were adamant that it was not possible to think about law or lawyering without also coming to terms with its moral dimension and normative purposes: law's social facts have inescapable moral components.

However, others saw Hart's failure to be more a deep-seated lack of positivist commitment. They contended that the disappointing fulfillment of Hart's endeavor did not point to fatal flaws in the positivist project itself. Hart's failure was more appropriately attributable to his diluted and softly-softly approach to positivism. If the promise and mission of positivism was to be realized, it demanded a much harder and more uncompromising adherence to the law/morality distinction. Once a student of Hart's, Raz has given his former mentor a run for his money in the jurisprudential sweepstakes of positivism.

Pushed hard by the naturalists and purposivists, the positivists conceded that law (whether in the form of constitutional provisions, legislative enactments, or common law rules) is shot through with moral terms, purposive conditions, and evaluative standards – reasonable care, fair dealing, honesty, good faith conduct, and so on. Consequently, modern positivists were obliged to make a much better fist of explaining and defending their defining 'separation thesis'. In particular, after Hart, the most pressing challenge was to demonstrate convincingly that "legal positivism is normatively inert"[3] – how can the existence of these obvious

[2] In earlier work, I have insisted that Raz's account of law is based on a series of evaluative and partial assumptions about society and its social arrangements. See Allan C. Hutchinson, *The Province of Jurisprudence Democratized* 115–20, 233–9, and 350–7 (2008).

[3] John Gardner, Legal Positivism: 5½ Myths, 46 *AM. J. of Juris.* 199 at 213 (2000).

moral occurrences in legal rules be squared with the positivists' insistence upon the conceptual division between law and morality?

Some took their lead from Hart, but offered a more nuanced account of law and lawyering. Although law and morality must be kept analytically distinct, moral values can still be incorporated and feature in determining matters of legal validity; their inclusion does not require any independent judgment about their moral truth and does not ask jurists to take a stand on their controversial quality. As such, law's identity can be still determined by its source-based pedigree, not its intrinsic moral merit. While this more 'inclusive' mode of positivism goes some of the way to accommodating the non-positivist critique, it does so at the considerable cost of reducing the supposed differences between positivists and non-positivists almost to vanishing point. Indeed, there is much merit to Dworkin's triumphalist claim that this version of positivism is "stunningly like my own" and that it is "hard to see any genuine difference".[4] Soft theorists maintained their positivist faith, but at the cost of their jurisprudential souls.

Raz was and is having none of this. If Hart preferred the softer view that there are no necessary connections between law and morality, Raz took the harder line that there are necessarily no connections between law and morality. He insists that legal norms must be capable of being identified strictly by their pedigree alone in terms of their social sources, not their moral merits. In regard to his softer colleagues, Raz is adamant that to allow the incorporation of moral standards in any way as part and parcel of legal rules would severely and perhaps fatally compromise the separation thesis. For him, it is axiomatic that the identification of law and its content be achieved "without resort to moral considerations" at all if positivism is to be secure against their critics' challenges. As such, Raz holds steadfastly to the claim that law's identity must be determined exclusively by reference to factual sources alone. The law's apparent incorporation of moral standards is nothing more than "an indication that certain considerations are not excluded".[5] For the hard-boiled Razians, it most certainly is not recognition that those moral standards are part of law *qua* moral standards.

[4] Ronald Dworkin, *Justice in Robes* 188 (2006). For other soft positivist approaches, see W. Waluchow, *Inclusive Legal Positivism* (1994), and Kenneth Himma, Inclusive Legal Positivism in *The Oxford Handbook of Jurisprudence and Legal Philosophy* 1235–6 (Jules Coleman and Scott Shapiro eds. 2002).

[5] Raz, supra, note 1 at 4 and 198.

More precisely, Raz explains that it is not that law excludes morality, but that it "modifies ... the way moral considerations apply". For instance, in the same way that conflicts-of-law rules give temporary legal effect to foreign laws in specified situations without making them part of the law itself, some constitutional rules give legal effect to certain moral norms without making them part of the law itself. In both cases, contrary to the claims of the inclusive, soft, or incorporationist positivist, foreign law and morality are not incorporated into the law and thereby do not become part of the law. Moral standards are treated much the same as rules of financial accounting or actuarial tables; they are relied on and resorted to by judges and lawyers, but they do not become part of law and, therefore, count as law by that fact. As such, law "concretiz[es] moral principles"[6] and, having done so, turns them into social facts, not moral values. In this way, issues of legal validity and moral legitimacy are kept conceptually separate.

When it comes to lawyering, therefore, hard positivists treat legal rules as strictly social phenomena that can be identified in an entirely objective and factual way by reference to an uncontested source of authority; there is an analytically unbridgeable chasm between formal pedigree and moral substance. From a Razian perspective, therefore, law exists and functions as both a fact and a norm. It is a social fact in that "its existence and content can be established ... without reliance on moral arguments"; there can be good and bad laws as well as morally legitimate or illegitimate legal systems. While law can by its nature be used to realize valuable ends and can be considered to have a variety of moral tasks to perform, law is not by its nature a morally valuable institution, even if its effects are morally significant. However, law is also normative in that "it aims to guide people's conduct and it claims authority to do so".[7] Although it may fail to make good on its claim, its authority flows from its theoretical capacity and ambition to do so.

It is the idea of 'authority' that lies at the heart of Raz's jurisprudence. For him, a legal system comprises those rules that seek to offer a rational and authoritative guide for human conduct. It is not so much whether that system and its rules have actual authority, but whether they can make a plausible and practical claim to legitimate authority in a particular society. As such, law is an institutionally backed set of reasons for people to do or not do things – 'no vehicles in the park'.

[6] Ibid. at 192 and 347. [7] Ibid. at 344 and 344.

Such legal rules operate as place-markers for substantive reasons. It is Raz's contention that people comply with rules rather than determine for themselves what would be the right thing to do in particular circumstances: "the law is a special kind of reason for it displaces the reasons which it is meant to reflect".[8] These rules must be identifiable as social facts and, therefore, be capable of identification without resort to non-legal or value-laden criteria. If the rules cannot be identifiable and followed in this way, they are no longer serving their primary normative function and, therefore, cannot make the practical difference that they are intended to make and upon which their authority is based. As such, law is an authoritative system of norms that must be identifiable and serviceable on its own terms. If it is not, then its authority would be illusory and such norms would no longer qualify as legal rules, whatever their appeal and authority as moral, religious, or other value-based directives.

There is, of course, much in Raz's work to admire. There is a reassuring sharpness to the distinctions made, an unflinching commitment to analytical rigour, and a welcome confidence in demarcating law's nature and operation. However, there is also much that is unconvincing and obfuscating. Raz tends to be philosophically extravagant in the claims that he makes for his analytical conclusions; this is especially so when he strives toward a universalistic account of law's nature. Moreover, he flaunts his own positivist criteria for separating law and morality when drawing lines between the existence of law, bad law, and no law at all.[9] However, for present purposes, the primary problem with Raz is that, when it comes to the practical elaboration of exactly how to go about identifying and applying law's rules, his minimalist approach is found to be seriously wanting. His account of the necessary technique of legal interpretation is woefully inadequate in its capacity to perform its central role. In short, Raz has no workable account of legal interpretation that can do the indispensable heavy lifting when it comes to making legal rules operational. Indeed, so deficient is his account that he has little to offer by way of guidance or advice in the resolution of so-called easy cases, let alone hard cases.

[8] Ibid. at 7. J. Raz, *The Concept of a Legal System* (2nd ed. 1980), *The Authority of Law* (1979), *The Morality of Freedom* (1986). See also Andrei Marmor, *Interpretation and Legal Theory* (1992).

[9] See Allan C. Hutchinson, Razzle-Dazzle, 1 *Juris.* 39 (2010).

Of Objects and Objections

Raz places great weight on the distinction between law-making, law's existence, and law application. In the Razian scheme of things, it is only law that is autonomous from moral considerations, not its making or its interpretive application: "the distinction between identifying the law and changing it is basic to the law, and central to any coherent understanding of judicial decision-making". For Raz, therefore, there is a sharp and crucial distinction between reasoning to fix the content of law at any point in time "without resort to evaluative considerations"[10] and reasoning to apply that law to particular circumstances and situations: one is reasoning *to law's premises*, whereas the other is reasoning *from law's premises*. This is a crucial distinction and goes some of the way toward vindicating his central positivist claim that law can be identified as a social fact. However, even if law application is interpretive and, therefore, fraught with values, Raz reminds us that, once interpretation is complete in a particular case, the resulting interpretation is absorbed into the law; this means that it can again be identified and fixed as a fact-of-the-matter. Therefore, while moral considerations will feature in the adjudicative application of legal rules, they do not become law until they are incorporated by way of a legal decision.

Understood in this way, it is obvious that Raz must be able to demonstrate that law's rules can be identified independently of and prior to their interpretation. He does this by drawing a comparison between interpretation and legal interpretation. To begin with, he acknowledges that "there is meaning in the world only where it was invested with meaning by human beings". Nevertheless, its human quality means that it is value laden, but this fact does not render it into an 'anything goes' free-for-all. While he concedes that there may well be no one fixed interpretive meaning available, "there is no conflict or tension between pluralism and objectivity as such". In interpreting art, music, or literature, he maintains that "a good interpretation is one that explains the meaning of its object." Most important, Raz insists that "interpretations explain and do not change their objects; ... what they affect is the meaning, not the object which it has". Consequently, all interpretation is a value-infused engagement with the original that gravitates inevitably between fidelity and fecundity. Innovative interpretations are still explanations of meaning, but "they show the object in a new light." He offers the

[10] Supra, note 1 at 239 and 378.

examples of Peter Sellars's interpretation of *The Magic Flute* and Jonathan Miller's *Rigoletto*. Yet when it comes to law, he comes to the strange conclusion that "there is no analogy for [personalized interpretation] in law . . . [because] in legal interpretation we value – other things being equal – continuity".[11] As I will show, this entirely begs the interpretive question in not only art, but also especially law.

By maintaining this strict distinction between the legal object to be interpreted and the act of legal interpretation, Raz claims to be able to preserve the vital positivist quality of law as something that can be identified as a matter of social fact rather than as an exercise in moral evaluation. This means that he carries a heavy onus to demonstrate that the identification of law and its resources can be effectively distinguished from their legal interpretation as practical matters. If he is unable to establish a factual basis on which to rest his interpretive forays, his central claim about law's existence as a social fact will be severely compromised. Yet for all his efforts to distance himself from Hart's softer positivism, Raz is caught in much the same bind – he needs some way to fix the meaning of the bulk of law's rules as a fact if he is to launch his positivist project.[12] Without such a platform, he will be in normative free-fall in which it is morality all the way down.

I contend that such a distinctive manoeuvre is not possible. One of the few examples that Raz gives seems to confirm this. He argues that "we can correctly say that 'sister' means female sibling, and add that everyone understands 'sister' to mean female sibling" to show a certain interpretive certainty.[13] But this entirely underestimates the socially dynamic and historically contingent character of language. Apart from offering little on what it means to be a 'sibling' (i.e., biological, adoptive, communal, etc.), it is surely the case that 'sister' can refer to a much broader group than siblings; it can easily embrace those females who share solidarity in a particular social struggle or who are part of a religious order. Also, it is now trite learning in law that references to 'sister' also include 'brother' unless the context dictates otherwise. None of this is to suggest that 'sister' has no meaning, only that its 'correct' or 'accepted' meaning has less to do with the factness of its existence and more to do with the shifting social conventions that underpin it at a particular place, time, and setting. This is nicely

[11] Ibid. at 230 (emphasis in original), 228, 301, 303, 321, 233, and 233.
[12] See supra, Chapter 3. [13] Supra, note 1 at 229.

illustrated by the Canadian courts' efforts to interpret 'persons' in the *Edwards* case; meaning shifts and changes over time.[14]

So, when it comes to determining the meaning of 'vehicles' or 'park', Raz has little to offer to those who must give specific meaning to its general orientation. Indeed, he seems to be left with the banal advice that judges are pretty much on their own in cases like *Lachapelle* and *Perron*. If anything, he falls back on the unconvincing ground of what Hart terms 'the core of ordinary meaning' and what Holmes in *McBoyle* calls "popular" and "everyday" meaning. These seem very flimsy and insubstantial footings on which to build and defend his unyielding positivistic edifice. Hard positivism seems to be grounded on soft foundations. The debilitating problem is that the value-infused interpretation of law bleeds into the factual identification of law to such an extent as to render the distinction untenable and workable.

No amount of wishful thinking can overcome the realization that there is no available method or means to identify law as a pre-interpretive matter. It is not so much that law does not exist: it does as a body of resources and a set of techniques. Nor is it that its likely development is entirely unpredictable: it has a certain predictability because it draws upon the general political leanings of the law itself (and its judicial interlocutors). But there is no one thing out there that is law, detached and distinct in its thereness and waiting to be interpreted. Legal history and practice strongly suggest that it is interpretation all the way down. Certainly in the common law tradition, interpretation is a thoroughly human and, therefore, value-laden activity that elides any maintainable distinction between rule identification and rule application.[15]

To begin with, there is no 'object' of law that exists before, after, or outside its interpretive apprehension. So, when talking about the task of legal philosophy generally, Raz postulates that the purpose of conceptual analysis is to explain "the conditions for minimal possession of the concept, that is those, essential or non-essential, properties of what the concept is a concept of, knowledge of which is necessary for the person to have the concept at all, however incomplete his or her mastery of it may

[14] See supra, Chapter 5.

[15] Raz ignores entirely the whole law-and-literary-theory debate of the 1980s and 1990s. See especially S. Fish, *Doing What Comes Naturally: Change, Rhetoric, and the Practice of Theory in Literary and Legal Studies* (1989). For my contribution, see A. Hutchinson, *Dwelling on the Threshold* 3–10 (1988), and A. Hutchinson, *It's All in the Game: A Non-Foundationlist Account of Law and Adjudication* 54–85 (2000).

be". As well as exploring art as an object, Raz talks about tangible things in the world, such as water, tables, snakes, and triangles to illustrate his point. For instance, he argues that, "if being made of H_2O is of the nature of water then this is so whether or not people believe that it is so, and whether or not they believe that water has essential properties".[16] This may (or may not) be so, but Raz fails to make the case for why water, art, and law should be considered as fungible or even similar entities for the purposes of conceptual analysis. Indeed, as socially created entities, laws are ontologically very different from tangible objects. Whatever the case for art, water, and the like, law demands a very different approach and understanding even in matters of conceptual analysis.

Moreover, it is true that, in law, there is a constant to and fro between fact and value. However, in contrast to Raz, I contend that this back-and-forth is not so much extra-legal, but is so integral to law as to be constitutive of it. It is not aside from law, but is law. Law is not something that exists before or after interpretive work, but is constituted by that interpretive activity. Whatever the case is in art and literature, legal object and legal interpretation merge so that one is not separable from the other in any sensible or persuasive way. This is particularly the case in regard to the common law tradition, whether the process involved is case law, constitutions, or even statutes. As such, lawyering is a thoroughly morally drenched activity that engages the law's resources as it creates and re-creates them over and across time; everything is permeated with an inescapable moral substance.

Raz is alert to the criticism that, without an interpretation-independent identification of the law's content, it will be incoherent to talk about fidelity or innovation in the interpretation of law. I would also add that, without such an interpretation-independent identification, the mainstay of his positivist jurisprudence – namely, that law can be determined exclusively as a social fact and not by way of moral evaluation – will be in great jeopardy. However, he has little to offer to deflect or defuse this criticism. His response that such a critical 'merging' claim is false is typically opaque and enigmatic. His explanation about constitutional law and interpretation is disquieting:

> It overlooks the fact that the reason fidelity and innovation are often mixed is that we often have reasons to interpret in ways that mix them.

16 Supra, note 1 at 22, 21–4, 67, and 27. Dworkin makes a similar move. See supra, note 4 at 154–5, and supra, Chapter 4.

> But this is not always the case. Sometimes we have reason to interpret the constitution in ways that simply elucidate its content at the moment, warts and all. Such an interpretation, I call it "conserving interpretation", will be successful if it is true to the existing meaning of the constitution. It will include no mixing of conflicting elements. It will display no dialectical tension, and it will establish the benchmark by which we can measure other interpretations to see whether they are more or less innovatory.[17]

This retort is as baffling as it is unconvincing. First, it is riddled with question-begging elements: the most telling is that it assumes that we can distinguish a mixing from a non-mixing. In other words, Raz posits that there is an 'existing meaning of the constitution' against which a conserving, innovatory, or mixing interpretation can be measured. Yet it is the very availability of this 'benchmark' that is at issue in contemporary debate in constitutional and legal theory. There is nothing in Raz's response that successfully undermines the critical claim that the law-as-it-is cannot be identified and fixed as an object without some interpretation or reference to the law-as-it-ought-to-be. Raz's assertion assumes that which is in contention and to be demonstrated. This is fatal for Raz because, so goes his theory of legal interpretation, so goes his whole theory of law.

Through the Park Darkly

As regards legal interpretation, Raz maintains a similar line by proposing that "the decisions of legal authorities are the primary objects, and through interpreting them we gain understanding of the content of the law, which they create". However, Raz is no mechanical formalist. He offers a powerful critique of those, like the originalists, who maintain that legal interpretation is necessarily and legitimately an exercise in retrieval. Instead, he insists that there is an unavoidable back-and-forth between innovation and preservation that allows the law to negotiate the competing demands of continuity and creativity. For Raz, therefore, legal interpretation is about the inevitably human and value-infused activity of giving meaning to those original legal resources of "constitutions, statues, precedents, the texts in which they were formulated, legal rules and doctrines, and the law itself". Moreover, when it comes to law, interpretation must be object-focused because of "the moral

[17] Supra, note 1 at 358.

respect for the law, and for its sources".[18] As such, Raz remains firmly within the formalist camp.

This approach seems to make light of the fact that, because many lawyers operate within a common law system, they are involved in a very organic and fluid process. In such a tradition, it is not so much that a rule is fixed beforehand and then applied to the facts of the case. Instead, a rule tends to be fixed in light of the outcome that it will bring about in the particular case. There is a constant mediation between rule fixing and rule application in the judicial decision-making process such that it becomes illusory to talk about there being two distinct stages as a practical matter; what-the-rule-is is as important as what-the-rule-means. Of course, the fact that the final judgment rendered in the case might not reveal this process or that it might work to actively conceal this dynamic process hardly counts against this explanation. This is doubly so when, in cases like *Donoghue v. Stevenson*, the court revises its previous stance and heads off in an entirely different direction. There, the House of Lords imposed a general duty of care owed by manufacturers to purchasers regardless of any contractual relationship: a new rule was fashioned that owed as much to the socio-political vision of Lord Aitkin as anything else. Rule-fixing and rule application were folded into one and the same process[19]

All this is by way of stating that law is always in the process of becoming rather than being – the law never simply is. In Raz's preferred artistic terms, it is not simply the interpretation of the legal painting that changes or that the legal painting is shown by interpretation in a new light. The legal painting itself changes. For example, the painting of American constitutional law in 2009 is not the same as it was in 1809 or 1909. It is not only that its interpretations have changed; the Constitution is much more than the constitutional document itself. It comprises doctrines, decisions, and principles that develop and change over time. There is never a finished painting; it is always a work-in-progress. In the process of establishing what it is, the judicial artists and legal commentators are always repainting and retouching it. The very act of interpreting law changes it and, on important occasion, redraws it substantially. Again, as in *Donoghue*, there is a whole new painting to be

[18] Supra, note 1 at 239, 273, and 235.

[19] See *Donoghue v. Stevenson*, [1932] AC 562. For an extended account of the dynamics of this case, see Allan C. Hutchinson, *Is Eating People Wrong?: Great Legal Cases and How They Shaped the World* (2010).

interpreted. It is sensible to talk about interpretations being 'conserving' or 'innovatory' only in terms of their political salience and moral effects. This, of course, is not an available move for the formalists unless they want to abandon their status as formalists.

This can also be true of even statutory or constitutional interpretation. Both textual sources are being read against the available principles and voluminous materials of the common law. This is not so much a fresh interpretation of an objective rule, but a remaking of the objective rule itself. Sometimes, words and phases are ignored; sometimes, words and phrases are added. These visible and the invisible processes work together to craft an evanescent and elusive object of interpretation.[20] For example, unwritten constitutional principles and conventions are considered to be of equal and occasionally greater weight than the written text itself. This can result in some sections of text being ignored entirely or being made subservient to larger, but unstated constitutional commitments: a particular and favored strategy is to graft the word 'reasonable' onto a statutory or constitutional mandate.[21] In the statutory context, unstated conditions and exceptions can be viewed as part of the relevant textual provisions. *Lachapelle*, *Perron*, and *McBoyle* each offer ample support for the informalist claim that the interpretive task is creative and uncontainable in scope and substance.

But to say more would be to take Raz's interpretive protestations too seriously and perpetuate a misleading depiction of law. He draws a false distinction between those who believe that there is objectivity and that interpretation is about retrieval and those who believe that there is only subjectivity and that interpretation is about creation; it is neither one nor the other. In the legal world, the judge is as much the artist as the critic or interpreter. Law/art is not simply created in the interaction between the materials, the artist and interpreter, but is found in the interplay itself; it is the process of painting as much as the resources and the product that counts as law. Indeed, law cannot be broken down into its constituent parts without losing the essential part of the dynamic interaction itself. Because the materials change, the artists change, and the interpreters change, the whole of law can be greater (and, on occasion, less) than the

[20] Laurence Tribe, *The Invisible Constitution* (2008). As Tribe insists, it is not so much "what's invisible" around "the Constitution [but] . . . what is invisible within it." Ibid. at 10.

[21] See, for example, *R. v. Sparrow*, [1990] 1 SCR 1075 (the Canadian Charter provision protecting aboriginal rights could be glossed with a reasonable limitation constraint).

sum of its individual parts. As such, law is better understood as an activity, not merely a thing. And as Raz himself would concede, if that is the case, then law is a human activity and inextricably bound up with the values and commitments of society.

Furthermore, Raz's elliptical aside that a demonstration that the law is "vague and indeterminate" still counts as a statement of what the law is only adds fuel to the fire.[22] If by this, he means that some rules will be 'vague and indeterminate', there is no cause for critical concern: it would be wrong-headed to dispense with any theory of law simply because it was unable to identify and fix all legal rules with complete precision and absolute determinacy at all times. However, it is another thing entirely if Raz is claiming that widespread or structural indeterminacy is compatible with his positivist account of law. At a minimum, it would seem that there would need to be some significantly substantial degree of operational determinacy to law if he was to make good on his crucial and fast distinction between law and its interpretation. I maintain that such a threshold cannot be reached and that, like the softer Hart, Raz's claims founder on the dangerous rocks of indeterminacy. This does not have to mean that law is so indeterminate that it cannot meet any jurisprudential standard of operational plausibility. It is enough to show that there is insufficient determinacy to support Raz's extravagant claims about law as a social fact of the matter.[23]

Accordingly, in the process of trying to salvage his claim that there is available an interpretation-independent identification of the law's content as a matter of fact, Raz has succeeded only in undermining further his positivist insistence on law's factual existence. If a conclusion that the law is structurally indeterminate (as opposed to concessions about the penumbral openness of individual rules) is counted by Raz as a valid and acceptable statement of what the law is, then he has given unwitting support to the withering assessment that "pure positivism comes close to pure emptiness".[24] By making the price of analytical accuracy to be the cost of practical worth, he has set the threshold of describing what "the law itself"[25] is in an interpretation-independent way

[22] Supra, note 1 at 359.

[23] That said, I will develop and substantiate the claim that law is thoroughly indeterminate in the sense that it is always and irreducibly open to destabilization and reconfiguration. See infra, Chapter10.

[24] James Boyle, Thomas Hobbes and the Invented Tradition of Positivism: Reflections on Language, Power, and Essentialist, 135 *U. Pa. L. Rev.* 383 at 400 (1987).

[25] Supra, note 1 at 273.

so low as to be virtually non-existent: what the law factually is can be whatever we morally want it to be. Indeed, Raz offers almost an apologia for the untutored and unreflective judge who, like Watkins L.J. in *Lamb*, simply goes with the conventional flow in identifying and applying rules: "a robust and sensible approach to ... remoteness will more often than not produce ... an instinctive feeling that the event or act being weighed in the balance is too remote".[26] However, as is so often the case, convention, let alone instinct, turns out to be an unreliable and flimsy basis on which to proceed when opinions diverge even slightly. All told, this approach is hardly a defence of legal positivism; it is more of a caricature and even contradiction of it.

Conclusion

The work of Raz is very much an acquired taste. While his work is celebrated as the epitome of rigorous analysis by his many supporters and acolytes, it will do little to convert those who are sceptical about the merits of a hard/exclusive rendering of legal positivism. In the same way that this spare and stripped-down depiction of legal philosophy will appeal to the converted, its barren and bleak portrayal will also disenchant the more critical. As one who is not persuaded by Raz's methodological approach nor its positivist product, I simply point out that law is a much richer, complex, and fecund territory than Raz's philosophical depiction can capture; the ravages and revitalizations of time and chance are inescapable on the moral terrain on which law exists and thrives. A full appreciation and understanding of law and lawyering warrants a much more colorful, sympathetic, and organic mode of representation and analysis than Raz encourages or allows. Accordingly, a harder line of positivism is no more successful at explaining law and lawyering than any other formalist account, positivist or otherwise. In such a 'rigorous' view, although touted as a solid and straightforward matter, legal interpretation remains a mysterious and almost mystical process.

[26] *Lamb v. London Borough of Camden*, [1981] QB 625 at 639.

8

Crossing Over

The Anti-Formalist Critique

Of course, the formalists' forces have not swept all before them. Critics of law and legal interpretation insist that there is no formalist methodology that can satisfactorily explain and justify what it is that lawyers do when they engage in acts of legal interpretation. While some recommend that judges' ideological preferences infiltrate their decisions in hard cases, there are others who take the unmitigated line that those ideological preferences are the main and, for some, the sole explanatory source of legal decision-making. These anti-formalists argue that, if you want to understand the legal or judicial enterprise, the best place to look is not the law's rules and technical methods but at the ideological preferences of the judges. In short, all the talk about legal rules and professional rule-applying techniques being at the core of the lawyering enterprise is considered to be so much distracting propaganda generated by lawyers and judges to legitimize their own power and authority. In the anti-formalists' frame of reference, legal doctrine is little more than 'shoveled smoke'; it hides much more than it can or does explain. For them, once the smoke is cleared away, it is ideology all the way through and through.

In this chapter, I will introduce and evaluate the claims that judges' ideological preferences are a much more (and perhaps the only) reliable guide to understanding their decisions than any other available mode of justification, including law and legal doctrine. Carried out mostly by social scientists, this work presents itself as a valuable corrective to the excesses and false optimism of the formalists. However, while I share their claim that ideology is a major and irrepressible force in driving legal interpretation, I maintain that it operates in a much less one-dimensional and more nuanced way than the anti-formalists allow. Therefore, the insights of the anti-formalists can and must play a part in improving any appreciation of legal interpretation, but they cannot claim to have solved its underlying puzzle; they offer an antidote to the formalist contagion, but they do not provide the cured condition. Much like formalism, the problem with the anti-formalists can be traced to their reliance on the same black-and-white view of the judicial world in which the explanatory choices are either law or ideology. In contrast, I am suggesting an informal account of legal interpretation that is more sophisticated in that it is not either/or, but is both/and when it comes to law and ideology.

The Charted World

In recent years, theoretical debates about law and legal interpretation have become laden down by the weight of their own abstract convolutions and technical contrivances. As well as seeking to respond to vigorous criticisms from outside the formalist citadel, there has been extensive in-fighting among formalists that has raised severe doubts about the way forward. However, as formalist theoreticians have tended to take debates down ever more obscure cul-de-sacs and blind alleys, another group of scholars has entered the fray. Deploying the more sophisticated and objective methods of the social sciences, a cadre of empirical scholars has sought to illuminate what it is that judges actually do. Rather than rely on what judges say they do or what jurists think they do, these scholars have turned away from traditional softer tools of legal theory. Instead, they have called upon the harder methodologies of statistical and quantitative analysis to generate and make sense of the data on judicial decision-making. In short, there has been an empirical turn in jurisprudence by way of a 'new legal realism'.[1]

The basic approach has been to correlate judicial decisions with political ideology; theirs is a descriptive, not prescriptive brief. Much of this work looks at the courts as one more political institution in which political actors and values vie for control and influence in decisions reached and policies promoted. The general empirical method taken is to isolate a judge's' political identity along a simple conservative/liberal measure by drawing upon his or her background, career, judgments, speeches, publications, and other pertinent information. While there is far from unanimity on design or detail in these studies, there is a general acceptance among interdisciplinary scholars that a judge's political ideology does play an important and perhaps exclusive role in explaining why judges decide as they do.

[1] *See* Thomas Miles and Cass Sunstein, The New Legal Realism, 75 *U. Chi. L. Rev.* 81 (2008). See also Victoria Nourse and Gregory Shaffer, Varieties of New Legal Realism: Can a New World Order Prompt a New Legal Theory?, 95 *Cornell. L. Rev* 61 (2009), and Larry Solum, The Positive Foundations of Formalism: False Necessity and American Legal Realism, 127 *Harv. L. Rev.* 2464 (2014).

Indeed, it is insisted that any effort to understand adjudication, especially of the appellate kind, will be flawed if it does not seek to incorporate judges' political values; matters of legal philosophy are decidedly secondary. Of course, the challenge remains of explaining exactly when and how judges rely on their ideological values and commitments.

The overall and unsurprising conclusion of these empirical and behavioral studies by political and social scientists is that, whatever judges think or say that they are doing in terms of the law's materials and interpretive techniques, the overwhelming evidence is that their work and decisions are influenced and often determined by their own ideological commitments and moral values. However, while all studies share that general conclusion, there is considerable disagreement over two important matters. One area of disagreement among empirical scholars is what counts as the most persuasive explanation why there is such a divergence between the appearance and reality of judicial making. Whereas some think that it might be knowingly understood and hidden, others maintain that it has more to do with cognitive biases or motivated reasoning.[2] Although this is not an insignificant issue, it is the other area of disagreement that has garnered most attention.

A serious source of disagreement in the social science literature is the extent of the influence of the judges' ideological preferences on their decision-making. There is a whole range of responses to this crucial issue. While some take a more measured and cautious approach, the bulk of available studies reaches the conclusion that such ideological values are the primary, dominant, or even exclusive factor in explaining or predicting judicial decisions. The role of 'law' is considered to be very much secondary or ancillary.[3] So, in

[2] See, e.g., Jeffrey A. Segal et al., *The Supreme Court in the American Legal System* 33–5 (2005). This is an important matter, but has more to do with psychology than jurisprudence.

[3] See e.g., Jeffrey A. Segal and Harold J. Spaeth, *The Supreme Court and the Attitudinal Model* (1993) and *The Supreme Court and the Attitudinal Model Revisited* (2002); Cass R. Sunstein et al., *Are Judges Political? An Empirical Analysis of the Federal Judiciary* (2006); Andrew D. Martin et al., Competing Approaches To Predicting Supreme Court Decision Making, 2 *Persp. on Pol.* 761 (2004); Frank Cross, The Significance of Statutory Interpretive Methodologies, 82 *Notre Dame L. Rev.* 1971 (2007); Richard Pacelle, Jr., Brett W. Curry, and Bryan W. Marshall, *Decision-Making by the Modern Supreme Court* (2011); and Lee Epstein, William Landes, and Richard Posner, *The Behaviour of Federal Judges* (2014). On Canada, see Daved Muttart, *The Empirical Gap in Jurisprudence: A Comprehensive Study of the Supreme Court of Canada* (2007); C.L. Ostberg and Matthew E. Wetstein, *Attitudinal Decision-Making in the Supreme Court of Canada* (2007); and Donald R. Songer, Susan W. Johnson, C.L. Ostberg, and Matthew E. Wetstein, *Law, Ideology, and Collegiality: Judicial Behaviour in the Supreme Court of Canada* (2012).

both *Lachapelle* and *Perron*, what an ideologically motivated judge would do is unclear; it will, of course, depend upon the particular cut of his or her own ideological affiliations. However, according to the anti-formalists, it is clear about how they would go about their task. Whether knowingly or otherwise, judges would consult their ideological preferences to discover what they might recommend in such situations. By way of generalization, it might be suggested that a more liberal judge would be more tolerant and a more conservative judge more restrictive in his or her interpretation of 'park' in order to give more weight to the convicted person's freedom of movement. While their judgments might be framed in more traditional formalist terms (as they were), this would be more by way of *ex post* rationalization than *ex ante* reasoning.

From the formalist perspective, this is a devastating conclusion if it can be justified as true and reliable. Moreover, it is also extremely troubling to anyone, including myself, who thinks that judicial decision-making is not simply a sham and that legal materials and techniques do play an important and serious role in the work of judges – are judges really so dishonest or deluded in their professional activities? Has law and legal doctrine no real salience in legal interpretation and decision-making? Fortunately, while empirical studies have much to offer, especially in undermining the grander and imperialistic claims of many formalists, they are far from beyond reproach or reservation themselves. The anti-formalist studies should not be read at face value. Being the mirror image of formalism, they are equally grand and imperialistic in their claims. As I will endeavor to demonstrate, the failings of an anti-formalist approach are equally large; they run from the methodological to the ideological.

Shift Happens

Until recently, the received view among these anti-formalists was that judges are thought to hold one particular set of general interpretive and substantive views about law and the Constitution; they do not tend to morph from one ideological or jurisprudential identity to another during their tenure. However, a surge of empirical studies on the relationship between judicial decision-making and judges' political values has begun to challenge that stance. Scholars now tend to conclude that Supreme Court judges exhibit 'ideological drift': whatever the political viewpoint of a judge on appointment to the Court, there seems to occur a noticeable change or modification over time. For instance, in studies of Supreme Court rulings, it has been concluded that, while a judge's location on a conservative/liberal grid can predict some future decisions, it cannot do so with any degree of consistency over time; justices shift and change in their political commitments. Indeed, according to the two leading studies, shift is seen to be the rule, not the exception: "Of the twenty-six judges who served on the Court for ten or more terms since 1937 [to 2007], all but four exhibit ideological drift over the course of their tenure – twelve moved to the left; seven to the right; and three in more exotic ways".[4] Drift is the apparent order of the judicial mind.

Notwithstanding important and subtle differences between results based upon varying research methodologies, Chart 1 shows that there is a general and similar pattern in play – judges' ideology tends to shift over time and there is no particular pattern or direction to that change.[5]

If judges were always true to their ideological preferences, the sense might be that they would be more consistent over time in their decision-making than Chart 1 suggests. In graphical terms, this would suggest that most judges would have a much flatter career trajectory. Of course, it would be silly to expect absolute consistency. Also, it would be equally silly to assume that judges might not change their ideological preferences as they develop and grapple with pressing social issues. Nevertheless, the drift (or what I would prefer to call 'shift')[6] is not trivial and needs some explanation.

[4] Lee Epstein, Andrew D. Martin, Kevin M. Quinn, and Jeffrey Segal, Ideological Drift among Supreme Court Judges: Who, When, and How Important? 101 *Nw. U. L. Rev.* 1483, 1504 (2007). These studies are generally confirmed by the sole Canadian study: "the clear story to be told, however, is that justices do in fact shift in their preferences over the course of their careers, and that it is extremely difficult to predict the manner in which the justices will shift." See Benjamin Alarie and Andrew Green, Policy Preference Change and Appointments to the Supreme Court of Canada, 47 *Osgoode Hall L.J.* 1, 61 (2009).

[5] The chart is drawn from Andrew D. Martin and Kevin M. Quinn, Dynamic Ideal Point Estimation via Markov Chain Monte Carlo for the U.S. Supreme Court, 1953–1999, 10 *Pol. Analysis* 134 (2002). There is debate about the efficacy of these studies in terms of their methodological shortcomings and political bluntness. See, e.g., Wade Farnsworth, The Use and Limits of Martin-Quinn Scores to Assess Supreme Court Justices, with Special Attention to the Problem of Ideological Drift, 101 *Nw. U. L. Rev.* 143 (2007), and Royce Carroll, Comparing Nominate and Ideal: Point of Difference and Monte Carlo Tests, 34 *Legis. Stud. Q.* 555 (2009). I am simply not qualified to enter that very technical exchange about data sources, coding, smoothing parameters, etc. Suffice it to say, the basic thrust of their analyses is sufficient for my purposes, whatever the reservations about the details of the studies. Daniel E. Ho and Kevin M. Quinn, How Not to Lie with Judicial Votes: Misconceptions, Measurement, and Models, 98 *Cal L. Rev.* 813 (2010).

[6] I much prefer the term 'shift' to that of 'drift'. Drift suggests that there is a lack of purpose or animus. While individual judges may not be entirely conscious of their shifts over time, it is unconvincing to imply that these changes are orchestrated by some unconscious or invisible hand

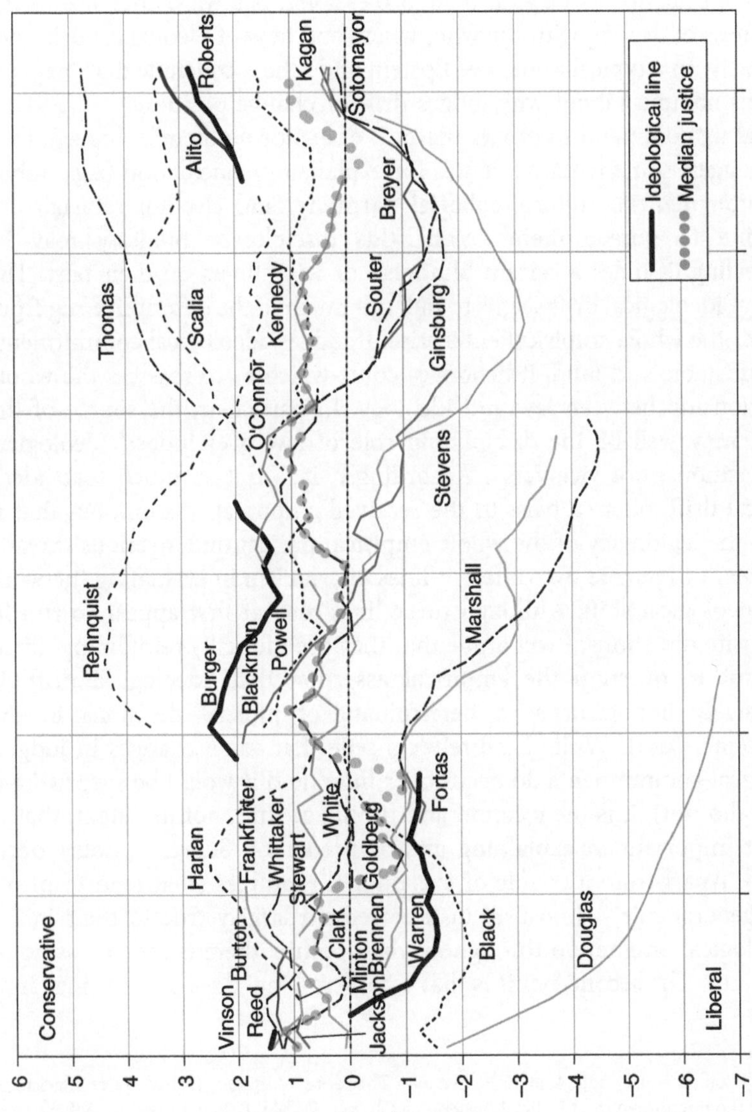

6
5
4
3
2
1
0
−1
−2
−3
−4
−5
−6
−7
1951
1961
1971
1981
1991
2001
2011
Conservative
Liberal
Vinson
Reed
Burton
Jackson
Minton
Clark
Brennan
Warren
Black
Douglas
Harlan
Frankfurter
Whittaker
Stewart
Goldberg
White
Fortas
Burger
Blackmun
Powell
Rehnquist
Marshall
Stevens
O'Connor
Scalia
Kennedy
Souter
Thomas
Ginsburg
Breyer
Alito
Roberts
Kagan
Sotomayor
Ideological line
Median justice

Chart 1

Unfortunately, most empirical scholars maintain that they can finesse or sidestep this compelling issue of explaining why judges appear to change their political spots over the duration of their careers. While they recognize the merits or importance of any such inquiry, they insist that such speculation is outside their professional bailiwick; they are in the business of dealing with the who, when, and how of ideological drift, not the why. In a typical aside, Lee Epstein and others conclude that "explanations abound [about why judges drift or change positions] ... and we certainly commend to others the task of exploring them".[7] Indeed, they do suggest some tentative routes for explanatory elucidation (e.g., public opinion, judicial culture, collegial harmony, and election returns) but decline to pursue them. While this disciplinary modesty may be appealing, it hides a certain blindness or willfullness on their part. The fact of ideological drift seems to pull out much of the descriptive rug from under the whole empirical enterprise. If judges' ideological commitments are unstable and fluid, it behooves court-watchers to reassess the whole relationship between law and ideology. In particular, the source of the shift may well be the disciplining role of law over judges' ideological dispositions, not vice-versa. Accordingly, it is not so much that 'ideological drift' offers a twist to the received empirical wisdom, but that it puts the legitimacy of the whole empirical project under serious threat.

I want to pursue two different lines of criticism in evaluating the work on ideological shift. Although these lines may at first appear to run in opposite directions, I will argue that they are mutually reinforcing. First, I want to question the empirical assertion that 'ideological drift' is decisively important as a determinant of judicial decisions in the Supreme Court. While I entirely concede that some changes in judges' political commitments do occur over time (and it would be surprising if they did not), it is the location and timing of shift, not its extent, that is most important in explaining and/or predicting Supreme Court decisions. Apart from a couple of exceptional examples (that tend to prove the general rule), almost all justices remain largely true to their initial ideological orientation throughout their tenure; there is little crossing of the lines. The second point is that what 'crossing' does occur brings into

[7] See Epstein, supra, note 4, at 1520. See also Theodore W. Ruger, Justice Harry Blackmun and the Phenomenon of Judicial Preference Change, 70 *Mo. L. Rev.* 1209 (2005); Lawrence Baum, *Judges and Their Audiences* (2006), and Neal Devins and Lawrence Baum, *Split Definitive: How Party Polarization Turned the Supreme Court into a Partisan Court* (2014).

critical focus the contested question of the role that is played by law and/ or non-ideological factors in judicial decision-making. A possible explanation for drift is that as 'law' changes over time, the resulting legal doctrine works to modify or diffuse the impact of judges' ideological preferences. I will pursue the first argument in this chapter and the second argument in the next chapter.[8]

Crossing the Lines

It seems to be assumed that this ideological drift has an impact on the decisions reached. In other words, the operating assumption is that, if judges were more consistent in holding and implementing their political values, the Supreme Court would have reached a different set of decisions and developed a different of body of legal doctrines. Yet this rather grand and unsettling finding is far from supported by the data that the empirical scholars rely upon. Indeed, it may well be contradicted by it. While the proven fact of some noticeable ideological drift among judges is unassailable, it has most definitely not had a significant or non-trivial effect on the development of the law, legal doctrine, and judicial decisions. This is not to say that there could not be an ideological drift of sufficient range and size that it would have a significant or non-trivial effect. It is only to say that any effect that can be convincingly attributed to the presently documented ideological drift is relatively insignificant and trivial.

For instance, if we pose two specific and pertinent questions of the data, they point to the fact that, even though there is a considerable amount of drift over time, any ideological variation has not had the substantial impact on the Supreme Court's decision-making that empirical scholars propose and defend. Those two questions are: how many judges have moved from one side of the liberal/conservative political spectrum to the other? and how many judges have moved across the line of the 'median judge'? This two-level inquiry puts the data in a very different light and recommends a very different set of conclusions. Indeed, the answers to these two questions are revealing and provocative on both a particular and general basis.

As regards the shift from one side of the liberal/conservative political spectrum to the other, Chart 2 is highly suggestive. Removing those

[8] See infra, Chapter 9.

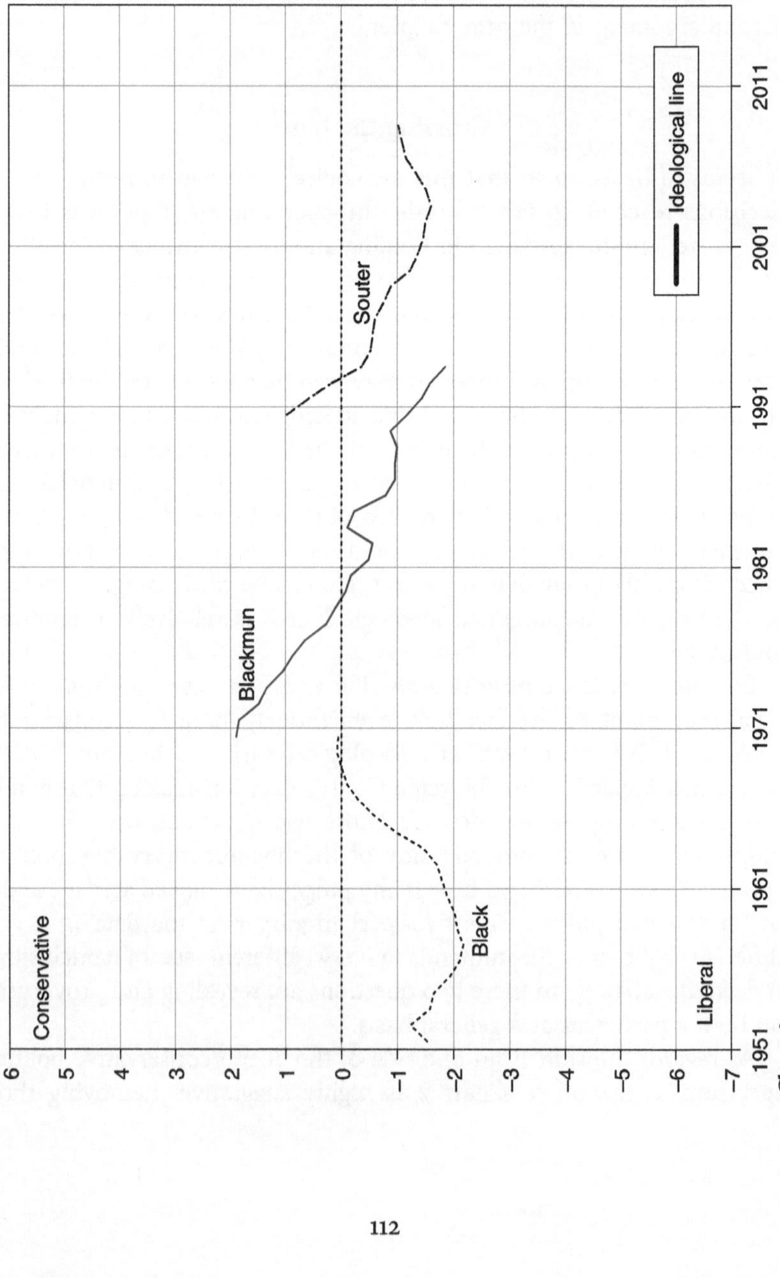

Conservative
Liberal
Black
Blackmun
Souter
Ideological line
6
5
4
3
2
1
0
−1
−2
−3
−4
−5
−6
−7
1951
1961
1971
1981
1991
2001
2011

Chart 2

judges whose values have drifted within the liberal or conservative sides of the spectrum, there are only three judges (i.e., Justices Hugo Black, Harry Blackmun, and David Souter) who have crossed the liberal/conservative dividing line. This means that, out of the thirty-four judges who served on the Supreme Court from 1937 onward, only these three have moved across the ideological divide in any significant or lasting way; this is less than 10 percent of the available sample. On the basis of such a finding, it is difficult to maintain the claim that ideological drift has played a decisive or significant role in Supreme Court decision-making or decisions.

As Chart 3 makes clear, the bulk of judges have tended to maintain the general ideological disposition from which they began. Of course, there have been deviations from their original ideological stance, some moderate and some less so. But liberals have tended to remain liberal (e.g., Justice Ruth Ginsburg) and conservatives have continued to be conservative (e.g., Justice Warren Burger). Moreover, some of those who have varied in their ideological disposition have hardened as much as softened in their views (e.g., Justices Thurgood Marshall and Clarence Thomas). Indeed, it would be surprising if judges did not make some alterations in the basic political values over the course of a long judicial career, especially where the political values of society at large were in flux.

Similarly, there is also a cluster of justices who have closely followed or straddled the ideological divide but have made no lasting shift from one side to the other. As Chart 4 reveals, some judges (e.g., Justices Byron White and Potter Stewart) who were in the middle of the road in political terms when appointed have tended to remain so throughout their careers. They have drifted in very small ways as the social times change, as the composition of the Supreme Court itself changes, and as their own political commitments recalibrate in emphasis and priority. Again, it would be surprising if judges, like most people, did not go through some developmental or reorganizational process as they dealt with the controversial subject matter of appellate litigation.

As regards the drift across the line of the median judge,[9] the story is much the same as that for the drift from one side of the liberal/conservative political spectrum to the other. As Chart 5 demonstrates, there are

[9] Put simply, the median judge is the real or hypothetical justice who would occupy the centre or average of the Supreme Court's ideological spread. As such, that position moves as the composition and orientation of the Supreme Court changes over time. See Andrew D. Martin et al., The Median Justice on the United States Supreme Court, 83 *N.C. L. Rev.* 1275 (2005).

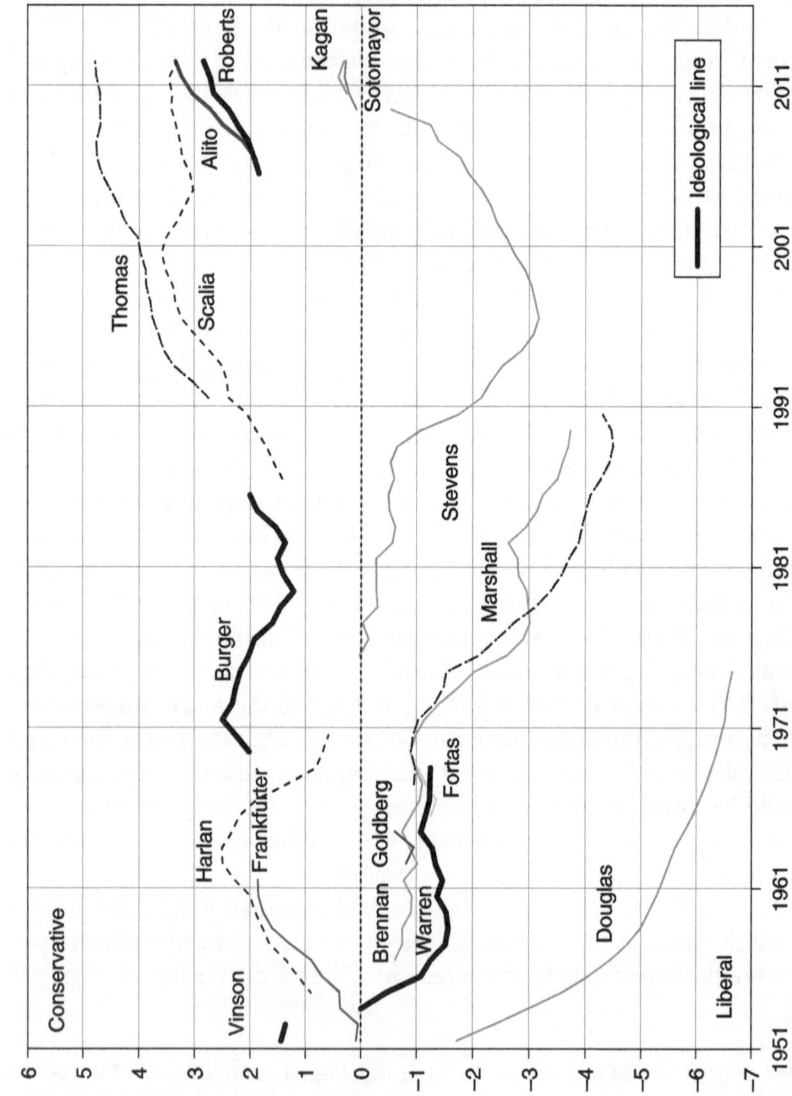
Conservative
Liberal
Vinson
Harlan
Frankfurter
Brennan
Goldberg
Warren
Fortas
Douglas
Burger
Marshall
Stevens
Thomas
Scalia
Alito
Roberts
Kagan
Sotomayor
Ideological line
6
5
4
3
2
1
0
-1
-2
-3
-4
-5
-6
-7
1951
1961
1971
1981
1991
2001
2011

Chart 3

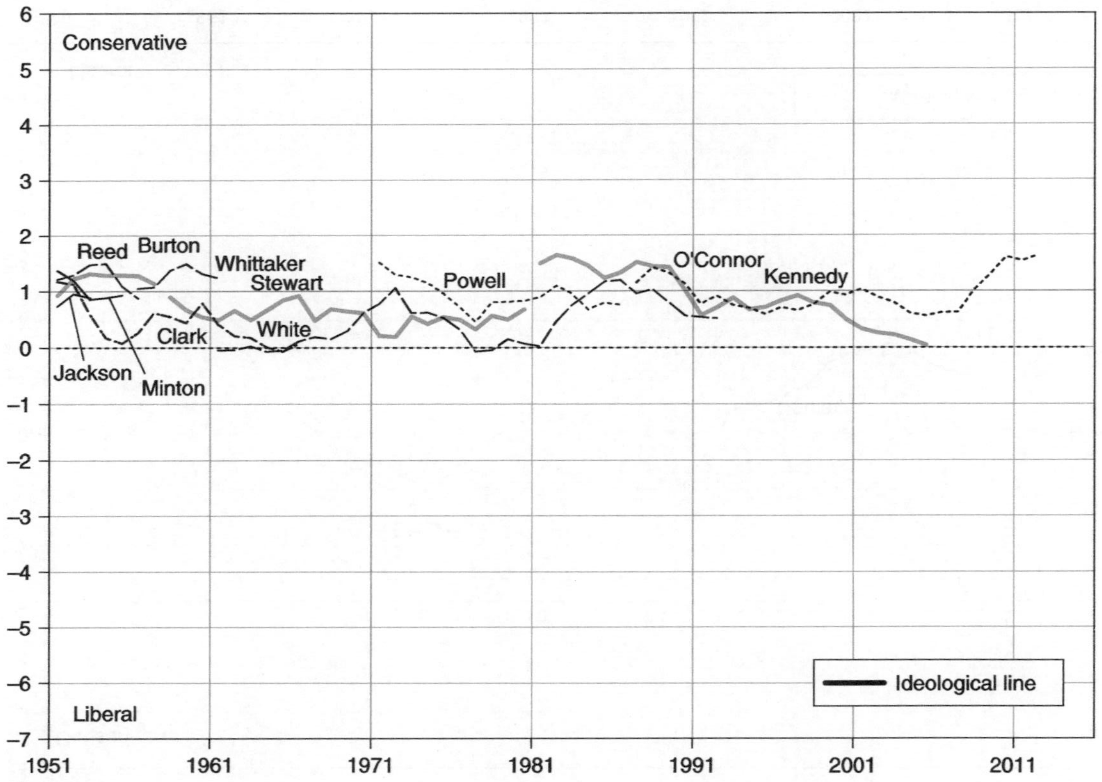

Conservative
Reed
Burton
Whittaker
Stewart
Powell
O'Connor
Kennedy
Clark
White
Jackson
Minton
Liberal
Ideological line
6
5
4
3
2
1
0
−1
−2
−3
−4
−5
−6
−7
1951
1961
1971
1981
1991
2001
2011

Chart 4

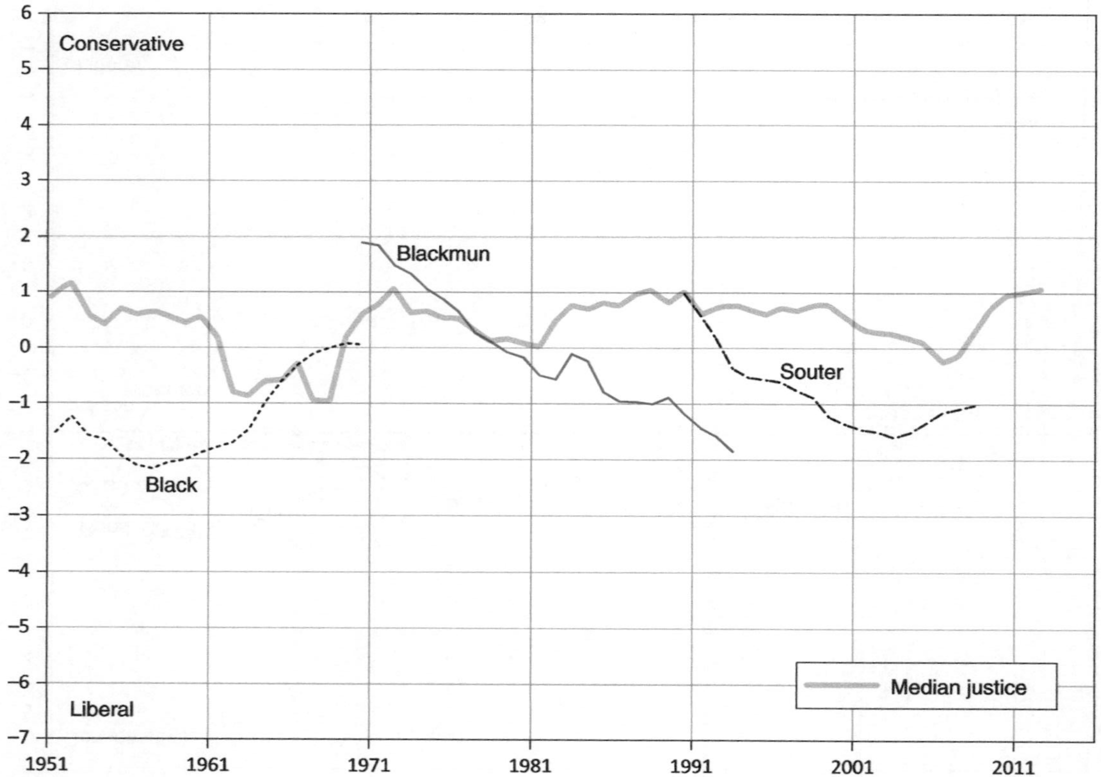
6
5
4
3
2
1
0
−1
−2
−3
−4
−5
−6
−7
Conservative
Liberal
Blackmun
Black
Souter
Median justice
1951
1961
1971
1981
1991
2001
2011

Chart 5

only the same three judges (i.e., Justices Hugo Black, Harry Blackmun, and David Souter) out of all the judges who served on the Supreme Court from 1937 onward who have moved across that line. Again, this amounts to less than 10 percent of the judges. The bulk of judges have tended to maintain the ideological position from which they began. Indeed, it is only one judge (i.e., Justice Harry Blackmun) who has made a marked switch in political allegiance from one side to the other

In the same way as with drifting across the political spectrum, most judges have tended to remain the same distance from the 'median judge' line or moved further away from it. Chart 6 confirms this phenomenon. Again, in much the same way, Chart 7 shows that there is also a cluster of justices who have closely followed or straddled the 'median judge' line but have made no lasting shift from one side to the other (e.g., Justices Byron White and Potter Stewart). It is the fact that they are ideologically middle-of-the-road that has been important, not the extent of their drift, if any. No judge has maintained a perfectly consistent and undeviating trajectory over the spread of his or her tenure. Again, it would be extraordinary if they had. Accordingly, any claim that ideological drift has made a significant impact on the work of the Supreme Court is hard to sustain as a general argument.

As far as my focus is concerned, the main point is that Justices Hugo Black, Harry Blackmun, and David Souter are the exceptions that prove the general rule – among the great bulk of judges, there is drift, but that drift is of contestable or limited significance. The fact that it has been asserted that "Blackmun very well may have undergone one of the most marked ideological changes the United States has seen in a public figure during [the twentieth] century" merely confirms my assessment. In order to be of great significance in the overall direction of Supreme Court decisions and legal doctrine, any ideological drift not only has to be extreme, but also has to move across the ideological divide as well as over the median line.[10]

The upshot of all this is that, while there might well be changes or shifts in judges' political commitments over time, their extent and effects are far less significant than the empirical scholars claim them to be. Almost all judges remain largely true to their initial and general

[10] Jeffrey B. King, Now Turn to the Left: The Changing Ideology of Justice Harry A. Blackmun, 33 *Hous. L. Rev.* 277, 277 (1996). See also Note, The Changing Social Vision of Justice Harry A. Blackmun: The Conscientious Conscience, 96 *Harv. L. Rev.* 717, 717 (1983) ("Harry A. Blackmun has undergone a remarkable transformation").

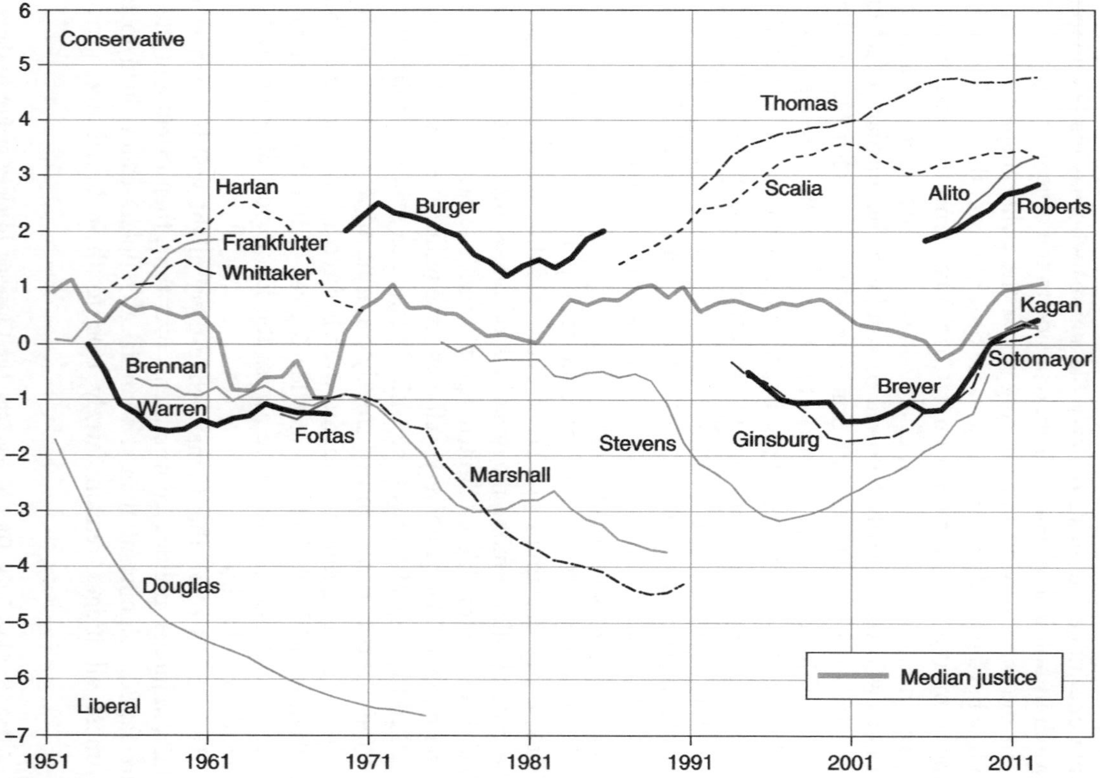

Conservative
Liberal
Thomas
Scalia
Alito
Roberts
Harlan
Burger
Frankfurter
Whittaker
Kagan
Brennan
Sotomayor
Breyer
Warren
Fortas
Stevens
Ginsburg
Marshall
Douglas
Median justice
6
5
4
3
2
1
0
−1
−2
−3
−4
−5
−6
−7
1951
1961
1971
1981
1991
2001
2011

Chart 6

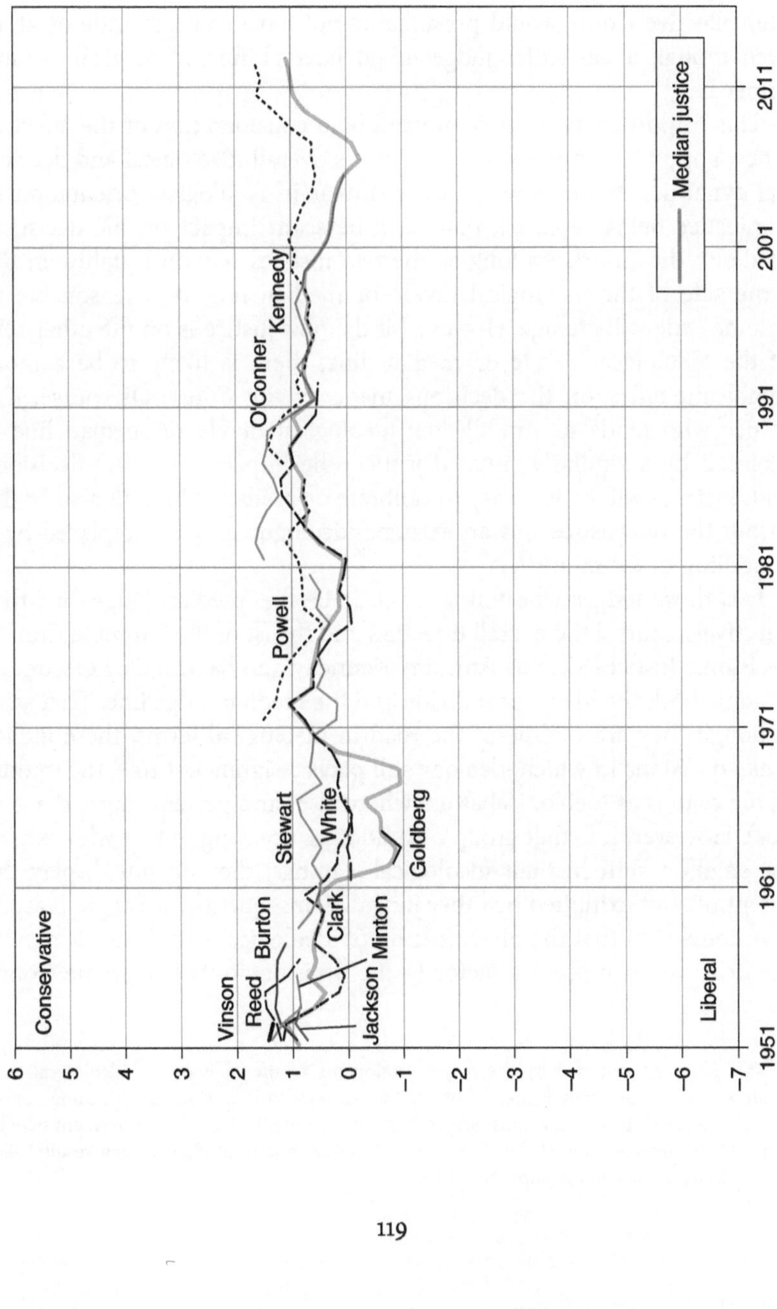
Conservative
Liberal
Median justice
Vinson
Reed
Burton
Jackson
Minton
Clark
Stewart
White
Goldberg
Powell
O'Conner
Kennedy
6
5
4
3
2
1
0
−1
−2
−3
−4
−5
−6
−7
1951
1961
1971
1981
1991
2001
2011
Chart 7

ideological commitments as conservatives or liberals throughout their tenure. Although their ideological leanings may become weaker or stronger over time, they do not change to such an extent that they will likely result in that judge making decisions or voting in such a way as to effect great change in the decisions made by the Court: the decisions of the collective Court would presumably not have changed little or at all even though a particular judge might have shifted ideological ground somewhat.[11]

This important point is reinforced by a consideration of the effect of a new appointee on the Supreme Court's overall ideological and decisional dynamics. If the new justice is similar in ideological orientation to the justice being replaced, there will be scant impact on the decisions made by the Court. As long as the two justices remain roughly on the same side of the ideological divide or median line, it is reasonable to assume little will change. However, if the new justice is on the other side of the ideological divide or median line, there is likely to be a more significant effect on the decisions made by the Court. Of course, if a justice who tends to straddle the ideological divide or median line is replaced by a similarly situated justice, the impact on future decisions and doctrine will be less easy to calibrate or predict. This will also be the case if the old justice was an extreme ideologue and was replaced by a straddling or swing justice.

It is those judges who follow or straddle the 'median judge' line that effectively control the overall direction and thrust of the Supreme Court's decisions. Justices such as Anthony Kennedy and Sandra Day O'Connor straddle both the ideological divide and the median judge line. That said, although they are middle-of-the-road in ideological terms, these judges make decisions in which ideology still plays a significant role; the middle of the road is as ideological as anywhere else (and perhaps more dangerous). However, it is that group of straddling or swing judges who exhibit the smallest shift in their ideological leanings; they do not display the extent of shift exhibited by other judges. Consequently, it can be reasonably concluded that the phenomenon of ideological shift is not generally the decisive or important factor in the decisions of the Supreme Court.

[11] This point is conceded by the major proponents of the existence of ideological shift among Supreme Court justices. But they do so only to ignore its undermining consequences for their overall claims. See Epstein, supra, note 9, at 47 ("the movement may be relatively inconsequential, but in others substantial doctrinal change may result"). See also Martin and Quinn, supra, note 10.

Those judges that shift most tend to do so away from, not across the ideological divide; they have little effect on the overall direction of decisions made.

Ironically, those justices who shift least have the most effect on the overall direction of decisions made. In other words, it is not so much the extent of shift that is important, but its location along the liberal/conservative ideological spectrum. Whereas large shift may have no impact nearer the poles of the liberal/conservative spectrum, small and even temporary changes in position can have substantial and even decisive impact along the median line (see Chart 7). Within polarized courts, the middle ground will prove to be the most influential. Accordingly, the common rap against statistical studies holds true for studies on judges and ideology – statistics hide as much as they disclose; it is the parts that are hidden that are as important as the parts that are revealed.

It is not so much that ideological shift occurs from some fixed ideological position, but more that a justice is working through and fine-tuning his or her ideological commitments, legal orientation, and relationship between the two. Indeed, it may well be that it is in the decisive region of the 'median judge' that legal considerations as well as political influences will have their most impactful influence. In most other circumstances, the crossing of the lines is limited. In light of this finding about ideological drift, I want to offer a more satisfying explanation of the relationship between judges' ideological leanings and their decision-making. Within the empirical literature, there is little serious or sustained debate about why the putative ideological drift occurs: some off-hand or speculative opinions are offered, but no consensus has come close to emerging. By filling that important gap and providing a fuller account of judicial decision-making, it becomes clearer why there is actually little tension in judicial decision-making between a reliance on political values and a respect for legal considerations. When properly understood, Supreme Court adjudicative behavior is revealed as being inevitably about the integration of ideology and law into an overall mode of decision-making.

Conclusion

There is much to learn from quantitative research into law's operation and effects; it can enrich and inform the understanding of law as a social phenomenon. This is particularly true about the empirical work done on judicial decision-making. However, this rich body of research has only a limited and inconclusive part to play in answering the pressing challenges of explaining the whys and wherefores of judicial decision-making; more empirical legal study is a necessary but an insufficient component of a revitalized jurisprudential project. If there is to be a more complete and satisfying account of the role of ideological values in Supreme Court adjudication, it will demand a more direct and full-on engagement with the theoretical challenge of providing a persuasive jurisprudential account of legal interpretation and judicial decision-making. One place to begin that important task is with a more subtle and nuanced account of ideology.

9

Moving On

An Ideological Inquiry

The strength of any scholarly contribution is to be found not only in the illuminating power of its central insight, but also in its awareness of that insight's reach and limitations. For all their strengths and corrective force, the anti-formalist studies on judicial decision-making rely on methodological assumptions and operating premises that are flawed and contestable. Although empirical scholars claim to be able to circumvent and thereby improve upon the theoretical debates about judicial decision-making, they actually rely on those debates and are obliged to take controversial positions within them. That said, much can be learned from detailed and rigorous studies of judicial behavior in different legal arenas (e.g., administrative tribunals, courts, and bureaucracies) about the overall structure, function, and form of judicial decision-making. Nevertheless, a considerable measure of caution must be exercised in placing too much reliance on them. To be more convincing, such studies must attend more closely to the theoretical framework within which their data are identified, generated, and understood; the facts unearthed or confirmed will need to be analyzed within, not aside from a particular theoretical account of the behavior studied.

In regard to judicial decision-making, this means that empirical scholars, like philosophical theorists, must deploy some initial theoretical hypothesis that allows them to identify and study the behavior under scrutiny: what is law? what is ideology? and what is it to be a judge? Although the anti-formalists are on the right track in moving beyond the formalist paradigm, they fall into the dangerous trap of exaggerating the importance of their central insight (i.e., that the work and decisions of individual judges is an exclusively ideological exercise). They fail to acknowledge that there is much going on that cannot be accommodated in their two-dimensional view of the world (i.e., law or ideology as the explanatory basis of judicial decision-making). The anti-formalists' failings fall into three categories: the extent to which their own ideological biases affect the objectivity and scientific status of their empirical studies, their very dated and unconvincing understanding of law that they employ, and their impoverished view about what counts as ideology and how it can play out in the judicial arena. These critical observations will be developed with an eye on establishing a better and more compelling informal account of judicial decision-making as a professional practice of law and ideology.

On the Bias

In a post-Kuhnian world, it is no longer acceptable or feasible to talk about facts as something that exist entirely outside of the disciplinary or theoretical paradigm within which they are apprehended and through which they are supposed to be validated. There has to be some resort to an informing context of theoretical and methodological values, whether implicit or explicit, that allows a necessary degree of filtering, weighting, and evaluation to occur before the existence of 'facts' can be identified and confirmed.[1] As such, facts are nothing on their own; they are unable to stand on their own feet. In order to provide insight and knowledge, they need to be understood within a particular framework of analysis. If theory without facts is empty, then facts without theory are meaningless. Consequently, in dealing with social and intellectual inquiries, there simply are no brute facts of the matter. The anti-formalists seem to proceed in willful ignorance of such concerns. While they are quick to highlight the ideological determinants of judicial decision-making, they are slow to appreciate the ideological context and forces that influence their own work and the conclusions that they reach. In short, quantitative research must attend to its own ideological status and standing.

Whatever the case in the natural sciences (and it is much contested), the 'factual' challenge is even more acute in the social sciences. When it comes to social facts, there is no form of pure scientific analysis that passively catalogues without also actively contributing to the construction of those facts to be catalogued and the creation of the catalogue itself. In other words, social practices cannot be fixed or objectified without

[1] Thomas Kuhn, *The Structure of Scientific Revolutions* (3rd ed. 1996). As Ronald Coase quipped, "torture the data and it will confess to anything." See Gordon Tullock, A Comment on Daniel Klein's "A Plea to Economists Who Favour Liberty, (2001) 57 *E. Econ. J.* 2, 203, at n. 2. For my own extended analysis of this challenge in legal theorizing, see Allan C. Hutchinson, *The Province of Jurisprudence Democratised* (2008).

a background matrix of theoretical assumptions about the intentions, motivations, vocabularies, and self-understandings of social actors. As such, there can be no external check on social inquiry other than another set of social practices that comprise the background matrix. Indeed, it is hard to imagine how it is possible to identify and catalogue the ideological dispositions of judges without some informing account of who judges are and what judicial behavior entails. If judicial attitudes and dispositions are to be jurisprudential grist for the empirical mill, they must at least be fixable and understandable within some rudimentary account of what it is that judges do. Without such an account, there would be no activity or behavior that could be isolated from other modes of activity and studied in any sensible way.

After all, empirical work on judicial decision-making is all about outcomes and results, not about arguments and justification. Yet to ignore that dimension of judicial behavior is to misrepresent the 'facts' to be studied and analyzed. Empirical researchers, especially those who study ideological shift, treat judicial decision-making as if it were only an exercise in ideological imposition by political actors; the role of legal considerations remains vague or non-existent. However, any explanation of a social practice, like judicial decision-making, must take seriously the self-understanding of its practitioners and participants. This does not mean that what such actors say about their work should be taken at face value, far from it. But the reflections and rationales offered by judges do need to be incorporated into any study of judicial decision-making that claims to provide a convincing and valid account of judicial behavior. And this is far from an easy or value-free undertaking.

The world of empirical scholars is one in which law and ideology are separate and apart; the one is not connected to or part of the other in any substantial or serious way. While this is far from being an indefensible position, it is neither self-evident nor uncontroversial. More important, its contested status undermines the stability and force of the scientific foundations on which empirical legal work tends to be based. Law and ideology do not stand in stark contrast to each other; ideology can be inside law.[2] If the law is a product of judges' ideological preferences, the law will come to resemble those preferences. This means that the perceived divide between law and ideology will not be as abrupt or

[2] See supra, Chapter 8.

obvious as many suggest. This will be particularly the case if there is greater homogeneity among judges; the gap between what judges' personal ideology might demand and what the law requires would be shaved very close. Consequently, it becomes important to generate a more sophisticated account of judicial decision-making that is less dichotomous in form and function. There needs to be a better and fuller appreciation of the relationship between law and ideology in the performance of the judicial task.

To this end, the preliminary task is to unpack the hidden ideological components and commitments that comprise the foundations of the empirical studies on judicial decision-making. Indeed, there are two sources of operating assumptions that reveal the soft value-laden underbelly of the hard fact-based shell that encases much empirical work. The first is the rudimentary and frankly simplistic account of 'law' that is relied on: empirical research on judicial decision-making draws on a highly formalistic and discredited theory of the nature of law and lawyering. The second is the equally frail and flat understanding of 'ideology' that guides and informs the empirical analysis of judicial behavior; it is so one-dimensional in content and thrust that it crumbles under the weight of its users' expectations. When the weaknesses of these two central props of the empirical project are combined, they demonstrate the overall fragility and unreliability of the empirical approach to evaluating judicial decision-making. Despite the recommendations and protestations, it is a house built on sand.

Flipping Coins

In offering an account of judicial decision-making that plays up the ideological causes of such activity and downplays the role of legal considerations, empirical scholars need to have some understanding of what judicial decision-making would look like if it were a result of exclusively legal factors.[3] In turn, this demands that such anti-formalists assume and develop a theory of law that can point up the

[3] Some work does argue that, in different ways, at different times, and for different justices, legal considerations are decisive. See Michael Bailey and Forrest Maltzman, Does Legal Doctrine Matter? Unpacking Law and Policy Preferences on the U.S. Supreme Court, 102 *Am. Pol. Sci. Rev.* 639 (2008); Michael A. Bailey and Forrest Maltzman, *The Constrained Court* (2011); and Paul H. Edelman, David E. Klein, and Stefanie A. Lindquist, Consensus, Disorder, and Ideology on the Supreme Court, 9 *J. Emp. Legal St.* 129 (2012).

materials that comprise law and the techniques that can be used to handle those materials. While they are far from forthcoming or open about what such a theory would look like, there are hints and clues as to what that might be. Once these are brought to light, the upshot is that the anti-formalists adopt a very dated and almost caricatured position on what law is and what it would mean to follow it exclusively. Indeed, they implicitly rely on a very traditional understanding of law and lawyering that is more formalistic than almost any contemporary and serious formalist scholar offers or defends.

In general, the empirical anti-formalists treat law as if it should function as a finite and seamless body of rules that should be able to be applied directly and uncontroversially to resolve any dispute. In this account of law, the judge is seen as being entirely detached and almost robotic in his or her capacity to locate, select, and use these pre-established rules as problem-solvers; the content of rules and their application to discrete disputes is considered to be something that does not implicate or involve the judge personally in their creation or merit. Not surprisingly, it is a jurisprudence that owes much to empirical scholars' status as social scientists and their reverence for a scientific mind-set that celebrates, in this instance, the virtues and possibilities of a neutral and impartial vision of law, lawyering, and judicial decision-making. For the anti-formalists, therefore, judges should be something of institutional automatons whose personal identity and ideological commitments should have no role at all in their deliberations or professional performance.

Yet such an image of the judge is almost laughable. Even a dyed-in-the-wool Hartian positivist would reject such a representation; the day of mechanical or slot-machine jurisprudence is over.[4] Indeed, there is no jurist or judge today who holds to such an implausible account of law and lawyering. As such, the anti-formalists allow themselves to be defined by an untenable account of formalism. They run the unconvincing line that, because judges and jurists must make some resort to moral values and ideological preferences, the formalistic mission of jurisprudence is entirely invalid as an account of law and legal interpretation. Yet once it is accepted that formalism is not defined by such a mechanical and formulaic sense of itself, the anti-formalist critique loses much of its bite. In the either/or universe of empirical

[4] See supra, Chapter 3.

studies, evidence that something is not one thing is taken as incontrovertible proof that it is the other. It is simply unconvincing to maintain that any evidence that judges are not performing their role in an ultra-formalist fashion is supportive of a claim that judges are exclusively or primarily ideological actors.

Of course, there are few actual jurists (and certainly even fewer judges) who adopt such polarized and unalloyed stances. Almost all legal actors maintain that there is some seepage from one category to the other. The most common position is that, in so-called hard cases, judges will inevitably have to stray into the ideological fray and allow political values to inform their legal analysis. Nevertheless, it is usually emphasized, even by those with a definite distaste for formalism, that it is possible to do law without being weighed down by inappropriate ideological baggage. For instance, although judge and jurist Richard Posner maintains that "judging is political" in that it cannot be done without resort to a whole slew of ideological desiderata (e.g., understandings about human behavior, moral values, economic logic, and sociological insights), he does not equate the particular reliance on such materials as being idiosyncratic or personal to a particular judge. At least as he sees it and does it, judging is "impersonal and non-political in the sense that many, indeed most, judicial decisions really are the product of neutral application of rules"[5] and based upon "modern analytical and empirical methods ... [and] scientific theory".[6]

Accordingly, judges are taken to be inescapably involved in the ideological game; the claim that adjudication can be undertaken without reference to values is exposed as descriptively inaccurate and normatively unappealing. However, while they insist on the legitimate role of values in the performance of the judicial task, they maintain that this can be done in an objective and neutral manner. Again, it follows from this that the anti-formalists are able to attain traction for their stance only by offering a caricatured representation of the formalist project. Modern formalists (and even some semi-formalists) maintain that the resort to values is not the death-knell for a defence of judicial decision-making as a relatively self-contained and professional activity.

[5] Richard A. Posner, *How Judges Think* 369–70 (2008). As the naturalist Ronald Dworkin emphasizes, "law ... is deeply and thoroughly political, ... [b]ut not a matter of personal or partisan politics." Ronald Dworkin, *A Matter of Principle* 146 (1985). See supra, Chapter 4.

[6] Richard Posner, *Reflections on Judging* 353 (2013).

This similar attitude to the connection between law and community or popular morality (i.e., ideology) is also reasonably commonplace among judges. The most well-known example of this jurisprudential approach is the judgment of Lord Atkin in *Donoghue v. Stevenson*. In his famous phrasing, he insisted that "I do not think so ill of our jurisprudence as to suppose that its principles are so remote from the ordinary needs of civilized society and the ordinary claims it makes upon its members as to deny a legal remedy where there is so obviously a social wrong".[7] In so proceeding, he did not simply hold up his finger to gauge which way the social winds were blowing and align the law with it. He surveyed the relevant legal materials and doctrine and came to the conclusion that "there must be, and is, some general conception of relations giving rise to a duty of care, of which the particular cases found in the books are but instances".[8] This was a decidedly formalistic approach to the judicial task. Lord Atkin was not simply legislating his own ideological preferences, but making a good-faith effort to make sense of the existing legal materials. As such, he managed to be both formalistic and ideological in his judicial decision-making; the ideology was both inside and outside the law. His was not an either/or stance, but an effort at a both/and approach to law and adjudication.

Accordingly, the anti-formalists are simply the flip-side of the same jurisprudential coin as the formalists – if not arch-formalism, then all and only ideology. Each relies on the other to make its case by casting both law and ideology as antithetical entities. So the anti-formalists' claim that law and legal interpretation involve a controlling deference to the judge's ideological preferences cannot win the day without more. It has to be shown that the judicial resort to ideological values and their incorporation into legal doctrine is done in a way that cannot be explained by the contemporary and more sophisticated theories of the formalists themselves: it must be demonstrated that ideology is outside law, not inside it. For the anti-formalist critique to become fully persuasive, anti-formalists must develop and work with a much more sophisticated account of legal formalism. By hitching their justificatory wagon to such a discredited model of formalistic interpretation, they unwittingly discredit not only their own critique of it, but also their own account of adjudication as a thoroughly ideological affair. When it comes to the anti-formalists, it is a case of 'so goes arch-formalism, so goes anti-formalism'.

[7] *Donoghue v. Stevenson*, [1932] AC 562 at 583. [8] Ibid. at 580.

Into the Ideology

In much the same way that the anti-formalists' theory of law and adjudication is found seriously wanting, so is their understanding of ideology. It is both too thick and too thin. It is too thick in that it attempts to shoehorn a range of different substantive values and commitments into only two possible ideological categories, liberal or conservative. But it is too thin in that it fails to incorporate a whole set of competing institutional values that work to temper or displace judges' more substantive ideological preferences on important occasions. All in all, although anti-formalists are on the right track in highlighting the importance of ideological factors in any explanation of appellate adjudication, their appreciation of what counts as ideology is blinkered and, therefore, misleading, especially in regard to the role of legal interpretation.

Almost everyone has some kind of ideology. Even if it is ill-formed or simplistic, it is something that people rely upon explicitly or implicitly in engaging with the world and making their way through it. There are many different understandings of what counts as 'ideology'.[9] But, for present purposes, it is sufficient to think about it as the medium through which people make sense of the social world and their place in it; it contains ideas and understandings about the nature of the individual, the organization of society, the relationship between an individual and society, the role of government, and so on. Although this ideology might vary and change as people develop or reflect upon it, its assumptions and values push people toward different opinions and conclusions about a whole range of moral issues and political controversies (e.g., taxes, abortion, gender, education, homosexuality, immigration, and law and order). It will rarely function as a clear-cut and detailed template for living (except for the most dogmatic and uncritical people), but it will orient people in a general direction when confronted with particular social challenges or moral controversies.

Like everyone else, judges have an ideology. Due to the nature of the job, Supreme Court justices are more likely to be more conscious of their ideological dispositions; they spend a large part of their working lives reflecting upon a range of moral and political dilemmas and (hopefully) developing a more refined sensitivity to ideological contestation and their own predispositions. And, like everyone else, their ideology might change or drift over time. This change will usually be

[9] For a good introduction and survey, see T. Eagleton, *Ideology* (1991).

less marked as justices are already middle-aged and usually have a career of choices and commitments under their belt. Exceptions to this, such as Justices Blackmun and Souter on the U.S. Supreme Court, serve to prove the general rule.[10] However, to imagine that labelling justices either liberal or conservative is sufficient in order to fix their ideological commitments in anything other than a general way and to explain the details of their adjudicative career is clearly unpersuasive. Such a shallow and black-and-white understanding of judicial ideology can be more obfuscating than illuminating.

While there is no doubt that ideology has a major influence on judges and their decisions, it is mistaken to imagine that a judge's ideology maps directly onto that of a simple political ideology, liberal or conservative, let alone that of a contemporary political party. Both abstract political principle and partisan political posturing are in the judicial mix; they inform judges' thinking in important and indistinct ways. However, there is no one liberal or conservative line on 'gay marriage'; a libertarian conservative might be for it, but a social conservative might be against it. Also, judges may be liberal on some issues and conservative on others; there is no one party line that runs consistently across social and economic issues. Moreover, these ideological predispositions do not easily or straightforwardly cash out in some of the complex issues that present themselves for decision in the Supreme Court – civil procedure, state rights, presidential powers, administrative tribunals, and even free speech. A person's ideology is not a template for resolving difficult moral or political issues but a framework or an orientating set of resources for thinking about and through them.

All this is especially so for those 'median judges' who do not hew to any marked or more extreme ideological stances; they shift back and forth as the details of the case at hand and the broader social context push and pull them in different ideological directions.[11] This is not in defiance of ideological influences, but in response to their middle-of-the-road ideological loyalties. Furthermore, as well as judges' broader political values playing a formative role, their different approaches to what they think the role of a good judge is in a constitutional democracy will need to be taken into account. This so-called judicial philosophy might well cut across the dictates of their more general ideological leanings. A liberal might join a conservative, not because of any substantive

[10] See supra, Chapter 8. [11] See supra, Chapter 8.

ideological affinity, but because they are both believers in 'judicial restraint' or 'judicial activism'.[12] While such judicial philosophy will play a significant role in some instances, it will more often bow to more direct ideological influences.

Nevertheless, Supreme Court justices are not entirely free to indulge those political preferences and decide all cases as they wish; they are not politicians or pamphleteers. They are obliged to work with the law, hear legal arguments, appreciate public sentiment, listen to law clerks, and be parts of a judicial collegium; these different influences will oblige good-faith justices to challenge themselves and their ideological dispositions. To explain all this away as so much background noise or professional dissemblance is to impugn the whole integrity of the judicial process and its personnel. Of course, this is not to say that some rogue judges do not act in bad faith and indulge directly and wantonly their ideological leanings. However, any account of judging that wants to be taken seriously, especially by the legal community at large, needs to accept that the craft skills of legal argument and judicial reasoning are not only self-serving exercises in convenient window-dressing. Even if legal considerations and techniques do not explain all that judges do, it is equally fallacious to assume that they have no influence or effect at all.

The concession that legal considerations have some effect on judicial decision-making does not mean that the role of ideological preferences will be severely reduced. While Justice Jackson may have overstated the influence of his judicial colleagues, his assessment is not far off the mark: "Why is it that the Court influences appointees more consistently than appointees influence the Court?"[13] In the same way that Supreme Court judges cannot freely indulge their ideological preferences, they cannot set them aside either. In fulfilling their judicial obligations to do justice through law, judges work with their ideological preferences in grappling with the extant legal materials. There are many reasons why judges may shelve their ideological preferences on particular occasions. However, it is not because 'the law' demands a different result. Although judges may make a big deal of being seen to uphold precedent and preserve the law's stability, the reality belies such intentions: the one constant in law is change.[14] As such, judicial decision-making is an exercise in legal and ideological decision-making.

[12] Cass Sunstein et al., *Are Judges Political?* (2006).

[13] Robert H. Jackson, *The Struggle for Judicial Supremacy* vii (1941).

[14] See Allan C. Hutchinson, *Evolution and Common Law* (2005).

Institutional Concerns

Judicial ideology is focused and calibrated differently from general or partisan political ideology. The political or moral substantive components of a judge's ideology are given prominence in jurisprudential debate, but they are supplemented by another set of values and commitments that have a more institutional or professional slant. The fact is that judges might well work hard to "mask their ideological goals in order to promote them more effectively".[15] There are several groups of factors that will be balanced against achieving preferred ideological outcomes. As in any other profession or job, these can include a whole host of influences – careerism, laziness, psychology, personality, collegiality, and so on. However, there is one particular institutional concern that can and does operate as a definite check on judges' temptation to indulge their substantive ideological preferences in resolving particular disputes or controversies: the legitimacy of the courts.

For judges on both sides of the liberal/conservative political divide, an overriding concern will be the standing and authority of the courts themselves, especially Supreme Courts. Whatever the broader political values that connect or divide individual judges on substantive matters, judges as a group are often devoted to ensuring that the courts' own integrity and influence on the governmental and political process is maintained. In certain circumstances, some justices will set aside political leanings and partisan sympathies when a Supreme Court's political authority and stature as a forum above the political fray is at stake. Consequently, it is misleading to treat the Supreme Court as being only a collection of nine individuals; it has a collective identity and works in ways that are sometimes more and sometimes less than the sum of its judicial and ideological parts. If the Supreme Court loses its veneer of institutional legitimacy, the judicial game will be up according to the lights of traditional theory and practice: its moral and popular authority will be undercut and its prestige sullied.

A couple of examples will illustrate and confirm this important point. In two celebrated instances, two Supreme Court Justices both named Roberts put the judicial cat among the jurisprudential pigeons. In 1937 in *Parrish*, Justice Owen Roberts defied his own undisputed conservative record to complete a liberal majority of five in favor of upholding a

[15] Lee Epstein, William Landes, and Richard Posner, *The Behaviour of Federal Judges* 70 (2014).

minimum wage law as being constitutionally valid.[16] In so doing, he is considered to have saved the Supreme Court from President Roosevelt's New Deal threat to pack the Court by increasing its membership from nine to fifteen judges. In 2012, a self-proclaimed conservative Chief Justice, John Roberts, surprised court-watchers in *Sebelius* by joining his four liberal colleagues to uphold the constitutionality of President Obama's healthcare initiative.[17] Whether the justices made these decisions for principled or expedient reasons, these occurrences throw into sharp relief the deeper jurisprudential debate over the role that judges' disclosed ideological dispositions play in judicial decision-making. Nevertheless, Roberts's actions were entirely explicable in terms of preserving the institutional integrity and public legitimacy of the Supreme Court. As such, there is an important lesson for both those formalists who prioritize the role of strictly legal considerations and those anti-formalists who give prominence to the ideological make-up of the judges.

Judicial ideology is different from general ideology in that judges will factor into their general ideological bent the stability, status, and overall standing of the Court in achieving the overarching public good of institutional legitimacy in a constitutional democracy. It is not simply political ideology that plays an important role in judicial decision-making, but 'judicial ideology' in which political ideology is only one, albeit important, component. The pull of judicial legitimacy helps to explain why a justice, like Owen Roberts in 1937 or John Roberts in 2012, will occasionally defy the odds and decide in a way that is apparently inconsistent with their general voting pattern and ideological orientation. That they do so on the odd or special occasion does not alter their general substantive ideological orientation. Yet the record shows that judicial ideology does play a frequent role in Supreme Court decisions.

For example, despite divided opinions within the Court (and the Court-centred commentariat) on the constitutional validity and political merit of controversial and high-profile decisions, like *Roe*,[18] there is a marked tendency not to overrule them or, at least, not with undue haste. To do otherwise would be to expose the Supreme Court to public censure for its failure to do law, not politics; it is considered that the Supreme Court's prestige as a privileged forum of non-partisan decision-making

16 *West Coast Hotel Co. v. Parrish*, 300 U.S. 379 (1937).

17 *National Federation of Independent Business v. Sebelius*, 567 U.S. __ (2012).

18 See *Roe v. Wade*, 410 U.S. 410 (1973). On the institutional dimension of judicial ideology, see Lee Epstein and Jack Knight, *The Choices Justices Make* (1988).

in a constitutional democracy would be severely jeopardized. However, none of this has prevented the Supreme Court from whittling away or hedging the sweep of these earlier decisions, but it has not been prepared to abandon those rulings when American society remains so divided around them.[19] In contrast, when the Supreme Court has sensed that public opinion has shifted considerably, it has been willing to reverse itself even after only a few years; this is the case with gay rights.[20] Of course, this imperative to preserve the non-ideological reputation of the Supreme Court is especially ironic in light of the fact that all, not only occasional, Supreme Court decision-making is ideological in nature.

Indeed, the present Chief Justice of the American Supreme Court, John Roberts, is very attuned to the need to preserve the legitimacy of the court and to neutralize any threats to it. Although *Sebelius* is strong evidence of this, his extra-judicial remarks bolster the argument. Recognizing that there is much riding on the court's institutional status if it is to retain its authority in the eyes of American society, he has made it clear that all judges should be "worried about the Court acting as a Court". So committed is Roberts to this idea that he urges his colleagues to "factor in the Court's institutional role" when they are tempted to write separate opinions and to succumb to their personal ideological preferences.[21] For Roberts, therefore, consensus and stability are the best underwriters of the Court's credibility as an impartial and professional arbiter of contested social and political issues. Once the Court fragments and fractures, the Court's vital legitimacy will have been severely compromised. Judges will be revealed and condemned as little more than ideologues who talk law but actually do politics.

Accordingly, the fact that judges, even Supreme Court justices, make decisions that do not seem to chime squarely or fully with their substantive ideological preferences does not mean that ideology is not in play. It is because judges sometimes allow institutional concerns to trump substantive preferences. This is not to be taken as evidence that ideology is not part of the judicial function. This occasional occurrence actually reinforces the claim that ideology is an integral component of judicial

[19] See *Webster v. Reproductive Health Services*, 492 U.S. 490 (1989), and *Planned Parenthood of Southeastern Pa. v. Casey*, 505 U.S. 833 (1992).

[20] See *Lawrence v. Texas*, 539 U.S. 558 (2003).

[21] Robert Rosen, Robert's Rules, *The Atlantic* (Jan/Feb, 2007). See also Dan Balz, Roberts Health Care Ruling Sends a Message to Politicians, *Washington Post*, June 30, 2012, and David L. Franklin, *Why Did Roberts Do It? To Save the Court, Slate*, June 28, 2012.

decision-making. Of course, this is as long as ideology is appreciated, as it should be, to encompass more than moral or political preferences. Understood in this way, an account of law and ideology provides a more convincing explanation of what Justices Roberts and Roberts did in their famous and exceptional 'switch in nine': they put the general legitimacy of the institution ahead of their own substantive ideological preferences. In so doing, they confirmed, not confounded, the idea that judicial decision-making is a practice of law and ideology. Law and ideology are not separate spheres of influence; they are integral and mutually reinforcing features of judicial decision-making. With a better understanding of both law and ideology, it will become apparent that they are not separate sources of influence in judicial decision-making, but combine to present Supreme Court judicial decision-making as a law-and-ideology enterprise.

Conclusion

As my consideration of the anti-informalist critique reveals, the way forward in jurisprudence is to combine the empirical and theoretical approaches in a practical study of judicial decision-making. This will not result in some grand integrated theory of judicial decision-making that can pull together the descriptive and prescriptive challenges of jurisprudence. There is no one method or approach to solving the puzzle of when 'no vehicles in the park' should and should not apply. What an informalist account will do is deepen and broaden the discourse so that the legal and ideological dynamics of judicial decision-making are appreciated not as being in opposition but as working with each other; they interact in complex and contingent ways. By understanding judicial decision-making as an enterprise in law and ideology, jurisprudence can reorient itself and offer richer explanations of how law and ideology work together at different times, in different venues, and in different ways. This would represent a genuine and worthy focus for future jurisprudential study and empirical research. It is to this informalist task that I now turn.

10

Law and Ideology

The Informalist Approach

So what does an informalist account of legal interpretation look like? What insights can it offer? As I have been at pains to explain and illustrate, traditional legal theory juxtaposes law and ideology in its manifold efforts to understand and evaluate legal interpretation. In contrast, I have been building toward an informal account of legal interpretation that is more cogent and more in line with actual experience of legal interpretation and adjudication. At its theoretical heart is the central claim that legal reasoning and judicial decision-making are themselves a specialized form of ideological practice. This does not mean that judges simply legislate their own preferences or advance their own ideological agenda under the charade-like guise of legal reasoning. The reality of judicial decision-making is much more complicated and sophisticated than that. In order to engage in the craft of legal reasoning and deliver legal judgments, judges must rely upon contested values and ideological preferences in reaching their decisions. While this is true of all judicial decision-making, it is particularly so for justices in a legal system's highest courts. Judicial decision-making is an exercise in law and ideology.

The first challenge is to show how an informalist account can get beyond the false foundations of either/or thinking that both formalism and anti-formalism seek to build their accounts. By so advancing, it will become possible to shift the jurisprudential discussion from issues of truth and accuracy to those of merit and utility. Also, a blending of law and ideology into one integrated account allows for a more satisfying and less strained grasp of judicial decision-making; this will be one in which doctrinal forms and political substance will be explicable in both an independent and conjoined fashion. As the informalist views it, law and legal interpretation can be understood as both determinate and indeterminate practices in equal shifting and contingent measure. Finally, an informalist account reveals that the process of resolving cases, be they perceived as easy or hard, will occur in much the same way; the dynamic of legal interpretation can be more or less on view in some cases than others, but it is still very much always in play. So rendered, an informalist account incorporates as it goes beyond the formalist and anti-formalist accounts of judicial decision-making. It synthesizes as it transforms the dominant modes of theoretical explanation.

After 'Theory'

So much traditional theorizing about law and judicial decision-making is caught up with an either/or way of thinking – theory and practice, natural science and social science, facts and values, philosophy and conversation, public and private, and, of course, formalism and anti-formalism. The classic gambit is to identify an activity or event as being one thing or another and then to draw certain important inferences from that divisive categorization. In so doing, there is generally a hierarchical dynamic at work that privileges or gives greater prestige to one category over another. This is exactly the situation with formalism and anti-formalism. For a host of reasons (i.e., institutional, democratic, professional, etc.), formalists draw a distinction between law and ideology and then highlight the superiority of law as a confining resource for judicial decision-making over judges' free-ranging indulgence of their ideological preferences. In this way, judicial decision-making is considered to be more principled and less partisan.

In contemporary circumstances, it is no longer feasible to claim that judicial decision-making is entirely a matter of legal considerations, not an occasion for some ideological intervention. As I have said, this has given rise to a variety of interpretive theories – originalism, literalism, purposivism, positivism, naturalism, and so on – that claim to solve the dilemma of how judges can either bridge the gap between law and ideology or build an adequate firewall between them. The key move, of course, is to claim that the preferred interpretive theory is a viable hedge against political ideology, not a reflective or reflexive manifestation of it. Although this manoeuvre is particularly prevalent in constitutional law where the stakes are so high and the need to preserve some degree of ideological neutrality is considered to be so pressing, it is prevalent throughout the common law. By relying on an interpretive theory, judges and jurists claim to be able to insulate themselves from charges of ideological duplicity in reaching decisions that align with their own partisan agendas.

Despite the popularity of this jurisprudential approach, it is by no means established or clear that theory has such an other-worldly authority in providing an epistemological warrant for judicial decision-making. Informalists (such as myself) would strenuously resist such claims. Instead, the whole distinction between theory and practice should be dismissed as one more diversion or distraction. There are no bright-line boundaries or essential methodological differences between theory and practice, facts and values, and, of course, formalism (law) and anti-formalism (ideology). It is not that these categorical distinctions collapse in on each other and have no relevant differences at all, but that such differences are contingent and social; they always arise from and within, directly or indirectly, their sustaining historical and political context. There is no available higher ahistorical ground from which to judge historical practices than the contested social terrain of history itself. Because there is no Method of methods and no Context of contexts, there are only situated arguments and reasons that have passed or acquired social muster. Moreover, because these social conversations and philosophical conventions are themselves open to the changing and dynamic forces of historical contestation, they are at least vulnerable to and often affected by political and social values. In short, no theory is innocent of historical or political significance.

Looked at in this more critical fashion, the traditional enterprise of legal theorizing is better understood as not being something separate and apart from ideology. Instead, theories of legal interpretation can be more usefully apprehended as being part of competing political traditions that work to privilege different values and interests over others. As with almost all other social practices, the methodological strictures of interpretive theories themselves will be shown to be responsive to the push and pull of various social, economic, institutional, ideological, and cultural currents. While this process is evident in the whole history of formalism's expanding character and make-up, it is particularly apparent in the rise and prominence of both naturalism and originalism. Each developed in response to certain socio-historical conditions and facilitated, even if they did not necessitate, the advancement of certain ideological commitments.[1]

Consequently, what has managed to get itself accepted in the community of legal theorizing about the appropriate or correct mode of judicial

[1] See supra, Chapters 4 and 5.

decision-making will be attributable to something other than the simple force of a 'good idea'. There are no conversation-ending or truth-fixing theoretical interventions other than those that gain acceptance in engaged debate in particular historical circumstances. The epistemological dimension (i.e., what is the correct methodology to access the true meaning of law or the Constitution?) is intertwined with the ideological dimension (i.e., what political interests and values are promoted or prioritized by a particular interpretive or constitutional methodology?). This is not to suggest that they both collapse in on each other, but it is to demand that they are not understood separately from each other. As such, it is important to adopt an interpretive approach that appreciates and embraces that demand rather than glosses over it. So, while formalism and anti-formalism ground themselves on insisting that law and ideology can be understood separately, an informalist approach works toward developing an approach that allows law and ideology to be understood in tandem.[2]

An important upshot of my recommended way of thinking is not to dismiss law or legal theory as nothing more than ideology. Even more enlightened jurists take the stance that, "although the inherent limitations of human reasoning, legal rules and standards, and law allow ideological influences to seep into judicial decisions, these factors are not so pervasive or vicious that they defeat rule-bound decision making".[3] Such a sharp characterization is mistaken as it simply replicates and re-entrenches the either/or thinking of traditional formalist/anti-formalist thinking – if not law, then ideology; if ideology, then not law. In contrast, an informal approach takes much more seriously and realistically the practical operation of judicial decision-making as a combination of law and ideology. It comes at judicial decision-making, especially of the Supreme Court kind, as a both/and, not an either/or activity. Ideology does not infiltrate or taint judicial decision-making because law already embraces and instantiates ideology; it most certainly is not 'vicious'. As such, judicial decision-making is an inextricable mix of both legal considerations and ideological concerns.

[2] My informalist account draws upon a wide range of philosophical and political positions that might also be loosely grouped under the heading 'pragmatism'. See *Pragmatism: A Reader* (Louis Menand ed. 1997); Roberto Mangabeira Unger, *The Self Awakened: Pragmatism Unbound* (2007); and Allan C. Hutchinson, *The Province of Jurisprudence Democratized* (2009).

[3] *See* Brian Z. Tamanaha, The Several Meanings of "Politics" in Judicial Politics Studies: Why "Ideological Influence" Is Not Partisanship, 61 *Emory L.J.* 759 at 771 (2012).

A Good Night's Sleep

Much of the contemporary jurisprudential debate has centred on rules, broadly conceived, and their application. Whereas formalists insist that rules can be identified and applied by judges in a non-ideological manner, anti-formalists are equally convinced that the supposed existence and application of rules is a smoke-screen for the imposition of judges' ideological preferences. Indeed, one of the stock images of contemporary legal theory has been the perceived choice between the ignoble nightmare and the noble dream when it comes to accounts of legal interpretation.[4] On the one hand, there is a utopian vision of legal interpretation that treats law as a complex but integrated body of norms in which the whole is greater and more just than the sum of its individual parts. On the other hand, there is a dystopian view of legal interpretation that depicts law as comprising an entirely indeterminate mass of directives in which lawyers and judges run rampant in fixing meaning as and how they choose. This, of course, tracks the more general division between formalism and anti-formalism. In contrast to both, an informalist account offers the real possibility of 'a good night's sleep'.

By proposing an informal account of legal interpretation, I am suggesting that this traditional choice not only is unnecessarily stark but is also entirely unnecessary. Law is neither as determinate as formalists think nor as open-ended as anti-formalists maintain. As a matter of professional training and social custom, rule application does not lend itself to a definitive account of what it is to follow a rule. The question is not whether there are rules or whether legal doctrine is relied upon – they clearly are. But that is not a quality that inheres within them. Legal rules, individually and collectively, do not exist as canonical directives that can impersonally dispose of cases without interpretive intervention; the meaning of a rule and its application never simply *is*. Rules determine nothing except customary reactions and dominant practices. As a social practice, the application of legal doctrine is not an analytical issue of formal realizability or causal necessity; *conformity with* is not the same as *caused by*.

Meaning is to be found in the social practices that coalesce around rules and legal doctrine. The more broad-based that practice, the more that there is a sense that the rule speaks for itself. However, as that

[4] H.L.A. Hart, American Jurisprudence through English Eyes: The Nightmare and the Noble Dream, 11 *Ga. L. Rev.* 969 (1977). See supra, Chapter 3.

practice begins to fragment and disagreement becomes the social order of the day, then the rule will not be sensed to be speaking for itself. It is not the rule that settles disputes, but the agreed social understandings behind it. This agnosticism is what distinguishes the informalist from the formalist and anti-formalist. In matters of social behavior, the most that a rule can do is to help one understand whether the participants in such behavior believe that they are following such a rule. As Wittgenstein concluded about justifying rule-related behavior, "the rule is . . . what is explained, not what does the explaining".[5] Rules and legal doctrines are rough-and-ready indicators or markers of earlier values that other judges have been persuaded had sufficient agreement within or appeal to the relevant discursive community.

In a non-trivial sense, therefore, every application of a rule or legal doctrine is a remaking of it. It is an occasion on which judges acknowledge, consciously or unconsciously, the values that hold certain social practices in place. Even if legal doctrine has an important role in judicial decision-making, therefore, this is not proof that ideological factors are not at work: there has to be an argument that the doctrine itself is not ideological in its creation and thrust. As I have insisted throughout this book, such an argument is untenable. Judicial decision-making and legal interpretation is through and through about values, not facts, and about persuasion, not demonstration. Applying rules or legal doctrine is an ideological matter of taking sides; the only questions are *which* and *when*. There is no available method or means to identify law as a pre-interpretive matter. Legal history and practice strongly suggest that it is interpretation all the way down; law is a thoroughly human activity that envelops and infiltrates the legal resources to be interpreted. This constant toing-and-froing between facts and values is so integral to law as to be constitutive of it; it is law. Law is not something that exists before or after interpretive work but is constituted by and in that interpretive activity. While this is most evident in matters of common-law adjudication, it is also apparent in all modes of adjudication.

All this is by way of stating that the law is always in the process of becoming rather than in a state of being – the law never simply is. The very act of interpreting law changes it and, on important occasions,

[5] Ludwig Wittgenstein, *Zettel* 303 (G.E.M. Anscombe and G.H. von Wright eds. 2nd ed. 1981). See also S. Kripke, *Wittgenstein on Rules and Private Language* (1982), and Charles Yablon, Law and Metaphysics, 96 *Yale L.J.* 613 at 633 (1987).

redraws it substantially. Nevertheless, it is a mistake to draw a distinction between those who believe that interpretation is about objective retrieval and those who believe that there is only subjective creation; it is neither one nor the other. Law is not simply created in the interaction between the legal materials and the judge but is found in the interplay itself; it is the process of interpretation as much as the resources and the product that counts as law. Indeed, law cannot be broken down into its constituent parts without losing its essential dynamism. As such, law is less a thing and more an activity. And as the naturalists insist and the positivists might concede, if that is the case, then law is a human activity and inextricably bound up with the contested values and divergent commitments of society. Law is a site of activity that occurs within and against a set of ideological values.

In a State of Constant Flux

Law comprises both a collection of resources (e.g., rules, principles) and a set of techniques (e.g., analogical reasoning, precedential refinement) for working with those resources. Most important, these two components are not separate or independent; they interact and reinforce each other. The law is not simply there in its object-like givenness but is always waiting to be disassembled and reassembled by the active crafting of its judicial or legal technicians. Indeed, a marked feature of common-law adjudication, even of the constitutional variety, is not so much that a rule is fixed beforehand and then applied to the facts of the case, but that a rule is fixed with an eye on the range of likely outcomes that it might bring about on the facts of the particular case being decided.

There is a constant mediation between rule fixing and rule application in the judicial decision-making process such that it becomes illusory to talk about there being two distinct phases as a practical or even theoretical matter. It is not that there exists a rule that must then be reworked with more or less creativity, but that the rule itself is brought to life and given substance in the act of creative interpretation. The fact that the final judicial opinion rendered in a case might not reveal this dynamic process or that it might work to actively conceal this hardly counts against this explanation. Consequently, while I completely agree with the naturalists that law is a thoroughly value-drenched activity that engages the law's resources as it creates and re-creates them over and across time, I completely disagree with them that this interpretive activity can be done in any constrained, apolitical, or distinctively legal way.[6]

Consequently, all judicial decision-making occurs in and through the fluid and creative interaction between the judges and the materials. Law is not simply created in the interactions between the legal materials and judges but is located and energized in the interplay itself; it is the process of interpretation as much as the resources utilized and the result produced that counts as law. Indeed, law cannot be broken down into its constituent parts without losing its defining and constitutive dynamism. This overall process takes place within the shifting contexts of social conventions, institutional expectations, and normative values. And it is not only the law's resources that change, but also its working tools. Over time, different techniques become more and less established as part of the judicial toolbox. A reading of the American, British, or Canadian Supreme Courts' judgments over the decades reveals that today's judges have a much more varied set of tools – policy probes, economic analysis, institutional evaluation, social statistics, and so on – on which to draw than their counterparts of yesteryear. As such, law and legal interpretation is always in a state of continual flux.

Understanding judicial decision-making in this way helps to explain why determinacy and indeterminacy are not pre-interpretive features of the law but qualities that are generated in the process of legal interpretation itself.[7] An area of law can be both determinate and indeterminate in almost equal measure depending on the broad and immediate context of its availability, apprehension, and application. Even the most apparently settled areas of law are always vulnerable to being destabilized and thereby reconfigured. Moreover, once it is grasped that the law is never simply there, it becomes possible to appreciate that law's normal condition is to be in a state of constant about-to-be, not already-is. Judges are presented with a range of options and choices that are as much constrained by their capacity to rework the materials as by the materials themselves. The judge is an artisan or craftsperson who works law's nooks and crannies to cobble together the materials at hand so as to manufacture and remanufacture the law. Therefore, while judicial

[6] See supra, Chapter 4.

[7] *See* Duncan Kennedy, Thoughts on Coherence, Social Values and National Tradition in Private Law in *The Politics of a European Civil Code* 9 (Martijn Hesselink ed. 2006), and Duncan Kennedy, A Left Phenomenological Alternative to the Hart/Kelsen Theory of Legal Interpretation in Duncan Kennedy, *Legal Reasoning: Collected Essays* 154 (2009).

decision-making is very much an exercise in professional argumentation, law's resources are so capacious and its techniques so adaptable that it can easily justify a range of plausible and contradictory results.

This means that neither law's materials nor judges' interpretive methods foreclose the need for a judicial resort to ideology. Indeed, the very capaciousness of those materials and those techniques' adaptability demand that judges are obliged to consult directly or indirectly their ideological preferences. This is where the empirical work of anti-formalist scholars is important and insightful. For instance, studies of statutory interpretation strongly recommend that it is ideological preference, not judicial methodology, that best explains the decisions of judges; 'textualism' is no more or less restraining than 'purposivism' in determining outcomes reached in ideological terms.[8] Moreover, in constitutional matters, the reliance on one particular interpretive theory will not conclusively or determinately dictate one outcome over another. In this regard, the Supreme Court's decision in *District of Columbia v. Heller* is instructive because the majority opinion and the principal dissent both draw upon the putative authority of an originalist methodology to validate their differing interpretations of the Second Amendment.[9] An informalist approach is not fazed by this because it is not in the formalist and anti-formalist game of fixing law with a specific content and settledness: it appreciates that judges are part of a *justice* system, not simply a legal process.

Within this informal account of judicial decision-making, it becomes clearer to appreciate that what distinguishes good or bad judges is not simply professional competence. It is less about judges' depth of knowledge about the resources available or their grasp of the argumentative techniques in play. The good judge possesses the dexterity and imagination with which to work and rework the extant materials to achieve a more just and desirable decision. And this is where a judge's ideology kicks in. Without some sense (or, more grandly, vision) of the ideological ends that such continuing acts of artistic craft serve, the judicial function becomes a haphazard and unreflective shot in the dark. There is no two

[8] See William N. Eskridge, Jr., and Lauren E. Baer, The Continuum of Difference: Supreme Court Treatment of Agency Statutory Interpretations from Chevron to Hamdan, 96 *Geo. L.J.* 108 (2008); N. Eskridge, Jr., The New Textualism and Normative Canons, 113 *Colum. L. Rev.* 531 (2013); James J. Brudney and Corey Ditslear, Canons of Construction and the Elusive Quest for Neutral Reasoning, 58 *Vand. L. Rev.* 1 (2005); and Frank B. Cross, The Significance of Statutory Interpretive Methodologies, 82 *Notre Dame L. Rev.* 1971 (2007).

[9] See *District of Columbia v. Heller*, 128 S. Ct. 2783 (2008). See supra, Chapter 5.

ways about it – to judge is to take a stand. There is no 'nowhere' or neutral ground on which to stand when engaging in judicial decision-making. The only issue is whether judges know where they stand ideologically and why they are standing there when they fulfill their legal responsibilities. In other words, judges do act ideologically as judges; there is no way to do law that can escape or evade such ideological involvement. The problem is not the resort to ideology, but the failure to acknowledge or accept that fact.

Nevertheless, it might be noted that sometimes the materials and tools available are simply too limiting to be worked through convincingly in line with a judge's ideological preferences. In a manner of speaking, if a hammer and nails are all that are available, it is next to impossible to build a computer, at least in one go. However (and this is what makes Supreme Court judicial decision-making so special), the judges have a last-ditch manoeuvre available to them – they can effectively throw out the old materials and/or tools and start almost afresh. And this is exactly what happens in cases like *Brown* and *Lawrence* in the constitutional context and *Donoghue* and *Escola* that abandoned extant legal doctrine and reoriented it in a very different way and direction.[10] Some have criticized such landmark decisions as being flawed instances of judicial decision-making and, therefore, as lacking constitutional validity. But with the passage of time, precedential authority, and doctrinal integration, it is now generally accepted not only that they are established parts of the legal canon, but also that they are justified and showcased as exemplars of judicial decision-making. That being the case, it becomes increasingly difficult to maintain, where a decision that knowingly throws over old rules and principles is permitted (and often praised), that ideological values are not an integral and persistent feature of doctrinal change and legal interpretation in common-law and constitutional jurisprudence.[11]

Accordingly, it can be reasonably concluded that judicial decision-making is a thoroughly professional as well as thoroughly ideological undertaking. Law's meaning is always parenthetical and can never be grounded outside the contingent work of legal interpretation. As such, it is not only unhelpful, but also impossible to talk of law's meaning,

[10] See *Brown v. Board of Education*, 347 U.S. 483 (1954); *Lawrence v. Texas*, 539 U.S. 558 (2003); *Donoghue v. Stevenson*, [1932] AC 562; and *Escola v. Coca-Cola Bottling Co.*, 150 P. 2d 436 (1944).

[11] See Allan C. Hutchinson, *Evolution and the Common Law* (2005).

whether determinate or indeterminate, as objective or given in the sense of being something that is realizable without legal interpretation. For all their good faith, Justices Butler and Goudge in *Lachapelle* and *Perron* and Justice Holmes and Judge Phillips in *McBoyle* cannot perform their duties in any convincingly objective or tried-and-true way. The legitimacy of any particular judgment or act of legal interpretation is not about formal correctness or validity per se but about the substantive acceptability of the decision reached and the institutional cogency of the arguments made. From an informalist perspective, it follows that the standard of evaluation will combine both issues of legal technique and ideological appeal; it will be an amalgam of legal form and political substance. This is the appeal and promise of an informalist account of legal interpretation and judicial decision-making.

Neither Hard nor Easy

It should by now be clear that an informal account of legal interpretation has no truck with or need for the traditional distinction between easy and hard cases. In short, for the informalist, there are no hard cases or easy cases: there are only cases. 'Easiness' is not a property or quality that inheres within a case or a rule. Rules and their application do not arise or make sense outside of an interpretive context. The easiness or hardness of cases derives from background facts about agreements in judgments, historical contexts, and social stability. What goes on in easy cases is the same as in hard cases, only that its context is less contested and more taken for granted. In this sense, Hart is correct when he states that easy cases occur where "there is general agreement that they fall within the scope of a rule".[12] Of course, this holds only if the emphasis is placed firmly on the fact of 'general agreement' and not, as Hart seems to put it, on 'the scope of the rule'. The fact of this 'general agreement' (whether a matter of social consensus or hierarchical imposition) is important – the greater its extent and strength, the greater the existential experience of easy cases and legal certainty.[13]

In understanding law as a series of functional interpretations, it is important to see it less as a set of individual tools, like ratchets and screwdrivers, and more as social device, like a manufacturing process or

[12] H.L.A. Hart, *Essays in Jurisprudence and Legal Theory* 106 (1963).

[13] See Schauer, Easy Cases, 58 *S. Cal. L. Rev.* 399 (1985), and R. Dworkin, *Law's Empire* 351 and 352 (1986).

assembly line, that demands a high degree of collaboration and integration. It is in this sense that 'general agreement' is to be understood. The temptation to mistake dominant ways of thinking for natural necessity must be studiously resisted; the process is so ingrained and uncontroversial as to *appear* as if the process did not occur. When informalists claim that many cases are easy and agree with Hart that "general terms would be useless to us as a medium of communication unless there were such familiar, generally unchallenged cases",[14] they should be taken as demanding that 'unchallenged' be understood as being *unchallenged in the present social circumstances.* After all, easy cases are as much a product of interpretation and reasoning as hard cases. They are not an occasion to forego the need for such interpretation but only an occasion upon which there is considered to be no ideological reason or political will to disturb prevailing or continuing understandings. Because rules arise within social relations, they are subject to change and have any particular meaning only within a specific politico-historical context. Of course, context is never self-evident but requires an act of delineation that implicates values and power: "the question can be raised, not whether a politics is implied (it always is), but which politics is implied in . . . a practice of contextualization".[15]

For instance, the meaning of 'park' is protean and inconstant. Like with most words, its plain meaning shifts over time and context – what was once the core meaning of a park (e.g., the grounds of a stately home) can become a more penumbral feature, and what was once not thought of as a park (e.g., an industrial park or ballpark) can become part of its core meaning. Similarly, although it does not seem a stretch to designate private land as a 'public park' for temporary purposes (e.g., the holding of a carnival likely required a public license), it also seems sensible to treat certain public areas as not being a 'public park' on occasion (e.g., the holding of a private, invitation-only event in a part of Lansdowne Park). Judicial interpretation and its jurisprudential underpinnings are built on shifting sands, not firm bedrock. The differing judgments and decisions in *Lachapelle* and *Perron* offer evidence of that.

The same holds true for 'vehicles'. This word might sometimes include animals and toys, but it might also sometimes exclude ambulances and planes. Context is vital and itself is ill-mapped in its boundaries. There is no absolute or even contingent right and wrong answers, but only

[14] H.L.A. Hart, *The Concept of Law* 123 (1961).
[15] J. Derrida, *Limited Inc.* 147 (G. Graff and S. Weber trans. 1988).

continuing and inescapable choices that can be masked but not wished away or obviated. In the disagreement in *McBoyle* over the "popular" or "everyday" meaning of 'vehicle', its resolution has little to do with Holmes having better or more accurate insights than Judge Phillips. It is not about rightness but about authority. Holmes prevailed because he had the higher perch in the judicial hierarchy; the Supreme Court outguns the Court of Appeals. This important lesson is neatly captured by Justice Jackson's famous adage – "we are not final because we are infallible, but we are infallible because we are final".[16] Holmes got it right simply because he had the institutional privilege of speaking last, nothing more and nothing less.

None of this commits the informalist to the untenable or nihilistic position that it will always be possible to make the application of a rule come out in the way that the judge wants it to. Sometimes, cars are vehicles and horses are not, and sometimes, gardens are parks and marine parks are not. But this is a matter of imaginative insight or strategic calculation, not objective truth or ahistorical determinacy. The very fact that an informalist account accepts the existential experience of rule-boundedness is what makes it cogent and realistic. It may be that the judge or a majority of judges believe that it is important to preserve some continuity or maintain some certainty and to place such institutional values ahead of substantive justice in the particular circumstances. This way of proceeding is, of course, no less ideological than a decision to disrupt the received meanings of specific word or rule.[17]

Consequently, while the positivists are right to point out the experience that lawyers and judges have of the core of settled meaning, they are mistaken to treat it as a feature that rules have and that it is settled in anything but the most temporary, provisional, or contingent way. Similarly, while the naturalists are right to insist upon the ineradicable role of purposive reasoning and evaluative opportunity in applying rules, they are also mistaken to pretend that such judicial work can be done in the constrained and non-ideological way that they claim. As informalists recommend, there is neither constraint nor freedom, but only a dynamic interaction. Judges constantly work with and within the available materials such that their constraints are always in place, but never themselves outside of creative reinterpretation. So understood, judicial decision-making is a thoroughly professional and thoroughly ideological undertaking.

[16] *Brown v. Allen*, 344 U.S. 443 (1953). [17] See supra, Chapter 9.

So *What is a 'park'?* and *What is a 'vehicle'?* The answers will depend on who asks, why they ask, where they ask, and when they ask. Even if such matters are sufficiently clarified, there will still likely be scope for manoeuvre and choice. No interpretive theory can provide clear and correct answers to such hermeneutical conundrums because there are no such answers available. Justices Milne, Butler, Maisonneuve, and Goudge or Justices Phillips, Cotteral, and Holmes will not be relieved of their judicial discretion by following or deferring to a theoretical disciplinary device of any kind. Whatever some jurists suggest and some judges feign, there is no available formula or method that will relieve interpreters of the considerable task of creating, not finding, meaning in the application of particular rules or doctrinal materials. An interpretive theory may initially orient a judge in one direction, but it can never do more than that. The judge will ultimately need to select, not be taken to a particular destination.

Conclusion

Of course, an informalist approach provides no easy answers, only difficult questions and more difficult choices. Judges and lawyers will have no insulation against the incursion of political and moral values into their professional lives and activities. But when properly understood, they never have had. From both a judicial and juristic standpoint, this offers both a burden and a blessing – the burden of there rarely being an escape from personal responsibility for the decisions reached and the blessing that they are rarely obliged to make decisions that they consider to be unjust or unwarranted. Like so much in life, burdens can be made into blessings and blessings can be turned into burdens depending on who have them and how they carry them. In the final analysis, it is for all judges and jurists to make the best of it – to give up both the noble dreams of the formalists and ignoble nightmares of the anti-formalists. In short, it can be confidently asserted that *we are all informalists now.*

11

Looking for the Informal Judge

It should be apparent that my informalist account of law and legal interpretation has no grand plan or blueprint to offer in solving the apparent mysteries of legal interpretation and judicial decision-making. It does not speak in terms of what it is that judges should be doing in a particular case as a prescriptive or substantive matter. Instead, it offers an account of how judges go about their jobs across the board and over a series of individual instances of decision-making. As such, the informalist insistence that judicial decision-making is about law and ideology does not recommend or entail any particular ideological content to be drawn upon in performing that task: judges will still need to take personal responsibility for the cut of their ideological commitments and how they might square them with their judicial strategy. That said, it might necessitate that judges be more open and forthcoming about their ideological preferences and their implications for particular decisions; candour might become their watchword. Indeed, greater jurisprudential and political progress might be made if all participants were able to agree that the main action in regard to judicial decision-making ought not to be around abstract interpretive theory, but about practical substantive politics – what are the political values and ideological commitments that should animate and drive judicial decision-making? And who are the best people to perform such a task?

If that is the case, then a pressing institutional challenge for jurists is to decide who, in a world of inevitable and political judicial choices, is the most suitable set of people to do that job. When it comes to constitutional adjudication in particular, this is a very real and sizable task. For instance, the organizational corollary of the originalists' depiction of judicial decision-making seems to be the rather disturbing recommendation that Supreme Courts would be better served by a bench of historians (or, at least, an exclusively historically trained group of lawyers). On the other hand, those with more naturalist inclinations might push toward the development of more politically attuned sites and philosophically trained personnel for fulfilling their constitutional mandate. Indeed, exploring these available alternatives would be a much more productive use of jurists' time. It is reasonable, therefore, to demand that an informalist account of law and legal interpretation has some response to these institutional challenges. Accordingly, in this final chapter, I will sketch out what the adoption of an informalist position might imply for the role of a 'good judge' and what it might entail for the institutional processes in place to appoint them.

The Good Judge

A crucial factor for any theory of legal interpretation – be it formalist, anti-formalist, or informalist – is the sort of persons who are entrusted with the responsibility of being judges. Theoretical concerns often come to a practical head whenever a new judge has to be appointed to a country's highest court. In the general hubbub that surrounds such occasions, there is the usual chorus of many in the legal community, both academic and practicing, that considerations of 'merit' should be uppermost in the mind of those entrusted with making appointments. In parliamentary democracies, this is usually the Prime Minister and, in republican democracies, the President (along with some type of congressional oversight/approval). In particular, there is an urgent, almost desperate plea to ensure that issues of 'ideology' are treated as having no or little legitimate place in the selection of Supreme Court judges. For many, therefore, merit and ideology are antithetical notions that must be kept separate. As one critic put it, the prime concern in any judicial appointment process is to "prevent ideology from trumping merit in the appointment of judges to . . . highest court[s]".[1] This is not surprising in a milieu that is dominated by the formalist mind-set and its antipathy toward the ideological infiltration of the judicial process.

The ambition to appoint judges who are truly meritorious is unquestionably appropriate. It is the issue of what counts as 'merit' that is debatable. Of course, nobody would want to have judges on such an important tribunal who did not possess all the technical and professional attributes of a truly competent judge. This much is undeniable. However, for the informalist, the problems arise when people assume that this can be achieved by institutionalizing a studied indifference to the ideological

[1] Peter Russell, Letter to Editor, *Toronto Globe and Mail* (May 16, 2011).

leanings of any particular candidate. Of course, it would be folly to select an out-and-out ideologue, especially if he or she otherwise lacked (or even had) all the qualities of meritorious judges: Karl Marx and Friedrich Hayek would make for less than ideal judges. However, the assumption that merit and ideology are unrelated notions and that it is possible to attend to matters of merit without taking into account ideology is fundamentally mistaken. For the informalist, merit and ideology walk down much the same street. As I have sought to emphasize, any denial, formalist or anti-formalist, to the contrary flaunts both the historical record of judicial decision-making and any informed professional analysis of it. While merit and ideology do not collapse into each other, it is simply not possible to talk of one without the other. Good judges recognize that the resort to values (and contested ones at that) is an integral and inevitable part of the judicial task.

When the present American Chief Justice John Roberts was appearing before the Senate's Judicial Committee during his confirmation hearing, he confided that he did not have an "all-encompassing approach" to his judicial role or to constitutional interpretation particularly. He went on to say that "judges are like [baseball] umpires – umpires don't make the rules; they apply them". He sealed this modest portrayal of judicial virtue by insisting that "judges have to have the humility to recognize that they operate within a system of precedent, shaped by other judges equally striving to live up to the judicial oath".[2] The not-so-implicit message of Roberts's credo was that being a good judge required restraint and forbearance; judges, even and perhaps especially Supreme Court ones, were not in the justice or politics game in any expansive or direct way. Their mandate was to apply the law and to rest content with that; justice would best be served by such an institutional separation of powers and responsibilities.

While this humble depiction of the judicial role – "it's my job to call balls and strikes and not to pitch or bat" – will strike a reassuring chord with some, it fails to understand the history and nature of the judicial role generally. Judges are much more than umpires. Indeed, the whole analogy between judging and umpiring is misleading and inaccurate. As far as their judicial duties go, history demonstrates that judges are very much part of the political action. It is less about *whether* they change the rules than about *how* they do so. Staying with the baseball analogy,

[2] John Roberts' opening statement before the Senate Judiciary Committee, *USA Today*, www.usatoday.com/news/washington/2005-09-12-roberts-fulltext_x.htm.

while some umpires claim to call balls and strikes "as they see 'em", others assert that "they ain't nothin' til I call 'em." People might be fated to play a baseball of the judges' choosing, but the judges are also very much part of the game; they play by as well as change the rules as they go along. In legal terms, not only what counts as 'balls' and 'strikes', but also what counts as 'baseball' changes over time. And it is the judges, for better and worse, who are the purveyors and guardians of many of these changes.

That being said, if judges are not umpires, they are not godly figures either. They have no especial, let alone divine insight into the meaning of legal texts or the nature of social justice – judgeliness is not next to godliness. There is no way to simply read off the meaning of laws, especially constitutions, in an impersonal exercise of professional technique without resort to larger and contested issues of social and political values. Similarly, there is also no way for judges to negotiate that fraught terrain with a sacred certainty or supernatural wisdom. As Edmund Burke observed, "whoever undertakes to set himself up as a judge of Truth and Knowledge is shipwrecked by the laughter of the gods".[3] And the same might be said of those formalists who claim that judges can perform in such a grandiose way; they also court the gods' derision. Because law is a social practice and society is in a constant state of agitated movement, law is always an organic and hands-on practice that is never the complete or finished article; it is always situated inside and within, not outside and beyond, the society in which it arises. In short, law is always a *work in progress* and judges are its privileged artisans.

Having these experimental, evanescent, and anything-might-go qualities, law is best represented by an informalist account of law and legal interpretation that recommends that its judicial personnel must also exhibit and embrace some of those qualities. While it is clearly a great help to possess an excellent set of technical skills, these will not be enough in and of themselves; they are a necessary but not sufficient condition of good judging. The possession of an extensive palette of paints, a set of superior brushes, and a strong grasp of various artistic techniques does not in itself make anyone into a great artist; it takes more than technical skill. The battery of adjudicative tools for rule application does not amount to a self-contained or self-operating technology: they make sense only as part of a larger understanding of law as a rhetorical

[3] Edmund Burke, Preface to Brissot's Address to His Constituents in *on Empire, Liberty, and Reform: Speeches and Letters* (David Bromwich ed. 2000).

and dynamic enterprise. Being a practical activity, adjudication does not consist of a series of formulaic applications in an abstract space. Instead, it is more profitably understood as an organic and judgment-based engagement in real time and in real places; it is less an occasion for logical operations than an exercise in operational logic.

Nonetheless, while the learned knack of using legal materials with adroitness and dexterity is not to be underrated, the effect of such a limited depiction of lawyers' special and distinctive expertise is misleading. It can too easily be used to avoid the democratic responsibility of justifying their power and authority by reference to the real-world pressure of getting the job done. The depiction of the judicial craft as an inward and insular undertaking serves to cut off law and adjudication from the sustaining socio-political context and rich historical resources from which they gain their vigour and vision. Legal artistry demands more than technical proficiency. Especially at the level of a nation's supreme judicial tribunal, great judges do not simply reproduce mechanically and mindlessly old arguments and trite analogies; they are those who can rework legal materials in an imaginative and stylish way. A bare legal craft can too easily acquire the elite habits of a Masonic order and fail to meet or sabotage its civic obligations: a job well done is not always its own reward.

To be worthy of the highest professional prestige, lawyers and judges must nurture a sense of social justice and a feel for political vision. Without these decidedly ideological characteristics, they will more likely become only hired hands for vested interests. As one commentator succinctly put it, "technique without ideals is a menace; ideals without technique are a mess".[4] Values and commitments can be hidden, but they cannot be done away with altogether. Judges and jurists cannot so easily evade taking responsibility for the artifacts and outcomes of their crafted performances by taking refuge in matters of technical consistency and internal coherence. So while the good judge should have technical skills in abundance (i.e., merit), he or she also needs to possess a socio-political vision within which and on behalf of which they can deploy those technical skills (i.e., ideology).[5] As the informalist insists, judicial decision-making demands both skill and vision: it is about law and ideology.

[4] Karl Llewellyn, The Adventures of Rollo, 2 *U. of Chi. L. Sch. Rec.* 3 (1952).

[5] Although *all* judges should combine merit and ideology, the great judges can be characterized as those who rework the conventional standards of what it is to judge well. See Allan C. Hutchinson, *Laughing at the Gods: Great Judges and How They Made the Common Law* (2011).

Getting Active

Few judges and even fewer jurists subscribe to Justice Roberts's umpiring analogy; it is a throwback to more ultra-formalist fantasies. In the twenty-first century, it presents an almost farcically simplistic account of the judicial role. But its invocation does point up both the deeper aspirations of most formalist jurists and its profound failings as an account of contemporary adjudication. This yearning for an ideology-free understanding of the judicial task might be understandable, but its achievement is perennially elusive. Moreover, it is institutionally debilitating in societies that claim some attachment to the virtues of democratic governance. As I have sought to demonstrate throughout the book, it defies convincing explanation of what would it mean for judges to 'follow the rules' without making some resort to a range of political values and moral commitments. The only real choice is one of candour or subterfuge.

At a very general level, there are three critical observations that an informalist can make against this bare formalist instruction to 'follow the rules'. First, the ascertainment of legal norms is itself fraught with political judgement and content. Declaring that certain rules are 'established' is simply a shorthand way of saying that certain moral or political commitments are now accepted by the legal community as settled; this is less an endorsement of the principles' apolitical nature and more an acknowledgment that general acceptance is a form of political validation. Second, the range of established rules and principles is extremely broad and often encompasses competing maxims; there is no neutral or non-political way to select between contradictory norms. Third, even if it is possible to isolate a relevant and exclusive legal norm, it is far from obvious how that general principle can be applied to particular facts in an entirely objective or impartial manner. In short, despite the desire of Chief Justice Roberts and his ilk for a simpler and more professional age, there is no purely technical and non-political way to engage in a principled mode of adjudication. It is no longer (and never was) possible to simply 'follow the rules' because the questions of which rules are relevant and in play, what those rules mean, and what following them entails remain related and irredeemably contestable activities. It is the 'who' of judicial decision-making as much as the 'what' that matters most.

These more general criticisms can be better substantiated by considering the debate around so-called judicial activism. At face value, it sounds as if it is something positive – healthy, vital, and purposeful. But when used in connection with courts, many hear it as having only disturbing negative resonances – uppity, illegitimate, and uncontrolled. For them, courts that do the least are courts that do the best. Of course, the concern that courts are interfering too much in the political process is a valid one. However, while exhortations to 'stick to the law' or 'follow the rules' are seductive, they offer little suggestion of how such a seemingly prosaic practice can be achieved. The fact is that, whether we like it or not, judges cannot avoid making political choices. The line that they are expected to tread between law and ideology is shaved so thin as to be non-existent. Indeed, the drawing of the line is itself contested and political. It is not a matter of whether to make choices, but only a question of which choices to make and how to do so. Adjudication is about choice, plain and simple. And those choices implicate ideology at each and every turn.

When it is accepted that there is no one right or exclusive way to identify and apply legal rules, the charge of being political and activist loses much of its force. The only thing left to debate is whether a particular ruling is better or worse, not correct or incorrect, in its informing political ideals and its practical impact. And that is exactly what the formalist critics try to avoid: they want to occupy the neutral territory of legal technique rather than contested turf of substantive ideological alignment. But such ground does not exist. Those occasions on which the formalists raise the spectre of judicial activism and those on which they do not are determined by ideological differences. Those decisions that do not fit their political agenda are condemned as 'activist', and those that do fit are defended as appropriate. The dividing line is one of their own political making. Although claimed to be made in the name of merit and neutrality, it is ideological in origin, operation, and effect.

In general, those decisions which promote greater equality (e.g., gay rights, women's reproductive choices, and aboriginal land claims) are dismissed as activist and illegitimate, whereas those which defend greater liberty (e.g., unlimited election spending, private health care, and religious freedom) are showcased as valid exercises of judicial authority. Yet in terms of their fit with opaque constitutional texts and legal doctrines, there is nothing to choose between them. It is only that some substantive values are preferred over others. Accordingly, today's claim of 'activism' is simply a veiled criticism that the courts are being too progressive and making decisions that do not reflect desirable conservative values. At a different time, it might be that it is the conservative-leaning judges who are being too activist. Any court that stands by and lets constitutional values be ignored or belittled is at fault. But there is no technical or purely legal way to decide what those values are – law is politics by other means. Legal interpretation is a site for debate, not a definitive contribution to it.

Of course, we need to be vigilant about what the courts are doing. Any court that tramples too often and too easily on the policy-making prerogative of legislatures is asking for trouble. Judges need to recognize that they are part of democracy's supporting cast, not its star performers. But that democratic watch should itself be open and honest. It is what the courts are being active about that is the key. It is no more or less ideological to maintain the status quo than it is to subvert it; conservatism is as ideological as progressivism. It hardly advances the democratic cause to deploy subterfuge and to pass off political commitments as constitutional or legal mandates. Decisions should be celebrated or condemned for the substantive values that they uphold, not for their vague failure to respect some spurious formal distinction between making and applying law. The fact is that any judge who stands by and let his or her sense of basic constitutional values be ignored or belittled is at fault.

Accordingly, if there is to be a genuine debate about what makes a 'good judge', let alone a great one, it is essential that we understand and accept that merit and ideology are inseparable companions. This critical claim that 'judging is inescapably political' should not be taken as tantamount to suggesting that judges simply legislate their political preferences and camouflage them behind legal doctrine and rhetoric, as the anti-formalists claim. While the occasional judge might do that, those rogue officials are and should be roundly condemned. The great bulk of judges perform their allotted task with genuine integrity and good faith. Ironically, some of the most celebrated judges are praised not merely for their technical qualities or analytical prowess. Judges such as Lord Denning, John Marshall, and Bertha Wilson are justly celebrated for the way that they left their substantive mark on the law. It was because of, not in spite of, their ideological political views that they are remembered. How they creatively and politically interpreted the law is a mark of their greatness, not a stain upon it. Their merit as judges not only is indistinguishable from their ideology, but also is in large part attributable to it.

Of course, judges are rarely ideologues in the sense that they pursue a dogmatic or even consistent line throughout their adjudicative careers. Judges are divided not only among themselves, but within themselves about contested social and moral issues.[6] Their political commitments

[6] See supra, Chapter 8.

provide a context or framework within which they approach issues and nudge them in certain directions or give justifications. But those deep-seated preferences do not determine in any mechanical manner the cut or content of their decisions. Judicial decision-making is political, but it is not crude or arbitrary for that. Judges play with the law's norms as they work within them. It is not that they are entirely free to do what they want or are fully constrained by the law's norms; it is that judges are located and function within the dynamic tension between freedom and constraint. Judges must constantly work with and within the available doctrinal materials such that its constraints are always in place but never outside of creative reinterpretation. So understood, judicial decision-making and legal interpretation are thoroughly professional as well as thoroughly ideological undertakings.

Moving Forward

It should be clear that the merit/ideology debate is simply one more incarnation of the law/ideology distinction. As such, the informalist response to the merit/ideology debate is that, when judges are appointed, attention should be paid to their values. Pretending to do otherwise by ignoring them is not only a mistake, but also a ruse. If legal interpretation is and must be about ideological values and political ideals, a society owes it to itself to appreciate the values and ideals of those who are or who are about to be judges. This demands an institutional process that allows for and facilitates such inquiries. Mindful of the increasingly potent role of courts in the modern governance of society, it is incumbent on those committed to democratic openness that they ensure that this opportunity is not lost. The adoption and defence of an informalist account of law and legal interpretation demands and supports such initiatives in the appointment of judges.[7]

One of the better institutional initiatives to achieve that is by way of judicial appointments through a thoroughly democratic process. There is an inevitable politics to judicial appointments; there always has been and always will be, even if it masquerades under the dubious label of 'merit'. But the choice is not between a political and a non-political process of

[7] Of course, an uncompromising commitment to democratic governance might well demand that the influential role of courts be curtailed and be replaced by more popular and diverse forums of participatory decision-making. See Allan C. Hutchinson, A 'Hard Core' Case against Judicial Review, 121 *Harv. L. Rev. F.* 57 (2008).

judicial appointments. Rather, it is a straightforward choice about whether the politics of the judiciary or the politics of the public at large, as expressed by its elected representatives, should prevail. While many will consider this a weak or even dangerous reform, it is necessitated by the nature and performance of the judicial function when understood from an informalist perspective. Such a politically informed and politically charged process will not contribute to a greater politicization of the judiciary; judges are already and inevitably a thoroughly politicized group. Instead, it will bring those politics out of the shadows and into open view. By so doing, it will render them more available for public scrutiny. After all, the politics of the public has more democratic legitimacy than that of the judges.

While there are more radical measures which might be taken, there are several less extreme steps that could be adopted which would better incorporate the understanding that 'law is politics' and that judicial decision-making requires judges to make contested and controversial political choices, especially in the appellate courts. The most important innovation would be to create a more democratic appointments process. This could be achieved by establishing an independent commission. Any such body would need to be as diverse and as representative as possible. Accordingly, it might consist of about fifteen members, of whom five would be appointed from the legislative arm of government (e.g., a House of Commons or a Senate), five would be judges, and five would be citizens; tenure on the committee would be limited to three years and the chair of the commission would be one of the lay members. Confident that no particular constituency (i.e., judicial, political, or lay) had a lock on the commission's work or decisions, the commission's task would be to establish appropriate criteria for appointment that took seriously the need for a diverse and talented judiciary.

Candidates could be identified by application, nomination, or search: interviews would be held and candidates would be subject to an intensive vetting. There could be rules to ensure both geographical representation and demographic diversity in terms of women, visible minorities, aboriginals, and other historically excluded groups. Also, threshold rules for eligibility in regard to professional experience and legal qualification might be relaxed to ensure that otherwise meritorious candidates were not excluded. Contrary to the received view that it is at lower levels of the judiciary that the criteria might need to be re-examined, such innovations are best made at the highest level; this will confirm the sincerity and importance of the commitment to diversity and change. In all its activities, the commission would ensure that ideological diversity was not a secondary or distant consideration but a leading component of 'merit'. Like the judges themselves, members of the commission would realize that their task was about both law and ideology.

The recommendations of the commission would be final and direct. The diverse composition and democratic operation of the commission would obviate the need for approval by any other body or official. This is not because such procedures are inconsistent with the move to take the Supreme Court out of the political arena, but because the commission itself will perform such a role more effectively. So structured, it will be less likely to turn the appointments process into a media circus or an institutional cover-up. Also, there should be a public register of 'judicial interests' and a tougher set of conflicts rules under a comprehensive Code of Judicial Conduct, which could be administered by the appointments commission. Judges should also have a fixed tenure of appointment of no more than twelve years. While the commission would have the power to receive complaints and discipline judges, it would not be able to dismiss judges without formal approval by the system's elected representatives.

While this package of reform proposals will fully guarantee neither the democratic accountability nor the institutional independence of the judiciary, it will far better deal with the realities of judicial authority and institutional power in constitutional democracies. At a minimum, it will get beyond the simplistic dichotomy of the merit/ideology debate that presently holds the appointment process in its paralyzing grip. As an informalist account suggests, genuine progress in judicial appointments will be made only when it is accepted that acknowledging the irrepressible ideological dimension to good judicial decision-making will improve the democratic validity of the appointments process. Moreover, the fear that exposing judges or their politics to increased democratic scrutiny will undermine their legitimacy is a canard that has been promoted by formalists to further their own cherished agenda. The fact is that more, not less information and knowledge about those who exercise power, be it judicial or any kind, is the best route to nurturing an improved democratic polity – *Better the devil you know than the devil that you don't.*

This informal view of judicial decision-making and appointments that I have offered has little to say prescriptively on what judges should do in performing their duties. This is not a weakness but is the strength of such a stance: it provides a necessary recognition that there are no professional or programmatic proposals that flow from the insistence that judicial decision-making is an exercise in law and ideology. Supreme Court justices will keep on doing what they are doing, although they might attend more critically and openly to the political values and ideological commitments that animate and drive their work. This does not mean that the legal and craft aspects of their work should be shunted to the side or not taken seriously; it is that the ideological dimension should be made more apparent and as equally available for scrutiny as their strictly legal work. On the basis that openness and candour are more conducive to democratic governance than disguise and dissemblance, this might well enhance the standing of Supreme Courts, not decrease it as many seem to fear.

Conclusion

It behooves me to end by returning to the place where I began. I asked what is involved in answering the questions *What is a park?* or *What is a vehicle?* in a legal or judicial setting. It should now be apparent that there is and can be no definitive answer to those questions. This does not mean that there are no answers at all to those questions; it simply means that there is no one or right answer that endures across time, society, and individuals. In suggesting that it is possible or desirable to hit upon a method of legal interpretation that will relieve lawyers and judges of the personal responsibility for making difficult choices among plausible answers, the dominant formalist approach is found severely wanting. There simply is no reliable intellectual device that will demonstrate that 'law' has some distinctive and authoritative way to answer such questions as *What is a park?* or *What is a vehicle?* in any way that is separate and apart from the ideological orientation of the particular lawyers and judges doing the answering. The best that we can hope for is intellectual clarity and political justice, not moral or ideological certitude.

By explaining and defending an informalist account of law and legal interpretation, I have sought to show that the answers reached are contingent on the circumstances and contexts in which they are asked. Moreover, there is no definitive way of fixing those circumstances in any uncontroversial way. Much will depend on the identity of the person answering them. Legal interpretation and judicial decision-making are both thoroughly professional and political in style and substance. However, it is not my contention that, with formalism (and anti-formalism) out of the way, lawyers will be released from the constraints and discipline that comprise the law and be entirely free to indulge their own political preferences and ideological leanings. An informal approach has no truck with either the claims of the formalists (i.e., that law is something separate from ideology) or those of the anti-formalists (i.e., that law is nothing other than ideological posturing). Rejecting such a dichotomy as false and unhelpful, an informalist approach to law and legal interpretation insists that judicial decision-making is an applied exercise in law and ideology; law and ideology are both integral parts of any adequate understanding of legal interpretation.

Appendix 1

R. v. Lachapelle

British Columbia Supreme Court

March 19th, 2008

Reasons for Judgment – Mr. Justice Butler

[1] In the late afternoon on May 9, 2006 Jerry Lachapelle drove Margaret Brown to the travelling carnival in Gitanmaax. She was 92 years old and Mr. Lachapelle was employed to provide assistance to her on a daily basis. They decided to go to the carnival to have a hamburger and fries for dinner. The carnival was set up on a vacant piece of private land in a large field. The carnival was busy when they arrived. As Mr. Lachapelle would have expected, there were hundreds of people and many children enjoying the amusement rides and the food, and playing the games.

[2] The carnival was a magnet for young people and, at that time of day, for families with young children. Two RCMP officers were in attendance to keep the peace. They knew Mr. Lachapelle was a convicted pedophile and was subject to a prohibition issued pursuant to s. 161(1)(a) of the Criminal Code, R.S.C. 1985, c. C-46. That order, dated November 18, 1997, provided as follows:

> . . . Jerry George Lachapelle is hereby prohibited for life from attending a public park or public swimming area where persons under the age of 14 years are present, or can reasonably be expected to be present, or a daycare centre, school ground, playground or community centre.

[3] Mr. Lachapelle was arrested and charged with breaching the prohibition order. Following a trial last year, Milne P.C.J. found that the field in which the carnival was held was not a public park or playground and acquitted Mr. Lachapelle. The Crown has brought this appeal.

The legislation

[4] Section 161 of the Criminal Code provides as follows:

> 161. (1) When an offender is convicted, or is discharged on the conditions prescribed in a probation order under section 730, of an offence referred to in subsection (1.1) in respect of a person who is under the age of fourteen years, the court that sentences the offender or directs that the accused be discharged, as the case may be, in addition to any other punishment that may be imposed for that offence or any other condition prescribed in the order of discharge, shall consider making and may make, subject to the conditions or exemptions that the court directs, an order prohibiting the offender from
>
> (a) attending a public park or public swimming area where persons under the age of fourteen years are present or can reasonably be expected to be present, or a daycare centre, schoolground, playground or community centre . . .

[5] Subsection 161(4)(b) provides that a person who does not comply with an order of prohibition is guilty of an offence punishable on summary conviction.

Trial decision

[6] Mr. Lachapelle, Ms. Brown and the two RCMP officers testified at trial. There was little controversy in the evidence. The trial judge found that the carnival included amusement rides, food stands, carnival games and games of chance. There were young children present throughout the grounds and many of them were less than 14 years old. While the majority of the children were at the rides, there were children running and playing in the grassy areas and by the picnic table where Ms. Brown sat down.

[7] Mr. Lachapelle's stated reason for going to the carnival was to have dinner. He was aware of the conditions of his order of prohibition and did not believe that the private field with the travelling carnival fell within the prohibition. He said that if that area had been designated as a park he would not have attended.

[8] The trial judge decided that a travelling carnival set up on a private piece of land was not a "public park". In arriving at that conclusion he stated as follows at para. 43:

> I am not satisfied that the words "public park" in section 161 include a carnival located on private land even though the public had access to it. In

> my view, the intent of Parliament was to restrict the activity of persons subject to prohibition orders to specific geographical places where children under the age of 14 may be reasonably expected to be. Public parks are ordinarily considered to be places "set aside" by some authority for the use by the public. They are more than places that are just accessible to the public. There is no doubt that children under 14 would be expected at a carnival, but in the circumstances of this case, such a carnival is not a "park".

[9] The trial judge also found that the carnival was not a playground and explained that decision at paras. 46–47:

> When one thinks of playgrounds, one thinks of swing sets and other outdoor equipment, usually in relation to a park or a school ground or a community-based location that is not simply used as a playground, but is also set aside for or designated as such.
>
> If the submissions of Crown were to succeed, a vacant lot, a street hockey game, or many other activities in a public area could be interpreted as a playground, if one considers only its use by members of the public. In my mind, a playground for the purposes of s. 161 must be something more than someone playing on a piece of ground.

Issue

[10] Did the trial judge err in determining that on May 9, 2006 the travelling carnival in Gitanmaax was neither a "public park" nor a "playground" as those terms are used in s. 161(1)(a) of the Criminal Code?

[11] to [15] omitted

Discussion

[16] The question raised on this appeal involves the proper interpretation of the two terms used in s. 161. The standard of review is correctness.

[17] The proper approach to statutory interpretation is that "the words of an Act are to be read in their entire context and in the grammatical and ordinary sense harmoniously with the scheme of the Act, and the intention of Parliament": R. v. Clark, 2005 SCC 2, [2005]1 S.C.R. 6 at para. 43.

[18] There is no issue regarding the intention of Parliament. The purpose of s. 161 is to prohibit pedophiles from having access to specified locations where children under the age of 14 are likely to be present and thus to protect children from becoming victims of sexual offences. The

Crown stresses that its suggested interpretation of the section gives full effect to Parliament's intention. The respondent says that the Crown's interpretation stretches the ordinary meaning of the words and would unnecessarily create vagueness and overbreadth.

[19] The decision in R. v. Heywood, [1994] 3 S.C.R. 761 provides a useful starting point for the analysis. The accused had been convicted of sexual assault involving children and was charged with vagrancy under s. 179(1)(b) of the Criminal Code when he was found taking photographs of children in a public park. That section made it an offence for a convicted sexual offender to be found "loitering in or near a school ground, playground, public park or bathing area." The accused was convicted at trial but the British Columbia Court of Appeal overturned the conviction. The Supreme Court of Canada dismissed the appeal, finding that the section violated s. 7 of the Charter and was not justified under s. 1.

[20] In Heywood, the court found that s. 179(1)(b) suffered from overbreadth. Cory J. noted that the concepts of vagueness and overbreadth are related in that both are the result of a lack of sufficient precision by the legislature in the means used to accomplish an objective. He described the analysis that should be used to consider whether a provision is overly broad at pp. 792–93:

> Overbreadth analysis looks at the means chosen by the state in relation to its purpose. In considering whether a legislative provision is overbroad, a court must ask the question: are those means necessary to achieve the State objective? If the State, in pursuing a legitimate objective, uses means which are broader than is necessary to accomplish that objective, the principles of fundamental justice will be violated because the individual's rights will have been limited for no reason. The effect of overbreadth is that in some applications the law is arbitrary or disproportionate.

[21] In finding that s. 179(1)(b) was overly broad, Cory J. stated as follows at pp. 794–95:

> The section is overly broad in its geographical ambit. It applies not only to school grounds and playgrounds, but also to all public parks and bathing areas. Its application to schools and playgrounds is appropriate, as these are the very places children are likely to congregate. But its application to all public parks and bathing areas is overly broad because not all such places are places where children are likely to be found. Public parks include the vast and remote wilderness parks. Bathing areas would include all the lakes in Canada with public beaches. Prohibiting

> individuals from loitering in all places in all parks is a significant limit on freedom of movement.

[22] Cory J. found that his conclusion was strengthened when he compared the geographical ambit of s. 179(1)(b) with that of s. 161. At the time, s. 161 was a new provision that had been enacted in response to the British Columbia Court of Appeal's decision that s. 179(1)(b) was unconstitutional. At p. 802, Cory J. stated the following regarding s. 161:

> It can be seen that this section is limited to clearly defined geographical areas where children are or can reasonably be expected to be present. Further, the prohibition may be for life or a shorter period and a system of review is provided. Additionally, the order of prohibition is made part of the sentencing procedure so that the accused is aware of and notified of the prohibitions. It is thus apparent that overly broad provisions are not essential or necessary in order to achieve the aim of s. 179(1)(b).

[23] Thus, Cory J. referred to s. 161 with approval because its geographical ambit was limited to "clearly defined geographical areas where children are or can reasonably be expected to be present".

[24] The difficulty with the position taken by the Crown in the present case is that it is asking that the geographical ambit of the prohibition in s. 161 be expanded in a way that introduces vagueness and uncertainty. As noted in the trial judge's reasons, a "public park" is a place ordinarily considered to be set aside for use by the public. The Crown's suggested interpretation would significantly alter the analysis as to whether a geographical location is one that is covered by the prohibition. Instead of deciding whether a location has been set aside or designated as such, the analysis would require a consideration of the nature of the activities being carried on at a location at a particular time. This would necessarily insert uncertainty into the section as it would require the individual and the court to undertake an analysis to determine if the recreational use and the degree of access at the time in question would qualify the location as a "public park".

[25] In my view, the analysis in D'Angelo does not assist in the resolution of the issue raised in the case at bar. Here, the issue is not whether the travelling carnival in Gitanmaax was open to the public. Rather, the issue is whether the fact that it was open to the public at the material time is enough to qualify it as a "public park" as that term is used in s. 161.

[26] The determination as to whether a place has been set aside or designated as a public park would normally be uncontroversial. The

conclusions reached through the situational analysis required by the Crown's interpretation would be much less consistent. In other words, if the Crown's interpretation was accepted, the ambit of s. 161 would be difficult to define and would no longer be "limited to clearly defined geographical areas". Vagueness and uncertainty would creep back into the geographical ambit of a prohibition order.

[27] In Heywood, the court referred, with approval, to a passage from the decision of Maughan P.C.J. in R. v. Graf (1988), 42 C.R.R. 146 (B.C. Prov. Ct.). In that case, the trial judge found that the predecessor to s. 179 (1)(b) offended the Charter. To illustrate the overbreadth of the geographical ambit she described at p. 150 many of the places at which the accused could not loiter:

> He is, for example, banned for life from standing idly about Stanley Park, including the aquarium and the zoo area, Lost Lagoon, the playing fields, the beaches and the entertainment area. Similarly are included Queen Elizabeth Park, English Bay, the Planetarium, Vanier Park, the endowment lands at the University of British Columbia, the Courthouse gardens, Jericho Beach, Spanish Banks, Kitsilano Park, the Sky Train greenbelt, the multitude of small city parks, Manning Park, the marine parks in the province, waterfront parks, Cleveland Dam, Capilano Hatchery, Mount Seymour ski area, Lynn Valley Park, Lynn Canyon Park and all beaches, lakes and rivers in Canada capable of being used by people for bathing. Public parks and bathing areas are areas set aside and maintained by public funds for the health, refreshment, recreation and entertainment of all of the country's citizens. They are areas set aside for indolence and rest of the body and soul.

[28] It is not surprising that each of the examples of a "public park" chosen by Maughan P.C.J. is an area that is set aside or designated as a park by some authority. Any member of the public and anyone subject to a prohibition order would know that each of those locations is a "public park". This interpretation of "public parks" is the ordinary usage of the word and the usage that was applied by the trial judge in this case.

[29] There is a similar difficulty with the Crown's suggested definition of the term "playground". It would also require the individual and the court to analyze and assess the nature of the activity carried on or likely to be carried on at a location at a particular time. If it could be concluded that at the material time the location had been set aside or commonly used for recreation and play by children, or by children and adults, then the prohibition would apply. Again, this would insert vagueness and uncertainty into the language where none is present.

[30] As the trial judge found, a playground is commonly understood to be an area with swings, climbing equipment or other facilities designed for children. It is usually located in a park or school or other location established by a community and set aside or designated as such. If the legislature had intended that any field where a recreational activity involving children was taking place should fall within the prohibition, much clearer language would be required.

[31] In summary, prohibition orders issued under s. 161 are a significant limitation on the fundamental liberty of movement of convicted pedophiles. If the words of the section are given their ordinary meaning, the geographical ambit of the prohibition is clear and the offender will know with a high degree of certainty what locations must be avoided. The trial judge gave the words "public park" and "playground" their ordinary meaning and read them appropriately in context. It was not the intention of Parliament to prevent a pedophile from attending at all events involving some element of recreation or play where children may be present. It is the specific location that determines whether or not the offence has been committed, not the nature of the activity occurring at the time. The fact that a travelling carnival with amusement rides is being held on a vacant, private field does not turn that field into a "public park" or a "playground".

[32] The appeal of the Crown is dismissed.

Appendix 2

R. v. Perron

Court Of Appeal For Ontario

March 23rd, 2009

On appeal from the order of Justice Lise Maisonneuve of the Ontario Court of Justice

Reasons for Judgment - Goudge J.A. (on behalf of Cronk and LaForme J.J.A.)

Overview

[1] On August 18, 2006, the appellant was arrested while working in a game booth at the Super Ex, a fair being held on the grounds of Lansdowne Park in Ottawa. He was charged with breach of a prohibition order made pursuant to s. 161(1)(a) of the Criminal Code, R.S.C. 1985, c. C-46, which prohibited him from attending a public park where persons under the age of fourteen years were present or could reasonably have been expected to be present.

[2] It was conceded that the Super Ex at Lansdowne Park was accessible to the public and was a place where persons under the age of fourteen years were present or could reasonably have been expected to be present. The contested issue was whether the appellant was attending a park.

[3] In thoughtful reasons, the trial judge found that the Super Ex at Lansdowne Park was a public park as that phrase is used in s. 161(1)(a) of the Code. She convicted the appellant. The appellant appeals his conviction.

Facts

[4] The facts are essentially uncontested. In the spring of 2006, the appellant pleaded guilty to one count of sexual interference and one count of sexual touching. The complainants were between the ages of

12 and 14. The appellant's sentence included an order pursuant to s. 161 (1)(a) of the Code, prohibiting him from attending a public park where persons under the age of fourteen are present or can reasonably be expected to be present.

[5] Section 161(1)(a) reads . . .

[6] Lansdowne Park contains a football stadium, a civic centre with a hockey arena, and several other buildings. There are trees and grassy areas around the perimeter of the property, and surrounding some of the buildings. There is also an extensive paved area that serves as a parking lot for events. The grounds are surrounded by a fence and are accessible to the public through several gates. There is an admission fee to gain entry.

[7] The Super Ex at Lansdowne Park included mid-way rides, game booths, concert areas, food courts, and a petting zoo. The appellant was found working at a game booth that involved throwing darts at balloons. It was on the north side of the fairgrounds in a long corridor of game booths lined with stuffed animals and other trinkets that could be won as prizes. The corridor, like most areas where people walked during the Super Ex, was on the paved area. The Super Ex was attended by what was described as a very young crowd, with a lot of young people who appeared to be between 12 and 16 years of age or even younger.

Issue

[8] In this court, the appellant did not contest that he was found in a place that was accessible to the public, and that it was a place where persons under the age of fourteen were present or could reasonably be expected to be present. Nor did he suggest that s. 161(1)(a) was unconstitutionally vague or overbroad.

[9] The only issue he raises is whether the Super Ex was a "park" and therefore a place he was prohibited from attending because of the s. 161(1)(a) order. The appellant's position is that it was not. He says that "park" ordinarily, in its regular everyday use, refers to a green space, such as an area with lawns and gardens or forests and trees, which is set aside and maintained for recreational use by the public. What is in essence a parking lot cannot be turned into a park by virtue of the way it is being used.

[10] The respondent's position is that in light of the purpose of s. 161 (1)(a), the meaning to be given to "public park" cannot be circumscribed by the physical geography of the land but must be significantly informed

by the use made of it. Approached this way, the appellant was properly found to be at a public park on August 18, 2006, contrary to the prohibition order by which he was bound.

Analysis

[11] The issue in this appeal is whether the appellant was attending a "public park . . . where persons under the age of fourteen are present or can reasonably be expected to be present" when he was found at the Super Ex at Lansdowne Park on August 18, 2006. This requires an analysis of the meaning of these words, and particularly "public park" as that phrase is used in s. 161(1)(a) of the Code.

[12] The Code does not contain a definition of "public park". In construing the words in s. 161(1)(a), the well known approach described by Professor Driedger in his Construction of Statutes, 2nd ed. (Toronto: Butterworths, 1983), at p. 87, is to be used:

> Today there is only one principle or approach, namely, the words of an Act are to be read in their entire context and in their grammatical and ordinary sense harmoniously with the scheme of the Act, the object of the Act, and the intention of Parliament.

[13] The purpose of s. 161(1)(a) is to protect children from becoming victims of sexual offences at the hands of those who have previously committed certain specified offences. The protection of this particularly vulnerable group in Canadian society must inform the task of construing the phrase in issue in this appeal. See R. v. D'Angelo (2002), 8 C.R. (6th) 386 (Ont. C.A.).

[14] Section 161(1)(a) addresses the legislative objective by specifying a number of locations that an offender can be prohibited from attending. The context provided by the full list of locations is of assistance in construing the phrase in issue here. Some locations such as day care centers or school grounds are places where children will inevitably be present because of the activities carried on there. However, this is not necessarily so for other locations such as public parks. As the Supreme Court of Canada said in R. v. Heywood, [1994] 3 S.C.R. 761, not all public parks are places where children are likely to be found. Wilderness parks for example are public parks where nothing goes on that is likely to attract children. However, consistent with the legislative objective, only public parks where children are present or can reasonably be expected to be present can be included in a prohibition order. In other words,

Parliament has specified locations in s. 161(1)(a) because what goes on there makes it likely that young children will be present.

[15] The grammatical and ordinary sense of the words in s. 161(1)(a) is informed by the definitions of "park" found in the Canadian Oxford English Dictionary, 2nd ed. (Oxford University Press, 2004):

> **park**/ park/ n. **1** a piece of land usu. with lawns, gardens, etc. in a town or city, maintained at public expense for recreational use. **2** a large area of government land kept in its natural state for recreational use, wildlife conservation, etc. **3** a large enclosed area of land etc., either public or private, used to accommodate wild animals in captivity (wildlife park). **4** (usu. in combination) **a** an area devoted to a specified purpose (industrial park). **b** an area developed for a particular form of recreation (snowboard park; water park; theme park). **5** N. Amer. an enclosed arena, area, stadium, etc. for sports events (esp. ballpark). **6** an area for motor vehicles etc. to be left in (trailer park). **7** the gear position or function in an automatic transmission in which the gears are locked, preventing the vehicle's movement. **8** a large enclosed piece of ground, usu. with woodland and pasture, attached to a stately home etc.

[16] The first six are of relevance here. All are specified locations characterized by what goes on there. For most of the six, it is some form of recreational activity.

[17] Finally, in construing the phrase describing the location that the appellant is prohibited from attending, sufficient clarity must be given. An individual bound by a prohibition order should be able to know what it requires, since breach of the order constitutes a criminal offence. In R. v. Tremblay (2008), 89 O.R. (3d) 48 (C.A.), at para. 10, my colleague Sharpe J.A. put the point this way in interpreting a term in a long-term supervision order:

> That said, we must also be mindful that failure to comply with the condition constitutes a serious criminal offence carrying a period of up to ten years imprisonment and that it must be interpreted according to applicable legal principles. In particular, the appellant is entitled to the benefit of the principle explained by Dickson J. in Marcotte v. Canada (Deputy Attorney General), [1976] 1 S.C.R. 108, [1974] S.C.J. No. 142, at p. 115 S.C.R:
>
> > No authority is needed for the proposition that if real ambiguities are found, or doubts of substance arise, in the construction and application of a statute affecting the liberty of a subject, then that statute should be applied in such a manner as to favour the person against whom it is sought to be enforced. If one is to be incarcerated, one

should at least know that some Act of Parliament requires it in express terms, and not, at most, by implication.

[18] In light of these considerations how are we to construe the prohibition from attending a "public park . . . where persons under the age of fourteen years are present or can reasonably be expected to be present"?

[19] The appellant argues that only a green space qualifies. I cannot agree. The legislative purpose, the kinds of locations that can be included in a prohibition order, and the ordinary grammatical meaning of the words clearly focus on the kinds of recreational activities that the public can engage in at the particular location and whether they are likely to involve the presence of young children. There is nothing to suggest that a particular physical geography is a vital characteristic. Indeed there are many locations commonly referred to as parks which exhibit little if any greenery. Skateboard parks are but one example. While in a particular case the presence of greenery may help in identifying a location as a public park for the purposes of a prohibition order under s. 161(1)(a), I do not think that the absence of greenery necessarily excludes it.

[20] In my view, to breach this term of a prohibition order under s. 161 (1)(a), the person bound by it must be attending at a defined or discrete location that is accessible to the public for recreational use that involves or is reasonably likely to involve children under the specified age. In particular cases, other factors may also be relevant, such as the presence of greenery or the public designation of the location as a park. Construed in this way, the phrase "public park . . . where persons under the age of fourteen years are present or can reasonably be expected to be present" best serves the legislative purpose and is most faithful to the ordinary and grammatical sense of the words in their legislative context. Moreover, it provides the clarity necessary for the person bound by the order to know the locations that must be avoided.

[21] The appellant places significant reliance on R. v. Lachapelle, 2008 BCSC 511, where the British Columbia Supreme Court determined that a prohibition order in the same terms as the one in this case did not extend to a vacant private field where a travelling carnival with amusement rides was being held. As I read the decision, the determining factor seems to be that the location was a vacant private field. If so, I agree with the result. If, however, the decision stands for the proposition that the nature of the activities taking place at the location is irrelevant, then respectfully, I disagree with it for the reasons I have indicated.

Conclusion

[22] Construing the phrase in issue in this appeal as I have described above, I agree with the trial judge that the appellant was in breach of his prohibition order when he was found attending the Super Ex at Lansdowne Park on August 18, 2006. He was at a defined location to which the public had access for recreational use that included or could reasonably be expected to include the presence of persons under the age of fourteen years. Moreover, in this case, there was some greenery at the location although it was peripheral. Finally, the location itself was publicly designated as a park. A person in the appellant's position would reasonably know that he cannot attend that location in those circumstances.

[23] The appeal must be dismissed.

Appendix 3

McBoyle v. United States

10th Circuit Court of Appeals

August 18th, 1930

Appeal from the District Court of the United States for the Western District of Oklahoma.

Before COTTERAL, PHILLIPS, and McDERMOTT, Circuit Judges.

Reasons for Judgment - PHILLIPS, Circuit Judge.

1. William W. McBoyle was convicted and sentenced for an alleged violation of the National Motor Vehicle Theft Act, section 408, title 18, U.S. Code (18 USCA § 408). The indictment charged that on October 10, 1926, McBoyle caused to be transported in interstate commerce from Ottawa, Ill., to Guymon, Okl., one Waco airplane, motor No. 6124, serial No. 256, which was the property of the United States Aircraft Corporation and which had theretofore been stolen; and that McBoyle then and there knew it had been stolen.

2. The evidence of the government established the following facts: During the year 1926, McBoyle operated a commercial airport at Galena, Ill. On July 2, 1926, McBoyle hired A.J. Lacey as an aviator for a period of six months. In October, 1926, McBoyle induced Lacey to go to the field of the Aircraft Corporation at Ottawa, Ill., and steal such Waco airplane from the Aircraft Corporation. Lacey went to Ottawa, stole the airplane, and flew it to Galena, arriving there October 6th. McBoyle inquired of Lacey if any one knew the latter had taken the airplane at Ottawa. Lacey replied in the negative. Thereupon, McBoyle changed the serial number to No. 249, and painted it over in order to conceal the alteration. McBoyle and Lacey serviced the airplane and supplied it with gas and oil. McBoyle gave Lacey $150 for expense money and instructed Lacey to fly the airplane to Amarillo, Tex., and there lease an airport for

them to operate during the winter months. McBoyle arranged with Lacey to communicate with him en route by telegraphic code under the name of Pat Sullivan. Lacey left McBoyle's airport at Galena, Ill., on October 6th and flew the airplane to Guymon, Okl., stopping en route at St. Joseph, Mo., and Garden City, Kan. At Guymon, they communicated with each other by telegraph and McBoyle instructed Lacey to sell or store the stolen airplane and come back to Galena. Thereupon, Lacey returned to Galena. McBoyle then gave Lacey $250 for expenses and instructed Lacey to take an airplane of the same kind and make belonging to McBoyle back to Guymon and substitute it for the stolen airplane. The purpose was to deceive the officers when they found the Waco plane at Guymon. Lacey started back to Guymon with the second airplane but crashed near Inman, Kan. Thereupon, Lacey returned to Galena and continued to work for McBoyle until the following December.

3. McBoyle denied all of the facts incriminating him except the sending and receiving of the telegrams. He testified that the telegrams did not refer to the airplane but to liquor which Lacey was supposed to have had in his possession in the airplane.

4. The primary question is whether an airplane comes within the purview of the National Motor Vehicle Theft Act. This act defines the term "motor vehicle," as follows:

> "The term 'motor vehicle' when used in this section shall include an automobile, automobile truck, automobile wagon, motor cycle, or any other self-propelled vehicle not designed for running on rails."

5. Counsel for McBoyle contend that the word "vehicle" includes only conveyances that travel on the ground; that an airplane is not a vehicle but a ship; and that, under the doctrine of ejusdem generis, the phrase "any other self propelled vehicle" cannot be construed to include an airplane.

6. The Century Dictionary gives the derivation of the word "vehicle" as follows: "F. Vehicule, L. Vehiculum," meaning a "conveyance, carriage, ship." It defines the word as "Any receptacle, or means of transport, in which something is carried or conveyed, or travels."

7. It will be noted that the Latin word "vehiculum" means a ship as well as a carriage.

8. Webster defines the word "vehicle" as follows:

> "(1) That in or on which any person or thing is or may be carried, esp. on land, as a coach, wagon, car, bicycle, etc.; a means of conveyance."
> (2) That which is used as the instrument of conveyance or communication."

9. Corpus Juris, vol. 42, p. 609, § 1, defines a motor vehicle, as follows:

> "A 'motor vehicle' is a vehicle operated by a power developed within itself and used for the purpose of carrying passengers or materials; and as the term is used in the different statutes regulating such vehicles, it is generally defined as including all vehicles propelled by any power other than muscular power, except traction engines, road rollers, and such motor vehicles as run only upon rails or tracks."

10. Both the derivation and the definition of the word "vehicle" indicate that it is sufficiently broad to include any means or device by which persons or things are carried or transported, and it is not limited to instrumentalities used for traveling on land, although the latter may be the limited or special meaning of the word. We do not think it would be inaccurate to say that a ship or vessel is a vehicle of commerce.

11. An airplane is self-propelled, by means of a gasoline motor. It is designed to carry passengers and freight from place to place. It runs partly on the ground but principally in the air. It furnishes a rapid means for transportation of persons and comparatively light articles of freight and express. It therefore serves the same general purpose as an automobile, automobile truck, or motorcycle. It is of the same general kind or class as the motor vehicles specifically enumerated in the statutory definition and, therefore, construing an airplane to come within the general term, "any other self propelled vehicle," does not offend against the maxim of ejusdem generis.

12. Furthermore, some meaning must be ascribed to the general phrase "any other self propelled vehicle," which Congress wrote into the act. It specifically enumerated all of the known self-propelled vehicles designed for running on land. It used the word "automobile," a generic term, which includes all self-propelled motor vehicles that travel on land and are used for the transportation of passengers, except those designed for running on rails. 42 C.J p. 609, § 2.

13. We conclude that the phrase, "any other self propelled vehicle," includes an airplane, a motorboat, and any other like means of conveyance or transportation which is self propelled, and is of the same general class as an automobile and a motorcycle.

14. Counsel for McBoyle contend that the evidence failed to establish that he committed any crime in the Western District of Oklahoma, and that therefore the United States District Court of that district, because of

the provisions of section 2, art.3 of the United States Constitution, and the Sixth Amendment to the United States Constitution, was without jurisdiction.

15. The Motor Vehicle Act provides that "whoever shall transport or cause to be transported in interstate commerce a motor vehicle, knowing the same to have been stolen, shall be punished," etc., and that "any person violating this section may be punished in any district in or through which such motor vehicle has been transported or removed by such offender."

16. The crime of transporting a stolen motor vehicle in interstate commerce is a continuing offense. It is committed in each state and district through which such vehicle is transported. It was not essential that McBoyle should have been physically present in the Western District of Oklahoma. The constitutional requirement is that the accused shall be tried in the state or district where the crime is committed, but not necessarily in the state and district where the accused was at the time the crime was committed. It is sufficient if the crime was committed in the Western District of Oklahoma and McBoyle caused it to be committed there.

17. Salinger v. Loisel, 265 U.S. 224, 235, 44 S. Ct. 519, 68 L. Ed. 989; Burton v. United States, 202 U.S. 344, 387, 26 S. Ct. 688, 50 L. Ed. 1057, 6 Ann. Cas. 362; In re Palliser, 136 U.S. 257, 265–268, 10 S. Ct. 1034, 34 L. Ed. 514.

18. The jury was warranted in finding, from the evidence, that McBoyle caused Lacey to undertake to transport such airplane from Ottawa, Ill., to Amarillo, Tex., that Lacey started from Ottawa and succeeded in flying as far as Guymon, Okl., and that, upon telegraphic instructions from McBoyle, Lacey stored the airplane at Guymon and returned to Galena; and in concluding that McBoyle caused the offense to be committed in the Western District of Oklahoma.

19. At the trial, Mathey, a witness in behalf of McBoyle, testified as to the good reputation of the latter, after stating that he had made an investigation into McBoyle's character. Upon cross-examination, he was asked whether or not, through such investigation, he had learned of specific charges or reports concerning McBoyle. Objection to this line of cross-examination was overruled. Counsel for McBoyle contend that such ruling was error. It is within the discretion of the trial court to permit a witness, as to reputation, to be asked upon cross-examination as to particular charges against or reports concerning the person whose reputation is under investigation. Such evidence is admissible to test the

knowledge and credibility of the witness, but not as substantive evidence against the defendant. White v. State, 111 Ala. 92, 21 So. 330; Smith v. State, 103 Ala. 57, 15 So. 866, 871; McCreary v. Commonwealth, 158 Ky. 613, 165 S.W. 981; People v. Gordan, 103 Cal. 568, 37 P. 534, 535. We do not think the court abused its discretion in the instant case.

20. During the course of the cross-examination of McBoyle, he was interrogated by counsel for the government concerning matters that indicated he may have been connected, either directly or indirectly, with other offenses – a stolen automobile, another airplane stolen by Lacey, and some transactions concerning intoxicating liquor. These matters would have been immaterial and improper but for the fact that they were first injected into the case by counsel for McBoyle upon the cross-examination of Lacey and in the direct examination of McBoyle. Having opened up these subjects, McBoyle cannot complain because counsel for the government inquired concerning them in his cross-examination of McBoyle. State v. Ritter, 288 Mo. 381, 231 S.W. 606, 608; Olive v. State, 11 Neb. 1, 7 N.W. 444, 452; State v. Mott, 72 Mont. 306, 233 P. 602, 604; 40 Cyc. 2496.

21. Counsel for McBoyle contend that the court erred in admitting, over objection, copies of the telegrams which passed between McBoyle and Lacey while the latter was at Guymon. McBoyle admitted sending and receiving the telegrams and admitted the correctness of some of the copies. Lacey identified copies of the telegrams and stated that they were sent and received by him. The telegraph operator at Guymon testified that he furnished copies of the telegrams to the United States Attorney, and that the originals had been destroyed. A sufficient foundation was laid for the admission of the copies, and the evidence was material.

22. After the verdict, McBoyle filed a motion in arrest of judgment and for a new trial. Counsel for McBoyle contend that the court erred in denying these motions. Matters presented by these motions were addressed to the discretion of the trial court. We have examined the record and are convinced that the trial court did not abuse its discretion in denying such motions. A ruling on a motion for a new trial will not be disturbed on appeal, in the absence of an abuse of discretion. Gibson v. Luther (C.C.A. 8) 196 F. 203, 206; Hamilton & Sons Co. v. Moss-Jellico C. Co. (C.C.A. 6) 271 F. 237, 238; Capital Traction Co. v. Sneed, 58 App. D.C. 141, 26 F.(2d) 296, 301; Detroit United Ry. Co. v. Craven (C.C.A. 6) 13 F.(2d) 352.

23. The judgment is therefore affirmed.

COTTERAL, Circuit Judge (dissenting).

1. I feel bound to dissent on the ground that the National Motor Vehicle Theft Act should not be construed as relating to the transportation of airplanes.

2. A prevailing rule is that a penal statute is to be construed strictly against an offender and it must state clearly the persons and acts denounced. 25 R.C.L. pp. 1081–1084; First Nat. Bank of Anamoose v. United States (C.C.A.) 206 F. 374, 46 L.R.A. (N.S.) 1139.

3. It would have been a simple matter in enacting the statute to insert, as descriptive words, airplanes, aircraft, or flying machines. If they had been in the legislative mind, the language would not have been expressed in such uncertainty as "any other self-propelled vehicle not designed for running on rails." The omission to definitely mention airplanes requires a construction that they were not included. Furthermore, by excepting vehicles running on rails, the meaning of the act is clarified. These words indicate it was meant to be confined to vehicles that run, but not on rails, and it did not extend to those that fly. Is it not an unreasonable view that airplanes fall within the description of self-propelled vehicles that do not run on rails? The question is its own answer.

4. The rule of ejusdem generis has special application to this statute. General words following a particular designation are usually presumed to be restricted so as to include only things or persons of the same kind, class, or nature, unless there is a clear manifestation of a contrary purpose. 25 R.C.L. pp. 996, 997. The general description in this statute refers to vehicles of the same general class as those enumerated. We may assume an airplane is a vehicle, in being a means of transportation. And it has its own motive power. But is an airplane classified generally with "an automobile, automobile truck, automobile wagon, or motor cycle"? Are airplanes regarded as other types of automobiles and the like? A moment's reflection demonstrates the contrary.

5. Counsel for appellant have referred us to the debates in Congress when the act was pending as persuasive of an interpretation in his favor. House, Cong. Rec., vol. 58, part 6, pp. 5470 to 5478; Senate, Id., vol. 58, part 7, pp. 6433 to 6435. The proceedings are not permissible aids, apart from the journals or committee reports. But they may be referred to as showing the history of the period. Standard Oil Co. v. United States, 221 U.S. 1, 31 S. Ct. 502, 55 L. Ed. 619, 34 L.R.A. (N.S.) 834, Ann Cas. 1912D, 734. The discussions of the proposed measure are enlightening in this case from a historic standpoint, in showing that the theft of automobiles

was so prevalent over the land as to call for punitive restraint, but airplanes were never even mentioned.

6. It is familiar knowledge that the theft of automobiles had then become a public menace, but that airplanes had been rarely stolen if at all, and it is a most uncommon thing even at this date. The prevailing mischief sought to be corrected is an aid in the construction of a statute. 25 R.C.L. 1016.

7. I am constrained to hold that airplanes were not meant by the act to be embraced in the designation of motor vehicles, and that the indictment charged no offense against the defendant.

McBoyle v. United States,

United States Supreme Court

March 9th, 1931.

Mr. Justice HOLMES delivered the opinion of the Court.

The petitioner was convicted of transporting from Ottawa, Illinois, to Guymon, Oklahoma, an airplane that he knew to have been stolen, and was sentenced to serve three years' imprisonment and to pay a fine of $2,000. The judgment was affirmed by the Circuit Court of Appeals for the Tenth Circuit. 43 F.(2d) 273. A writ of certiorari was granted by this Court on the question whether the National Motor Vehicle Theft Act applies to aircraft.

That Act provides:

> "Sec. 2. That when used in this Act: (a) The term 'motor vehicle' shall include an automobile, automobile truck, automobile wagon, motor cycle, or any other self-propelled vehicle not designed for running on rails . . .
>
> "Sec. 3. That whoever shall transport or cause to be transported in interstate or foreign commerce a motor vehicle, knowing the same to have been stolen, shall be punished by a fine of not more than $5,000, or by imprisonment of not more than five years, or both."

Section 2 defines the motor vehicles of which the transportation in interstate commerce is punished in Section 3. The question is the meaning of the word 'vehicle' in the phrase 'any other self-propelled vehicle not designed for running on rails.' No doubt etymologically it is possible to use the word to signify a conveyance working on land, water or air, and sometimes legislation extends the use in that direction, for example, land and air, water being separately provided for, in the Tariff Act,

September 21, 1922, c. 356, 401(b), 42 Stat. 858, 948 (19 USCA 231(b). But in everyday speech 'vehicle' calls up the picture of a thing moving on land. Thus in Rev. St. 4 (1 USCA 4) intended, the Government suggests, rather to enlarge than to restrict the definition, vehicle includes every contrivance capable of being used 'as a means of transportation on land.' And this is repeated, expressly excluding aircraft, in the Tariff Act, June 17, 1930, c. 497, 401(b), 46 Stat. 590, 708 (19 USCA 1401). So here, the phrase under discussion calls up the popular picture. For after including automobile truck, automobile wagon and motor cycle, the words 'any other self-propelled vehicle not designed for running on rails' still indicate that a vehicle in the popular sense, that is a vehicle running on land is the theme. It is a vehicle that runs, not something, not commonly called a vehicle, that flies. Airplanes were well known in 1919 when this statute was passed, but it is admitted that they were not mentioned in the reports or in the debates in Congress.

It is impossible to read words that so carefully enumerate the different forms of motor vehicles and have no reference of any kind to aircraft, as including airplanes under a term that usage more and more precisely confines to a different class. The counsel for the petitioner have shown that the phraseology of the statute as to motor vehicles follows that of earlier statutes of Connecticut, Delaware, Ohio, Michigan and Missouri, not to mention the late Regulations of Traffic for the District of Columbia, title 6, c. 9, 242, none of which can be supposed to leave the earth.

Although it is not likely that a criminal will carefully consider the text of the law before he murders or steals, it is reasonable that a fair warning should be given to the world in language that the common world will understand, of what the law intends to do if a certain line is passed. To make the warning fair, so far as possible the line should be clear. When a rule of conduct is laid down in words that evoke in the common mind only the picture of vehicles moving on land, the statute should not be extended to aircraft simply because it may seem to us that a similar policy applies, or upon the speculation that if the legislature had thought of it, very likely the picture of vehicles moving on land, the United States v. Bhagat SinghThi nd, 261 U.S. 204, 209, 43 S. Ct. 338.

Judgment reversed.

INDEX